BEYOND THE STARS

Part II

SERGEI EISENSTEIN

Beyond the Stars

II. THE TRUE PATHS OF DISCOVERY

EDITED BY RICHARD TAYLOR

TRANSLATED BY WILLIAM POWELL

LONDON NEW YORK CALCUTTA

SEAGULL BOOKS, 2018

Originally published by Seagull Books and the British Film Institute, 1995

English translation © Seagull Books, 1995, 2018

ISBN 978 0 8574 2 524 9

British Library Cataloguing-in-Publication Data
A catalogue record for this book is available from the British Library

Typeset by Manasij Dutta, Seagull Books, Calcutta, India
Printed and bound by Hyam Enterprises, Calcutta, India

CONTENTS

PART TWO

THE TRUE PATHS
OF DISCOVERY

Fyodor Basmanov in a mask. Eisenstein's drawing for *Ivan the Terrible*,
Part Two. Alma-Ata, 30 May 1942.

The sucking sound of galoshes slapping against mud.

Our feet slipped out of them.

The mud was a mixture of wet clay and the first snowfall.

A zoo, completely deserted.

Alma-Ata.

Steppe eagles, with bedraggled crests, looked like my companion's aunt.

A deer without antlers and with large, moist black eyes looked very like my travelling companion (Kozintsev, the director).[2]

A bear lumbered in aimless circles.

There was an amazing snow leopard.

His terrifying tail twitched at our every movement; it looked like a furry snake distended after a good meal.

The whole body was still, idle.

The eyes were closed one moment . . .

but they would suddenly open wide: fathomless, grey-green.

You can just make out the narrowed pupil, like a second hand on the twelve.

The snow leopard lay utterly still beneath the roof of his cage.

Only the tip of his tail tirelessly, nervously reacted to our every movement.

The snow leopard was like the Japanese military attaché at the Red Army Parade on Red Square.

Bushido—the samurai code of honour—does not permit a Japanese from the elite caste (and this tradition later came to apply to all Japanese in general) to show any change of expression, come what may.

The face of the Japanese attaché was impassive.

But then a new class of combat aircraft cut through the sky.

His expression was set.

His hands were behind his back.

But what they did!

In their yellow gloves they flew like birds.

Just like the leopard's tail.

While the eye fixed on us did not so much as waver.

The next day I sent Misha Kuznetsov to study this leopard's eye for his role as Fyodor Basmanov.[3]

Kuznetsov's grey eyes were perfect for this.

He had to know how to capture their look.

We went further, into a sheltered enclosure.

There was a strong stench of urine.

A black Great Dane.

Flocks of green parrots—a mass. I saw parrots like that flying among the palms of the Mexican tropics.

Pelicans, too.

The lion smelt of dog.

The tiger smelt of mouse.

We went to see the monkeys.

The baboons were kept separately . . .

I tossed a bit of carrot in.

The monkey stopped what she was doing.

She was, of course, looking for fleas.

Three leaps brought her to the carrot; she did not take her eyes from it.

But then a piece of white paper came into her line of vision, lying not far from the carrot.

The white made a deeper impression on her than did the dull orange.

And the carrot was forgotten.

The monkey moved towards the paper.

But then, just nearby—a penetrating cry and the characteristic chattering of teeth.

The monkey turned away from the paper when she heard the cry.

Her gaze rested on the swaying branch.

A moving object is more eye-catching than a still one.

One jump and the monkey was already holding on to the branch.

The monkey's mate chattered up above.

The next second, the monkey was already obligingly deep in her mate's fur.

One's living companion is of course a much more attractive proposition than a simply mobile object.

The branch, paper and carrot were all forgotten.

. . . The difference between me and the Alma-Ata monkey is just this one fact:

I jump from object to object in much the same way, as soon as a new object surfaces in my memory.

But, as distinct from the monkey, I still occasionally return to the original object.

I dedicate the progress of the subject matter in these notes to my anonymous sister—the monkey in the Alma-Ata zoo . . .

THE HISTORY OF THE CLOSE-UP[1]

A branch of lilac.

White,

double-flowered.

With lush green foliage.

Hanging heavy in the blinding sun.

It spilt through the window into my room.

It swayed above the sill.

And became the first of my memories of childhood associations.

A close-up!

The close-up of white lilac swaying above my cot is my first childhood impression.

Actually it was not a cot at this stage; it was a small white bed, a nickel sphere crowning each post and a white crocheted net between them to stop me from falling out.

I was too old for the cot.

I was all of three or four!

My parents and I were at our dacha.

On the Riga coast.

In modern-day Majori, then called Majorenhof.

The bough of white lilac, cutting across a ray of sunshine, looked in at my window.

Swayed above my head.

My first conscious impression was a close-up.

So it was that my consciousness awoke beneath a spray of lilac.

Then it began nodding off again, for very many years at a time, beneath that same branch.

Only the branch was not real but drawn; half painted and half embroidered in silk and gold thread.

And it was on a Japanese folding screen.

I used to doze off looking at this branch.

I don't remember when it was placed near the headboard of my bed.

It was as though it had always stood there.

The branch was luxuriant and weighed down.

There were birds on it.

And in the distant background beyond—visible through it— were the traditional features of a Japanese painted landscape. Small huts.

Reeds.

Streams crossed by little bridges.

Small vessels with pointed prows, drawn with two brush strokes.

But the branch was not only a close-up.

The branch was a typically Japanese foreground, through which the background had been painted in.

And so I was aware of the beauties of foreground composition before I saw Hokusai[2] or was entranced by Edgar Degas.

A small foreground detail can attain such size that it dominates everything else in the painting.

Then somehow a chair was put through the screen in two places.

I remember it had two holes in it.

The screen was taken away.

I think these two branches brought two, organically connected ideas together—the idea of a close-up, and the idea of foreground composition—in one living impression.

And many years later, when I began to look for the historical precursors of the cinema close-up I automatically began searching not in isolated portraits or still lifes but in the fascinating history of how an individual element in a picture begins to move forward from the picture's general make-up and into the foreground.[3] As figures, in a general view of a landscape in which it is sometimes impossible to detect Icarus falling, or Daphnis and Chloë, begin first of all to approach the full height of the painting, and then gradually come so close that they are cut off by the edge of the canvas, as in El Greco's 'Espolio', and later—jumping forward three centuries—the French Impressionists, who were strongly influenced by the Japanese.

For me, it was two Edgars who encapsulated the tradition of foreground composition.

Edgar Degas and Edgar Poe.

Edgar Poe came first.

The vivid impression of the painted Japanese bough probably accounts for the strong impression left by Poe's story about how he was gazing out of the window and suddenly saw a gigantic monster crawling up the ridge of a distant mountain.

It then emerges that this is no prehistoric monster, but a little cricket crawling upon the pane.[4]

Only a camera lens can do this, and only a 28 mm lens at that;[5] it also has an amazing capacity for distorting the close-up, artificially exaggerating its size and shape.

I have reluctantly decided to set out some proposals concerning Poe's visual imagination elsewhere, in a small work on the elements of cinema in El Greco's *oeuvre*.

But I think it was probably the conjunction of that branch of white lilac and the plastic description from Poe's terrifying tale that decided my more effective and pronounced foreground compositions.

These are the skulls and monks, masks and carousels of the Day of the Dead in the Mexican film.

The spot of the white lilac branch became a white skull in the foreground.

And the terrifying element in Poe's story became a group of monks in black cassocks in the background.

It amounts to the Jesuits' Catholic asceticism, ruling, with a rod of iron, the sensual magnificence of Mexico's tropical beauty.

The carousels of the Day of the Dead echoed this deeply tragic theme with irony.

Here were those white skulls once more, flung into the foreground and almost tangible.

But the skulls were only cardboard masks.

Life-size carousels and Ferris wheels spun behind them, flashing through the empty sockets of masks which seemed to say with a wink that death is no more than an empty cardboard box that, come what may, the whirlwind of life will punch holes in without thinking twice.

Another good example is combining the profile of the Mayan girl with the entire pyramid of Chichen-Itzá, in one and the same frame. But I explored the model of this composition with particular thoroughness in *The Old and the New*.

The incomparable compositions by the second Edgar—Edgar Degas and Toulouse-Lautrec (whose compositions can be even more powerful) bring us back again to the realm of the purely plastic arts.

But the actual interweaving of these descriptive and spontaneously visual impressions meant something quite specific to me.

Here I sensed, probably for the first time, the link between painting and literature, seen as equally plastic.

That gave me my first inkling of how to read Pushkin from a visual, plastic and montage viewpoint and, when I needed an English equivalent, Milton too.[6]

Reading Pushkin and, later, Gogol strengthened my sense of this link.

If Poe showed us an essentially visual picture, described in detail like a visual picture and even as an optical phenomenon, then in

Pushkin we find a description of an actual event or phenomenon done with such absolute strictness and precision that it is almost possible to recreate in its entirety the visual image that struck him so concretely.

And I do mean 'struck', which applies to the dynamic of a literary description, whereas an immobile canvas inevitably fails.

Hence it was only with the advent of cinema that the moving picture of Pushkin' s constructions could begin to be sensed so acutely.

Tynyanov wrote about the concreteness of Pushkin's lyric poetry, saying that Pushkin's lyric poems were not an interaction of conventionally lyrical formulae, but in all cases were a record of genuine lyrical 'spiritual states' and emotional experiences, always precisely located and having a quite real source.

Analysis of Pushkin's poems (and prose) reveals the same precision in his description of quite real visual images that may be established or recreated from his exposition of them.

Arranging a passage by Pushkin for editing as a sequence of shots is a sheer delight, because each step shows how the poet saw and logically showed this or that event.

> And then as from above inspired
> Came forth the ringing voice of Peter
> 'To the task, in Heaven's name!' And from the tent,
> Surrounded by a swarm of favourites,
> Comes Peter . . .

The gradual way in which Peter is presented is remarkable. First there is the voice; after it, the crowd, with Peter in the midst of it but still invisible; only then is Peter revealed to us as he is, or, rather, as 'the thunder of God itself'.

No less original and Pushkinian is the 'micromontage', i.e. the combination of separate elements within one frame.

TOP. Eisenstein with his students on the first day of filming *Bezhin Meadow*. Moscow, May 1935. (Photographs: Jay Leda)
BOTTOM. Stills from the prologue for *Behzin Meadow* (first version, 1935–36).

Here, the same thing happens in the way the words are deployed within phrases.

And if you take it as read that the consistency with which words are ordered defines their position, as they move from the background of the 'frame' into the foreground (which is natural enough), then almost every phrase of Pushkin's coincides with a scheme of plastic composition, outlined with complete accuracy.

I say a scheme of composition, because the positioning of the words defines the chief and crucial matter of composition: the understood relationship and juxtaposition of the elements of the subject and the other values within the pictures.

This 'essential bone structure' can be dressed up in any type of personal artistic solutions.

And, while following the rigid plan of the author, this enables anyone who might try his hand at literary description in the plastic arts to interpret it in their own way.

The prerequisites and the limit of creative interpretation of a writer's works, as in any aspect of directing, are both to be found here.

A good example of how an author's compositional plan develops and how failure to notice it can wreck this structure, can be seen by comparing an actual extract from Gogol with a conventional adaptation for cinema. The example comes from Kuleshov's book and is the start of the attack in *Taras Bulba*—the appearance of Andrei:[7]

We have to think, when we are recording the shots for this sequence, how we are going to portray Andrei riding on his horse. If Andrei gallops through the middle distance, the viewer will not be able to see Andrei's face in sufficient detail; the expression in his eyes, the black curls streaming from under his helmet, etc. If Andrei is in the foreground or in close-up, we will then stop the viewer from seeing Andrei for long enough—the horse and rider will no sooner appear on screen than they will vanish off it.

So the frame of Andrei on horseback must be filmed by a tracking shot—moving the camera on a parallel course to the galloping horseman (filming from a truck or a car, etc.).

Let us record the shots for this sequence:

4m 3.   *Medium shot*: Andrei rides ahead of his regiment. Andrei is the most animated and handsome.

Tracking shot: He is covered in gold.

Sound: Music for the attack. The gleam of the gold.

4m 4.   *Close-up*: Waist upwards. His black hair streaming from under his helmet.

Tracking shot: A scarf he treasures is tied about his arm.

Sound: Music for the attack. The gleam of the gold.

6m 5.   *Medium long shot*: The walls of the fortress. Out comes the Polish woman.

Sound: Music for the attack. The Polish woman's theme.

3m 6.   *Close-up*: Waist upwards. The Polish woman on the wall.

Sound: Music for the attack. The Polish woman's theme.

'Andrei is the most animated and handsome.'

'The prized scarf, a present from the Polish woman.'

Andrei sees the Polish woman. We show Andrei's good looks and the Pole's scarf.

We say again: ' . . . So the black hair flies from under his bronze helmet . . . '

' . . . The prized scarf flutters from his arm . . . '

We show the Polish woman looking at Andrei.

We record the shots:

2m 7.   *Close-up*: Black curls streaming from under Andrei's helmet.

Tracking shot.

Sound: Music for the attack. The Polish woman's theme.

2m 8.   *Close-up*: The scarf fluttering from Andrei's arm.

Tracking shot.

Sound: Music for the attack. The Polish woman's theme.

4m 9.   *Close-up*: From the waist. The Polish woman watches.

Sound: Music for the attack. The Polish woman's theme.[8]

Reading Kuleshov's critique and explanations, you can only agree with his conclusions.

It is all logically correct; all the details are there.

There is, however, a nagging feeling that you cannot film Gogol in so trivial a way.

Here are these nine shots.

If you take the corresponding passage from the narrative, you will see that it diverges sharply from Gogol in the very first lines; that is to do with principle rather than mere appearances.

Whereas Kuleshov's chief aim right from the outset is to show Andrei going into battle (tracking shot, shot 3, close-up, shot 4 and so on are specifically so designed), Gogol on the other hand presents him quite differently:

> The gates were opened, and the hussars—the pride of all the cavalry regiments—flew out. Beneath the riders, the brown steppe horses raced as one. In front of the others there rode a knight more animated and handsome than the others. His black hair streamed from under his bronze helmet; his prized scarf fluttered from his arm—it had been embroidered by the hands of the greatest beauty.[9]

Where does it say here—where is it indicated, even—that this is Andrei?

Is it accident that Andrei is neither named nor shown at the start?

Of course not.

The next phrase makes the author's intention plain: 'Thus was Taras struck dumb when he saw that this was Andrei . . .' The author's plan was to reveal Andrei's identity as this remarkable knight through Taras' eyes.

So the viewer should be 'dumbfounded' with Taras.

The author's plan was for the foremost, flashing, fabulous soldier to turn out suddenly to be Andrei.

And Gogol does not let Andrei start hacking and chopping immediately. He first devotes many lines of description to his easy and brilliant gallop, using the simile of a young borzoi, before saying how keenly he brandishes his sword.

Whatever impression we have of Andrei in his Polish armour, we gained it a few pages earlier, from the description Yankel gives Taras—Yankel had seen him in the town:

> Now he is such an important knight. I almost didn't recognise him! Golden shoulderplates and golden armlets, golden breastplate and golden helmet and gold around his waist and gold everywhere, everything is made of gold. Like the sun in springtime, when all the birds sing in the garden, and there is a scent of grass—that is how he gleams in his gold . . .

That is our first impression of Andrei!

Andrei should be shown first as he was when still an unknown knight, shining like the golden sun, before Taras recognized him.

To do this with film shots is extremely simple. Without even having to take the lens cap om

(Incidentally, this appearance of the radiant knight would make a fine contrast with his death, as told by Taras two pages earlier: 'He fell, fell ignobly, like a vile cur!')

Interestingly, the Polish woman is also not 'personified', only indicated: 'The scarf, embroidered by the hands of the greatest beauty.'

This type of indirect presentation was a favourite device of Pushkin's, too. That is how Peter leaves his tent in 'Poltava', or Istomina exits in *Eugene Onegin*.

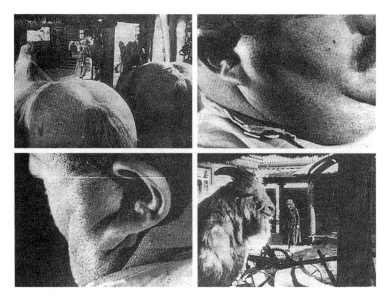

ABOVE. Stills from the episode 'Marfa Lapkina in the kulak's house', from *The General Line*.

BELOW. Long shots from *Que Viva México*!

Here he is also concerned that the reader should recognize Andrei at the same time as Taras. This is also connected fundamentally to the fact that the viewer must identify right to the end 'with Taras', who in everything he does is the embodiment of the patriotic idea!

We observe exactly the same thing when we see how one montage group follows the next.

And incidentally, the cross-cut to the woman on the fortress wall is here really a 'silent-film' device.

Andrei's 'curls' etc., 'he saw before him'

—she still cannot make up her mind.

And of course the musical leitmotif should have been worked out here, weaving this theme of the drunk, stupefying passion that possesses Andrei in battle and especially in death, when this theme in the music, growing in strength, might cut across the magnified titles and clearly merge, mixing with Andrei's pronunciation of her name before his death.

This would have been an example of the development of a theme, not only plastically but also aurally, and finally in an interrelated, audiovisual way.

Of course, the Chinese provide the most interesting examples in this area too: the unity of painting and writing technique, which evolves uniquely from an original visual perception and its specific characteristics and which defines the unexpected characteristics and forms of both painting and writing conventions.

I think that, just as Pushkin's word order turned out to be the ultimate stimulus from my first impressions, so Pushkin himself represented a stepping stone to the theme that absorbed me most—audiovisual counterpoint.

The fact is that Pushkin often splices the intonational and melodic progression of the phrase itself and so creates a visual equivalent to the word order.

The melodic graphics are so distinct and correspond so precisely to the verbally sketched subject of a scene that sometimes it looks like an outline of actual details, or a *mise en scène* of events, or a motionless interweaving of everything in view.

Which is one step away from the case where the concrete subject disappears, leaving behind only the outline and the weave of the intonational progression that characterized it.

The melodics of the poetry have merged into music.

The problem of audiovisual combination arises from the possibility of audiovisual correspondence and unity.

(The key part of my only book to date, *The Film Sense*, is devoted to this and there is no point in repeating myself here.)

Here I am interested chiefly in the highways and byways that I have travelled on my journey to the central problems and that have excited me in different sectors of my creative practice.

The sweet poison of audiovisual montage came later.

Silent film was primarily concerned with montage and the role of the close-up.

But, curiously, even in silent film I often sought a way of conveying something through a plastic construction composed of purely aural effects.

I remember filming in the Winter Palace one night in October 1927 (for the film *October*). In the palace rooms I achieved a plastic recreation of the impressions made by a salvo from the 'Aurora's' guns. The echo rolled through the rooms and reached a room where everything had been covered by white sheeting and where members of the provisional government were awaiting the fateful moment— the establishment of Soviet Power—wrapped up in fur coats.

A system of 'iris' diaphragms, in a correctly gauged rhythm— an opening and shutting out of views of rooms—attempted to capture the echo's breathing rhythm as it resounded through the galleries. The crystal chandeliers tinkling in reply to the rattle of machinegun fire on the square was more successful and remained in the audience's memory.

There was also a purely subjective association here apart from the visual and motor equivalent of the swaying crystal pendants. The attempt to capture the graphic equivalent of the echo was, of course, more interesting from the point of view of method!

The close-up in the form that silent pictures handled it—a close-up, that is, which is actually separate from the rest of the picture and no longer connected with it, but entirely abstract in its own right, the *pars pro toto*—is also linked to a vivid impression I had several years before I even began working in theatre!

I associate the close-up of a monosemantic sort, as a part of possible combinations of tempo alone, with a real saraband of noses and eyes, ears and arms, belts held up high by safety pins, earrings and coiffes entwined with flowers and ribbons.

Day-time vision is quite different from night-time.

Day-time, in the sense of being awake.

Night-time, in the sense of dreams.

The interlacing of details and general form is typical of daytime vision and is so harmonious that you need either a highly developed special skill, like Pathfinder's eye,[10] or that of his great-nephew, Sherlock Holmes, or an unusually acute sensitivity of attention, to be able to select at a moment's notice an isolated detail in close-up, from the harmony of the whole.

You need a particularly well-trained analytical visual sense to pick out the detail.

You need a particular aptitude for synthesizing thought, to discern among the data of analytical vision the crucial, characteristic detail, the detail which can, as a fragment of the whole, recreate the idea of the whole.

Curiously, when we are asleep, the entirety and the part are blended just as harmoniously, but in such a way that both are equally noticeable.

It is hard to find a better description of this than in Dostoyevsky, in the conversation Ivan Karamazov has with the Devil, where, characteristically, references to the 'highest manifestations' lie next to 'the last button on the shirt-front'. We might also mention Lev Tolstoy in this connection; he is equally at home handling the huge canvases of war or describing unexpected details' like the curls of hair against Anna Karenina's neck and it has been said that even 'quite mediocre folk' see similar things in their dreams; that there are such people for whom, in the waking hours, the 'whole' is an amorphous, complex and undifferentiated picture.

But the most rewarding states are those between dream and reality.

The leap from one state to the other seems to splinter both one and the other harmony: fragments of perception or impressions from the perceived object are shaken like dice or shuffled like a pack of cards.

It was at this juncture that I saw the above-mentioned saraband in close-up.

It was not a dance at Bald Hills.

Not on any hill at all, come to that.

It was on a beaten-down space in front of a few large huts somewhere in the old Kholm District, part of what used to be the Pskov guberniya.

This was on another occasion.

During the Civil War, I found myself quite unexpectedly thrown into military construction work in the town of Kholm in Pskov, even though this town was 95 kilometres from one railway line and 70 from the other. We were building defences: trenches, ramparts, blockhouses. Although we had not the faintest idea whom we were defending the town against . . .

It emerged much later that it was a self-interested whim on the part of the sappers' commander that sent us to Kholm; after the retreat from Dvinsk or Polotsk he found himself on the other side of the abandoned positions, and his wife's former estates were somewhere in the Kholm region.

This commander was noted for his crazy motorcycling, brilliant expertise as a sapper, and also, perhaps for always doing handstands on his chair whenever you went in to see him with your report each morning.

And at the sappers' amateur dramatics, during our operations around Velikie Luki, this engineer brilliantly acted a taciturn servant with a napkin, in a sketch of *The Double* performed from memory, taken from the repertoire of the prewar theatre of miniatures (on Liteiny Prospekt, I think).

(That was one of my first-ever attempts at writing on amateur directing.)

And in the rich variety of my terribly vivid impressions of that shifting epoch there resides that small, fleeting memory that had nothing to do with the scale of the epoch and events, but simply emerged somewhere incidental to and remote from the general course of the historical events of those years. In fact, it does not even count as an event. The only requirements were a very narrow bench.

An accordion.

With our feet soaking wet, we had 'to warm up' with swigs of home brew.

Crossing the river to where the girls danced.

Before that, we ate a hearty meal in a peasant's house (yet to be de-kulakized); the family was ready to demonstrate its friendship in any way we asked, just as long as we retained the only son as foreman in the sappers' division where a student technician was on an equal footing with the other foremen.

We slumbered fairly heavily after the unusually rich meal—I think it was the first one I had ever eaten in a peasant's home—and from the communal round bowl.

There was an amazing sunset.

And an unhealthy sleep at sunset lying on a very narrow bench running the length of the lean-to.

While the girls danced.

And the accordion played uproariously.

And the other members of our 'expedition' kicked out their heels on the beaten square before the spacious hut; below was the silted river, stinking and brackish, where our boat floated (she leaked slightly, hence our wet feet), the rowlocks and chains clinking . . .

I have dozed off many times in my life.

And in all sorts of different situations.

Dying from heat, in a skiff among the pointed-tailed skates in the lagoons in the bird sanctuaries of Campeche.

High up (!) in trees growing in narrow tributaries, their branches trailing in the water and their roots greedily sucking moisture out of those veins which the Pacific Ocean sends, tendril-like, into the impenetrable palm forests of Oaxaca. In the distance, a crocodile's beady eye and upper jaw lay on the surface of the water.

I have been rocked to sleep by an aeroplane flying from Veracruz to Progreso, above the azure waters of the Gulf of Mexico. Flamingoes cut smoothly through the sky like pink arrows, passing between us and the emerald surface of the gulf.

Sleepiness has overcome me among the sun-scorched bushes around Izamal; bushes which have grown from fissures in the immeasurable expanse of rock with its marvellous carvings, which were once the proud cities of the ancient Toltecs and which might have been tossed and scattered by an angry giant.

I also felt tired sitting at a red checked tablecloth in a lot of black clubs around Chicago.

My eyelids began drooping in the *bal-musettes*, the Parisian dance halls—'Le Java', 'Boule Blanche', 'Aux Trois Colonnes' . . . young labourers, little older than Gavroche, danced amazing waltzes, holding their partners close and spinning, their feet never leaving the ground.

But for some reason it was only then, long ago, after the rich meal provided by the Pudyakovs, in the cool, damp sunset above the unknown stream that I sensed this strange phenomenon, a marvellous farandole before my eyes—now a gigantic nose, the only one of its kind; now the peak of a cap, leading an independent life; now a whole line of dancing faces; now an exaggerated moustache, now just the little crosses embroidered on the collars of a Russian shirt, now the distant view of the village swallowed up by the twilight, now again the too large blue tassel of silk cord hanging around a waist, now an earring entangled in some hair, now a flushed cheek.

Oddly, when I embarked upon the theme of peasants and collectivization for the first time, just over five years later, I did not lose sight of this vivid impression. The kulak's ear, and the fold of skin on his neck filled the entire screen; another's massive nose was as big as a hut; a huge hand hung limply above a jug of kvass; a grasshopper, the size of a reaping machine—all these were constantly being woven into a saraband of countryside and niral genre pictures, in the film *The Old and the New*.

The last, and perhaps the most purely plastic and also ornamental was the visual impression I experienced in the rarefied, mountain air of Alma-Ata, my entire field of vision suddenly shattering before my exhausted eyes (or brain?) and part of it (the lower left hand side) dissolving into bright zigzags, like a fan of clearly defined stripes of white, dark blue and dense brown.

Its pattern and range of colour were in precisely the style of Peruvian ceramic painting, and I had found that so overwhelming precisely because its graphic and tonal stylization made it quite impossible to guess the nature of the external impressions that had given rise to them . . .

Such random, ornamental forms could only have been realized in multiple visual shifts, in dreams in twilight states, whether they were originally visual, or had been initially produced (the laws of weaving transcribed for decorating cylindrical vessels).

Here, on the lowest level, as everywhere where the levels of cultural advancement are still moving upwards, we find this conjoined unity of seeing and perception—a reflection of reality, refracted through consciousness, and a reflection of reality refracted through the prism of sensual thought.

On the lowest rungs of development, this occurs primitively and directly—in the representation itself and in early, stylized attempts at forming that representation. At higher levels, it is more refined, involving that organic dyad of perception in increasingly complex problems of form, until eventually separate chance manifestations of formal solutions and 'discoveries' are synthesized. Individual stylistic mannerisms are even found both to be elements of studying a method of art as it comes together and as elements of the actual method of the arts.

THAT'S JUST IT[1]

There are some wonderful phrases in Russian.

'It takes all sorts.'

'It's anyone's guess.'

'That's just it.'

The best,

the most versatile, is of course: 'That's just it.'

It comes in handy on all occasions in life.

Such as, when a conversation has to be kept alive but there is nothing to say.

This is akin to Abraham Lincoln's famous judgement on a book: 'People who like this sort of thing will find this the sort of thing they like.'

Saying 'That's just it' has points of similarity.

It is very versatile.

It was particularly versatile during the Civil War, which was where I picked it up, together with the knack of rolling up my puttees quickly, putting on foot bindings and disregarding even the most basic creature comforts.

'We've got this Soviet power,' a ruddy peasant might say, his eyes screwed up slyly, 'but we haven't got any salt. Hmm?'

'That's just it,' you say brusquely.

'I've heard the south is swarming with Whites,' another says with an innocent expression but looking at you beadily out of the corner of his eye.

'That's just it,' you sigh.

'You just don't understand our way of life, dragging us off here to dig trenches for you when there's hay to be made.'

'That's just it,' you say, in anguish.

The more ambiguous the remark, the more provocative the question, the more anguished, sensitive or brusque the 'That's just it' will sound.

Try it for yourself; you will find it so.

'That's just it' became a part of my routine in Kholm.

A broad river cut the town of Kholm in two. The Lovat.

Defences were being built along the Lovat's banks; the deep rear passed through this point.

It was so far to the rear that mere strategy cannot explain why we were building reinforcements here.

Like all good Russian rivers, the Lovat has two banks.

One is high, the other low-lying.

Geography textbooks attribute this natural phenomenon to the earth's rotation.

The water is said to flow slowly and cannot catch up with the high bank that is ahead of it.

Just like brother Moon going to meet his sister, the Red Sun.

And the low bank is behind the river and chases the high bank for ever.

I expect this is a feature typical of Russian rivers.

I never observed it in Colorado riverbanks.

In fact, rivers there flow so quickly to bore their bed deep between the sheer walls that they have no time at all for worrying about the differing heights of the banks.

Both rims of the Grand Canyon are extremely high, if you measure from the bottom of the gorge gouged out by the river.

But quite low, if you measure from the average surface of the desert; they do not rise so much as one foot above it.

There was an endlessly long wooden staircase leading to the top of the high bank of the Lovat.

It rose upwards in a series of zigzags and it had railings.

Girls hoisted buckets full of water up the steps, carrying two on a yoke.

Meeting full buckets[2] was hardly a sign that one's life would be a full one. Full buckets were all too frequently met with here.

There was a game the lads would play.

They would let a girl reach the top step.

Then they would tip the bucket over . . .

The aim being to drench the shrieking girl.

The Shelyapins' dwelling ran along the high bank.

It was a big family and their house took up the whole length of the bank.

The Shelyapins were the local grandees.

Millers and corn chandlers.

Having said that, they varied enormously.

Some lived in town, others in the country.

Some were well-to-do, others poor.

There were close relatives and distant cousins.

There were masters in their comfortable stone houses and owners of wooden cabins from outlying villages which the town had swallowed up.

The Krasilnikovs lived on the opposite bank.

They were a small family.

A family which ran a certain brewery.

Which also made kvass.

The head of the firm, Krasilnikov, a young man, was the typical outcome of a boy who had been considered an 'awkward' child.

By the time he was twenty, he had managed to 'experience all that life had to offer'.

Even the attempt the marshal of the nobility made to abuse him.

He spoke as proudly of this as he did of his success in repaying the debts his parents' brewery had run up: taking advantage of inflation, he used worthless banknotes without even stopping to consider the firm's honour.

His small factory had not yet been nationalized.

But it would be, of course.

Although this was subject to delay because of Eglit, an engineer in our military construction unit.

Eglit was a well-fed Lithuanian of pinkish-grey complexion.

He had a shaved head, grey eyes, and wore a soft brown leather jacket with a velvet collar.

Eglit married Krasilnikov's sister.

The Eglits had a daughter.

They called her their *dotter*.

My clerk of works, Sasha Stroyev, lived with the *dotter's* mother.

I learnt the expression 'That's just it' from him.

There was also Grandfather Krasilnikov.

He was seldom to be seen.

He was senile.

And he spent whole days in the grey outdoor privy.

He futilely expended what remained of his masculine energy as he looked through a crack, watching the girls playing in the sun.

Krasilnikov, or his wife, hit him about the hands with nettles a few times a day.

The nettles did not help much.

I expect they even had the opposite effect of heightening his excitement.

'This seems more like a setting for a possible story or novel, wouldn't you say?'

The river.

The Krasilnikovs and Shelyapins on opposite banks.

The Revolution broke out in Kholm.

The military construction corps moved in.

Eglit served under Stroyev.

Stroyev slept with Eglit's wife.

Eglit knew about this.

But Sasha Stroyev stood for the brewery's inviolability. The works made kvass too.

The lads pouring buckets of water on the girls.

And Grandpa Krasilnikov, looking in his white beard like Father Christmas idle during the summer months, peeping at the little girls through the crack.

'It's a wonderful place, a lovely place—a perfectly Russian place!' Peitsch the sapper sang, throwing a section of the military construction corps into this backwoods.

But I am not writing a novel or a story.

Why have I written all this?

Why?

'That's just it.'

I read Otto Weininger in Kholm.[3]

I had already had a thorough grounding in Freud.

So *Sex and Character* did not produce the effect it otherwise might have done.

I no longer remember when and where it was that I read the funny notion that creation (one's work) was first and foremost a division of oneself, a separation.

This was entertainingly demonstrated by the Lord God's activity in the first week of restless existence when he created the universe from chaos.

Indeed: he divided light from dark.

Land from sea.

And, finally, Eve from Adam (Eve was made from Adam).

Chaos began to assume a sort of constant appearance.

Moreover, thanks to that constancy, a certain dynamic necessity for a subsequent reunion was implanted—a necessity for what had been torn asunder, rent in two by divine will, to merge again.

This happened with the most consistent results in the case of Cain, Abel and Seth who (apart from Abel who died at a tender age) triumphantly passed their parents' experience on to their descendants.

Striving as far as possible to blend into a unity, polarized opposites penetrate each other; in the process they create the wealth of forms found in nature, making her powers manifest.

Ancient Jehovah, floating above primeval chaos before there was this type of activity, was only the humanized embodiment of the remote and mysterious Dao which (according to Chinese mythology) itself split into two opposing origins. These also 'always strove to come together, and they gave rise to all natural phenomena, processes and objects in the attempt.'

It is highly suspicious that it is none other than Chinese mythology that provides the source of the legend of Adam and Eve; and equally Plato's enthralling legends of living creatures joined by their backs, subsequently to split and doomed to search for their right half in order to complete the cycle of their earthly existence, forming what Rabelais picturesquely described as '*la bête à deux dos*'.*

* French: 'the beast with two backs'.

Using a contrary hypothesis, there is a charming proof that 'halving' is no less important and necessary as 'unifying' in this interesting process.

The horror of indivisibility: a state of permanent bonding or proximity without the means of parting to come together again later.

One of Henri Barbusse's *True Stories* about the atrocities of the Sigurança is *The Two of Them*.[4] People who love each other are tied together, face to face, for an unlimited period. 'Abide with me.' The horror of this position lies in the transition from empathy and sympathy for each other to torment and bestial hatred.

This story seemed incongruous to me then; the others seemed actually realistic.

But the formula reminded me of something I had read long ago in *Mir priklyuchenii* [The World of Adventures], where villainous inquisitors condemned a man to 'be with himself': he was left in a room where all the walls were mirrors. There is a room like this in Gaston Leroux's *The Phantom of the Opera*. In any amusement park in the West. And of course, as a philosophical derivation, by Skovoroda (see the epigraph to *The Hare's Forfeit* by Leskov).[5] But the precursor of this style is of course Edgar Allan Poe in *The Pit and the Pendulum*.

Anyway, I asked Barbusse (we were very good friends) whether this tale was true.

He burst out laughing and said he had of course made it up.

But it is none the worse for that! That makes it a psychological approach to the problem: what would have happened with the striving for unity, had there been no division into two, resolved here with the classically 'primitive' opposition of man and woman.

(Bernard Shaw wrote an ironic passage somewhere about the dream of never parting and remaining for ever in each other's embraces, and the 'inconveniences' that would ensue if this were to happen.)

Interestingly, the 'horror' when confronting such an 'indivisibility' (depriving you of the opportunity of joining together as opposites)—but on a cosmic scale—comes from Indian folklore: in the story of the meddlesome jackal who once wanted to marry, to reunite earth and sky. Luckily, he was persuaded otherwise by the cost of so doing—the cost of everything on earth (as I have said, they arose by division—the halving of the whole, according to oriental mythologies: Taoism, Judaism, Hinduism, Yesidism, etc.).

The *contrepart** of this is the Maori myth of the cutting in two of the Sky-Earth, and all her sons rushing out into light and life.

* In French in the original.

MONSIEUR, MADAME ET BÉBÉ[*1]

Mama lived at No. 9 Tauride Street in St Petersburg.

Her front door opened on to a yard.

It had a lift.

There was a white-marble fireplace downstairs.

A fire crackling cheerfully in the grate.

For me, it was always winter here.

Year in, year out, I went there only for Christmas.

The fire always crackled cheerfully.

A soft red carpet ran up the staircase.

Mama's boudoir was hung with a pale cream brocade, decorated with tiny garlands of roses.

So were the portieres.

The carpet was pale pink to match the roses.

The boudoir was also her bedroom.

Two curtains screened Mama's bed.

Those portieres were also decorated with roses.

Many years later, when I was a student living permanently with my mother, I was laid up there with my second attack of measles.

The windows were curtained.

The sun shone through the curtains.

The room was bathed in a bright pink light.

Was it the fever?

Not just the fever: the lining of the curtains was also pink.

Sunlight turned pink as it shone through them.

* In French in the original.

When you turn your head towards the sun and shut your eyes, or hold up your hand in front of a bright light, there is the same pink shining through the skin.

There is the same warm glow when you think of the nine month-long state of bliss in the womb . . .

The pink light of the room blended with the heat and delirium of my fever.

Grandma's bedroom—I remember being in that room when I was very small—was all light blue.

Blue velvet on low armchairs and long blue hangings.

Did Grandma have a blue period?

And Mama a pink one?[2]

The hangings and furniture from Mama's boudoir are now in my dacha and coming to the end of their life.

The garlands are barely visible.

The upholstery has turned grey.

The fringe is missing in places on the chairs; at the bottom it looks like an upper jaw with missing teeth.

A grey period?

The divans, settees, couches—whatever they are called—were littered here and there with books.

Most of them were the yellow books published by Calmann Levy.

Library books, taken out by a woman of decisive and independent views.

First of all: *La Nietzschiéenne*.[3]

Then the obligatory *Sur La branche* by Pierre Coulevain.[4] And of course Bourget's *The Semi-Virgin*,[5] replacing *Twilight* by Dumas *fils*.

I did not open those yellow covers.

But suddenly, breaking the run of books about semi-virgins, I found somewhere a small book called *The Stages of Vice*.[6]

This is nothing less than a sympathetic story of a country girl who 'fell'; first on the Paris 'street', then in a *maison close*.*

Circumstance. Life. Morals.

What makes the book interesting is that it is full of photos.

Illustrations such as those that, *um die Jahrhundertwende*,† as the Germans say, might fill an edition of Maupassant, Colette and Willy or Gyp.[7]

The ridiculous poses made the pictures charming—they showed these mistresses expecting 'visitors', falling asleep in their wretched mansards after 'work', drinking their morning chocolate, or at their toilette.

And there are a few documentary photographs—luxurious beds with cheekily naked, gilt cupids at each corner.

I have loved photographic illustrations of the nineties since I was in nappies. Papa had masses of albums from Paris.

And a particularly large number were to do with the Exposition Universelle in 1900.

I knew my Exposition Universelle from cover to cover by heart, no worse indeed than I knew the 'Our Father'!

These were probably the first photomontages I ever held.

The principle of these photographs consisted of shooting the models one at a time in different poses, then mounting them all on to a background which was either a photograph or had been painted.

There was 'Offstage at the *café-chantant*', where the figures represented famous stars, in the extremely revealing costumes of queens of the night, cats with fluffy ears; a jockey, or a marquis.

---

* French: literally 'closed house', meaning 'brothel'.
† German: 'at the turn of the century'.

And of course the fireman—le *pompier*—with a huge false moustache.

Or it was 'Le Foyer de l'Opéra', crowded with men in *hauts de forme** and high-society ladies in silk wraps, in a sea of lace flounces.

Sometimes it was a carnival; then everyone wore a mask.

Or a general view of a firework display.

Then the characters were enraptured and it was quite clear that the lighting and the source of light did not match and that they were looking in quite a different direction from where one might have expected.

These 'montages' were printed in different tones:

pale orange, lilac, sepia, greyish-green.

Perhaps my interest in montage began growing from that point, although the actual type of composite picture is significantly older.

The twenties and thirties of the last century had seen charming patterns of pictures made out of parts of engravings.

Folding fireside screens and flat fireguards were typically decorated in this manner.

Such screens, made in the forties, I remember, were still in use in 1927, in the parts of the Winter Palace that were not a museum.

And Lord Byron once had screens like that—with the portraits of the best English actors playing their best roles.

The fascination with making these composite pictures, together with the art of cutting out silhouettes, began in the middle of the *dix-huitième siècle*† with Moreau Ie Jeune, Eysen and Gravelot.[8]

This pastime was called *découpage* and pictures showing ladies doing this have survived.

* French: 'top hats'.
† French: 'eighteenth century'.

Another sort of photo album was constructed on another principle.

As distinct from 'Paris La Nuit', 'Le Moulin Rouge', 'Le Casino', and so on, with Loë Fuller, Jane Avril, the cake-walk, the Matchish, can-can and so on—the sisters of those contemporaries of photography, the posters and lithographs of Toulouse-Lautrec—some albums had names like 'Le Rêve', or 'Le Rendez-vous', etc, etc.

These albums were as good as cinema.

Page after page of a girl—in bed.

The girl wakes up.

Stretches.

Daydreams.

There she is, washing.

Now she has thrown on a smart blouse.

There she is, doing up her corset.

Etc, etc.

Now she is waiting for her knight in shining armour.

He has not turned up.

The pictures follow each other with the same logical progression as that amazing series of six small canvases by Goya depicting the story of Margorotto, the robber.

Here, the robber is attacking a defenceless monk.

Here the monk suddenly puts up unexpected resistance. Here, even more unexpectedly, the monk throws the robber.

The robber is put under guard.

The photographic illustrations in *The Stages of Vice* followed the second sort of album.

The Stages of Vice is indelibly stamped on my memory.

(There are other books on this principle too, such as *Comment on nous vole, comment on nous tue*,* where these studio photographs show *ces demoiselles* robbing their clients, as well as elegantly murdering representative types of *ces messieurs* with a lump of lead in the heel of a stocking.)

And my imagination was troubled by *The Stages of Vice* until I realized, to my unspeakable surprise, in the rue Blomet in Paris, *chez* Madame Aline in Marseilles, or in the Maison des Nations in the rue Chabanne, that that is how life really is.

More surprisingly still, little has changed over these thirty to forty years.

And in the carved, gilt beds in the Maison des Nations one can discern the twin brothers of the shameless *bambini*† who laughed at you in your childhood from the pages of that book.

In fact, that is not entirely the case.

The corsets have gone, and so have the fluffed-up hairdos with the roller on the forehead.

The dazzling stockings, with the broad strip running round, have also gone.

And the awkward white knee-length *pan-pans*‡ have vanished for ever.

But these are only technical details.

Two other books turned up among Mama's settees and divans.

I glanced inside them.

More than once.

But with trepidation.

With a certain excitement.

* French: 'How we are robbed, how we are murdered!'
† Italian: 'children'.
‡ French: 'pantaloons'.

Mingled with fear.

And these books were carefully wedged between the back and the seat of the chairs and divans.

To make it seem more natural, cushions were placed on top. Mama's handiwork, richelieu embroidery.

(The patterns were cut out, and held together by a system of very thin strips. How many similar patterns did I stick together for Mama, from magazines! And how many did I later combine, or independently create, myself!)

. . . These books were hidden partly from embarrassment and partly from fear of what was within.

Not because I wanted to be able to put my hands on them at any moment . . .

There was something frightening about these books.

They were *The Garden of Torments* by Octave Mirbeau and *Venus in Furs* by Sacher-Masoch (the latter was even illustrated).[9]

These were the first pictures of an 'unhealthy sensuality' that I found.

I came across Krafft-Ebing somewhat later.

But I still have a morbid aversion to the first two.

I sometimes wonder why I never play games of chance. And I do not think it is because I am just not predisposed to gamble.

More likely, the very opposite.

Sometimes you are 'afraid of being scared'.

I used to find that, when I was a child.

I was not afraid of the dark; I was afraid I would wake up in the dark and be frightened!

Which is why I give games of chance a wide berth.

I am afraid that once I start playing, I will not be able to stop.

I remember very dearly being in this pale pink boudoir with the garlands of roses and taking an avid interest in the stock market reports, when Mama decided to stake a smallish sum of 'spare cash' on stocks and shares . . .

I was right to flee Mirbeau and Masoch, who were reaching out for me.

An alarming streak of brutality had been aroused within me even earlier in my life.

Strangely, it was a living impression. But a living impression from the screen!

It was one of the very first pictures I saw. Probably made by Pathé.

In the home of the blacksmith—a billet.

The time: the Napoleonic Wars.

The blacksmith's young wife deceived her husband with a young sergeant of the 'Empire'.

The husband found out.

He caught the sergeant.

Tied him up.

Threw him into the hay loft.

Ripped his coat.

Exposed his shoulder.

And . . . branded him there.

I remember it vividly: the bare shoulder, the huge square iron rod in the muscular hands of the smith with black sideburns and the white smoke (or steam) rising from the burn.

The sergeant collapsed, unconscious.

The smith brought the police.

Before them lay an unconscious man with a bared shoulder. On the shoulder was a convict's brand!

The sergeant was trussed up like a fugitive.

He was jailed, in Toulon.

The finale was heroic and sentimental

The forge caught fire.

The former sergeant saved the smith's wife.

The 'shameful brand' vanished as the flesh burnt.

When did the forge burn down? Was it many years later? Whom did the sergeant save: the smith himself too, or just his wife?

Who pardoned the convict?

I don't remember any of that.

But the scene with the branding still remains ineradicable in my memory.

It gave me nightmares when I was young.

I dreamt about it at night.

Once, I was the sergeant.

Another time, the smith.

I grabbed hold of my own shoulder.

Sometimes, I thought it was my own.

And sometimes, someone else's.

And it became uncertain who was branding whom.

For many years, I had only to see fair curly hair (the sergeant was blond) or black sideburns and Napoleonic overcoats for that scene to come to mind. Then I formed a passion for the Empire style.

For a time the ocean of brutalities in which my pictures are steeped could not drown (like the sea of fire which consumed the convict's brand) those early impressions of the vicious film and the two novels from which it doubtless in some way took its source ...

Nor should it be forgotten that I spent my childhood in Riga during the heat of the events of 1905.

And there are as many terrible and brutal impressions as you could wish for all around: the wild outburst of reaction and repression from men like Meller-Zakomelsky and his accomplices.[10]

Even more important, the brutality in my pictures is indissolubly tied up with the theme of social injustice, and revolt against it ...

Monsieur, madame et bébé.

Here is yet another title of a book which was very popular in those years.

But I beg your pardon!

I have not only not read or seen this book yet, I do not even know what it is about. I think it was slightly scandalous—at any rate *un peu risqué.*

I only knew it by its title.

I would like to group, under this title, some thoughts that have lately been occupying me a considerable amount.

This title fits them admirably!

But of course, as always, the title of the book brought with it the circle of books from which it was taken.

The books drew in their wake the small tables and chairs which they were scattered upon.

Carpets rolled under the chairs.

Windows appeared at the sides.

Curtains covered them.

The sun shone through them.

And the whole was bathed in the pink, warm opacity of memories.

The pink light between the drawn curtains evoked the image of a mother's bosom.

And strange though it may seem, it is only that and the heading '*Monsieur, madame et bébé*' that wholly suit what I want to write about.

But before writing about what I want to—about *Monsieur, madame et bébé* vis-à-vis myself—I want to talk about that in relation to ecstasy.

I came to the subject of ecstasy through that of pathos.[11]

The death of the Grand Princess Yelena Glinskaya. Detail by Eisenstein for the prologue to *Ivan the Terrible*. Alma-Ata, 5 October 1942.

I came to the subject of pathos when trying to rationalize my work on *Potemkin*.

The formula came about readily and of its own accord.

Pathos is when all the component elements are in a state of ecstasy.

In Russian, ecstasy—'ex-stasis' [*is-stuplenie*]—literally means 'stepping outside oneself', 'leaving oneself'.

I was then very interested in 'orthographism'.[12]

I supposed (wholly reasonably) that a true dynamic picture of a phenomenon is typically (very often) reinforced by the verbal definition of the act itself.

This began with the analysis of a mechanical formula for the dynamic of expressive movement.[13]

Here this proposition is proved exactly.

Because a symbol which we are used to considering as figuratively abstract in fact continues to be the symbol of movement which has been stamped by the dynamic process of this expressive movement.

When one has to analyse the motive (the general 'algebraic' formula) that corresponds to a given emotional condition, 'it is enough to read literally' the symbol that man has 'figuratively' reinforced by a verbal symbol for a particular condition.

Because of all the 'arithmetical' nuances of individual cases, 'aversion' [*otvrashchenie*] constitutes a comprehensive 'general' formula of the motive process, which expresses this condition internally: a-version (just as, invariably, *ot–vrashchenie, Ab–scheu*), su[b]-spicion, dis-dain and so on.

The expressive movement that spills out of the 'human system' into space becomes *mise en scène*.

Mise en scène is a spatial, metaphorical outline, the sense of which must be read by the viewer.

'Tailing' someone is expressed spatially by preserving the distance between the spy and the object.

The uniformity of the distance conveys the idea of the 'linkage', 'attachment' of one to the other, hence the figurative reading that the second is 'inseparable' from the first.

(N.B. Uniformity of distance may be roughly, crudely literal. But a 'correct' solution here of course will be a dynamically constant distance: that is, a constant average of changing physical intervals:

Not: But:

_____   _____

_____   _____ ___

_____   _____ ___

_____   _____

The first way is for analysis.

The second way, however, is for 'creation': correctly 'naming' the formula, then 'expanding' it into a construction.)

'Naming' it correctly is only possible when you have sensed it *precisely*, experienced it *precisely*, etc., etc.

All of this has been set out and described in the appropriate place.[14]

And this method later becomes applicable to all questions of form.

Finally, the form itself begins to be read as a 'literal' reading of the formula of the 'content'.

And I applied this device of etymological analysis—the return of the abstract term to the dynamic picture that gave rise to it—to the range of phenomena such as 'ecstasy' with the greatest excitement.

I tested it in practice.

And the accuracy of this reading (and of the actual mode of reading) was verified at each step.

In pathos, each element stands outside itself.

This has been set out in detail in three sketches 'On the Structure of Things'.[15]

I could here provide a quotation for the order of things:

Pathos is what makes the viewer leap from his seat. It is what makes him jump. It is what makes him throw up his arms and shout. It is what makes his eyes sparkle in delight, before that same feeling makes him cry. In short, it is everything that makes the viewer 'come out of himself'.

Put more elegantly, we could say that the effect of pathos in a work is to bring the viewer to ecstasy. Formulating it like that adds nothing new, for in the three lines written above is exactly the same ex-, which means exactly the same as our 'coming out of oneself, or coming out of one's usual state.

Princess Yvefrosiniya Staritskaya standing over Vladimir, her son who has
been murdered. The finale of *Ivan the Terrible, Part Two*.
(Photograph: Viktor Dombrovsky)

All the above-mentioned signs follow this formula faithfully: from sitting to standing; immobility to violent movement; silence to shouting; dullness to brightness; dryness to moisture. All of these are a 'coming out of oneself', 'departure from one state'.

Furthermore, 'leaving oneself' is not 'a departure into the void'. 'Leaving oneself' has to mean entering something different, something of a different quality, something contrasting with what came before (immobility into movement; silence into resonance, etc).

Thus, even from the most superficial description of an ecstatic effect which a pathetic construction may induce, it is clear what must be the basic indication marking the construction of a composition of pathos.

In this system, one must be able to observe the condition of 'coming out of oneself' in every instance, and of a constant transition into some different quality.

But this is just a part of the problem—the one I most need—the 'operational' problem.

I call my 'system of aesthetics', which I might eventually assemble, an 'operational aesthetic'.

How to do it.

How to 'do' the pathos clearly.

But for a full picture of ecstasy, you must be clear about the question of the psychological state that constitutes ecstasy.

It is accurate enough to call it the 'behavioural process' connected to ecstasy; that may not be the whole answer but it points us in the right direction.

The phrase we always use is 'bathed in ecstasy'. Despite the fact that ecstasy is a state of 'upliftedness', 'exaltation'.

Of course, a purely orthographic analysis is inadequate here.

To understand just how comprehensively precise is the verbal element of this procedural, dynamic symbol which goes with ecstasy, the first thing to do is undertake a huge survey of the works of the great masters who 'immersed' themselves in ecstasy.

There is the psychological repertoire adduced in commentaries for spiritual exercises; the equality between the mechanism of psychic meditation and the basic physical system in the practice of the Khlysts,[16] the dervishes or Mexican *danzantes*. Juxtaposing the Eastern to the Western practices. The Indian ecstatics, Buddha and Nirvana. The ecstasy of the prophets of ancient Judea and of the mass psychosis at Lourdes, etc., etc.

I soon hit upon the idea of Nirvana and how it might be explained as a psychological state: returning to the embryonic condition.

More time was spent on an all-embracing scrutiny of this than on an assimilation of the phenomenon itself.

My thanks to psychoanalysts who have preceded me on this path.

For here is the key which the verb 'immersed' holds to an understanding of the phenomenon.

And here is the key for the proper understanding of the verb itself!

A return to the embryonic state!

That accounts for the psychic picture of how one feels when in ecstasy.

But what is interesting is not the inert, lifeless condition induced by ecstasy.

The moment of 'illumination' is what is interesting.

Not the length of the 'stay'.

But the climactic flash.

Emergence.

Ecstasy can be very briefly formulated as participation in the 'emergence', and also as dialectic understands it: the moment of transition from quantity into quality; the moment of a (sensation) of unity arising in a multiplicity, the moment when a unity is formed from opposites.

When does this moment occur, within the parameters of a human individual's experience?

It is that point which, as personal experience, is contained with the whole of its original force, at each moment of analogous situations on later paths of the human individual's emergence and development.

Naturally, that point shoots out at the very first moment of life within the womb—at the lowest threshold and within it.

At the moment when the future human individual is implanted in the womb.

A fair amount has been written about being in the womb (for example, Doctor Alexander on 'Nirvana' in *Imago*).[17]

Rank, in *Das Trauma der Geburt* [The Trauma of Birth], has written beautifully about 'emerging into the light'.

I cannot remember anything of the divinity 'of the first spark'.*

But the 'illumination'—the moment within the limits of personal experience—is of course here.

And precisely here, in one moment, 'in the moment' . . . *monsieur, madame et bébé*.

According to Hegel, *monsieur et madame* destroy their own selves and their opposite qualities merge into one.

And the physical bearer of this unity—*bébé*—comes into being at this moment.

The question of illumination (and all ecstatics speak of memories of a blinding light) is explained with elegant simplicity.

It is one's first trauma and it always merges in one's conscious (preconscious?), sense (foresense?), memory (pre-memory?) with the

---

* In English in the original.

second chief trauma—the trauma of birth, the trauma of coming into the light (Rank has written on this exhaustively).

These traumas merge into one: after all, time has no meaning during the nine months spent in the womb! The starting point and the finishing point are the same!

(I omitted earlier to mention a most remarkable author Ferenczi[18]—who expounded all of this in his *Versuch einer Genital-theorie* and who also raised at this point the question of the death-wish. And also the regression, through 'aspects' of animate nature, to the level of the inanimate!)

Pathos can be very briefly read as a degree.

Not as something evolutionarily separate from other, less intense aspects of the state of poetic material.

But as something organically integral, having differing degrees and an inevitable quality of novelty at a certain level of quantitative intensity.

We can immediately draw conclusions from this.

The pathetic uplift, the explosion of pathos, is momentary—it is only a conjunction of those traits which, taken *legato*,* determine the general effect.

And the intensity turns out to be directly proportional to the degree of separation.

A crowd experiences unity at the (pathetic) moment of the outburst—pathetically.

But the unity of the crowd (for instance, the people) can appear gradually, in a leak (as opposed to an explosion!) from the volumi-nous work of history.

In both places there will be awareness of the unity.

The emotional coloration of this awareness and sensation will be of one and the same kind.

* Italian: 'smoothly'.

But the condition will be of a fundamentally different degree. The same thing happens with means and method.

And the gradual transition, let us say, from opposite to opposite, will be just as essential a basis for exerting influence; but the spirit of the explosive leap will flow not in the appearance (not in the form) in the pathetic work, but will 'fluidly' descend the scale of spontaneous intensity, in forms ranging from novel to short story and chronicle, from tragedy to drama and play . . .

A jump of the multiplier, from normal speed to a deceleration, 'slow motion',* as a dynamic, cinematic means, is a plastic interpretation of the function of this diminishing intensity.

Imagine all three of these types of filming successively applied to one and the same phenomenon—an explosion—and you will have the full picture.

The same clouds of smoke, the same girders and rails flying upwards, the same clouds of dust.

But an answering explosion of emotions in one (the first case) and fluid, perceptive contemplation in the other (the third).

The questions of the degree of immersion, of the degree of regression and of the degree of return to the 'zero' point, rest in the devices and means used.

And the explosion seems to have been fired with the camera running backwards to the starting point. Because only by returning to this zero can there be a new uplift; and the closer to the zero, the more complete and shattering will be the all-encompassing uplift!

The means of influence are like fragments from yet lower and lower-lying layers of consciousness (preconsciousness).

Neutral form is from the layers of consciousness on today's level.

Works have been deprived of their latent 'grip'* which is characteristic of works that do not appeal to the 'lower layers'* of consciousness and the emotions.

* In English in the original.

Orthodox form is like a fragment from the layers of primitive thought.

Pathetic form is buried in the 'profoundest layers'* beyond the limits of sensual thought: instinctive, vasomotive, electrical, chemical and physical phenomena.

A noter!† Here, form also embraces the concept of subject—one of the primary ways of realizing the desires to be expressed.

The Revenger's Tragedy, for example, can serve as a thematic example of the third case; the realization of an original, physical law of each action having an equal and opposite reaction. And the scene of the chase is born of instinct—the hunter's instinct.

As Herman Melville puts it so well in *Moby-Dick*: '. . . for I believe that much of a man's character will be found betokened in his backbone. I would rather feel your spine than your skull, whoever you are' (from the chapter about the actual extraction of spermaceti from a whale's head).[19]

And it is these very layers of my influence that I attack with my harpoon.

And I try to penetrate them more and more deeply.

But my means are fragments from those layers, for it is only through these fragments that I can make these layers vibrate in unison with my will.

But 'backbone' and 'spine'* are layers on a par with the embryonic state, repeating the general curve of development, modification and growth of forms and appearances as one grows into the other.

So much for the ways and types of an operational aesthetic. But maybe it is the same in a psychological sketch?

Perhaps a merging that is legitimate, natural, and crucial—*monsieur, madame et bébé*—at the crucial moment when life's mystery

* In English in the original.
† French: 'N.B.'

emerges, at the point of the conception, can also reach further; also be observed far beyond the limits of that moment, because of its *legato* reach, in life's slow current?

Which is what my elaborately expressed discourse has led to.

'That is how I feel!'*

It may be racial.

It may be individual, psychological.

My beloved *raza de bronce*—the bronze race of the Mexican Indian is just that.

The masculine frenzy of temper, the feminine softness of outline hiding a steel musculature and the outer muscles flowing around it; and the disposition to forgive coupled with a childish naughtiness—this combination of features in the Mexican Indian makes either him or her—*muchacho* or *muchacha*†—for ever a continuing unity of *monsieur, madame et bébé*.

Adult men and women seem adolescent in comparison with other races; a race of young people, where the men have not yet lost their early femininity, nor the women abandoned their puerile pranks and both seem charmingly childish.

I mean, of course, the ideal, pure, collective, synthetic type and the best examples of the women and men, youths and girls, who passed before my camera and before me during the long months of my wanderings about the strange and wonderful, harsh and tender, childishly delightful Mexico.

I sometimes think that I am, *tout à la fois,*‡ *monsieur, madame et bébé*.

Alas, not only at times of pathetic exaltation.

* In English in the original.
† Spanish: 'boy' or 'girl'.
‡ French: 'all at once'.

But even on occasional days of industrious productivity, when, like an inquisitive child, I break into the dense layers surrounding the secrets of my work with a decisive, masterful arm; and then, with the hands of a bustling housewife, I try to reassemble the fragments of the broken stratum to insert them block by block into the conception.

Bricks or blocks?

Into a serious matter or a childish plaything?

But more often I suffer from the melancholy infantilism of an overgrown child, ridiculous and helpless, pitiable and insignificant in his clashes with life.

Eternally tied to Papa and Mama (again, as I am)—to two people who were sick to death of each other, after living together as husband and wife; spouses whom neither tsar, God nor any hero could liberate and free from each other; who were not even able to kill each other and were doomed to pay for it eternally with a lacklustre, humdrum existence; the threefold portrait of *monsieur, madame et bébé*—a grotesque caricature of the divine moment when man's threefold nature comes into one, at the very moment of the explosion of ecstasy . . .

PRE-NATAL EXPERIENCE[*1]

*Il fut nourri par une chèvre et conserua longtemps des allures
brusques et sautillards de sa noumce . . .*[†]

And just think!

None, none of this might ever have happened!

None of the sufferings, searchings, heartaches or spasmodic moments of creative joy! And all because there was an orchestra playing at the Ogins' dacha at Majorenhof.

Everyone had drunk far too much that evening. A fight broke out and someone was killed.

Papa grabbed his revolver and dashed across Morskaya Street to restore order.

Mama, who was pregnant with me, was scared to death and almost gave birth prematurely.

A few days passed in the fear of possible *fausses couches.*[‡]

But that did not happen.

I made my entrance into this world at the allotted hour, albeit three whole weeks early.

And my haste and my love of gunshots and orchestras have remained with me ever since.

Not one of my films goes by without a murder.

---

* In English in the original.

† French: He was suckled by a goat and preserved for a long time the jerky, hopping gait of his nanny . . .' A. Dumas *pére*, 'Eugène Sue', *Les Morts vont vite* [The Dead Go Quickly], II.i. [E's reference]

‡ French: 'miscarriages'.

In the USA, 1930.

It is of course hard to imagine that this episode could have left any impression on me *avant la lettre.**

But a fact is a fact.

My interest in the pre-natal stage of being has always been very strong.

It quickly extended to the invisible aspect of being.

I became interested in the stages of biological development that preceded the stage of man!

More than that, my range of interests took in early forms of social relations; pre-class, primitive society and the forms of behaviour and thought peculiar to it.

It was because they repeated the surviving fragments of all the stages in our consciousness, thought and behaviour that I found these areas so rewarding.

* French: 'before the event'.

TO THE ILLUSTRIOUS MEMORY OF
THE MARQUIS[1]

'We're having pancakes today.'

'A soldier came to our house today.'

'So? We're having pancakes today!'

'And we had a soldier come!'

The two little boys in the old story boasted to each other long and hard.

'We're having pancakes today!'

'Well? We had a soldier!'

They boast long.

They boast hard.

Until one gives in and starts to whine.

Boasting like that is a typically boyish characteristic.

But, as we established at the outset that the little boy in me is still alive, it is only to be expected that all these pages should be full of boasting, either latent or overt.

I boast on one page that we are having pancakes today. On another, that a soldier came to our house.

I do not only boast about successes and 'merits'.

But equally about misfortunes and flaws.

People find all sorts of things to boast about.

Father's medal.

A cousin's wooden leg.

Uncle's sideburns. Grandpa's beard. Aunt Nadya's glass eye. A missing finger.

A pulled tooth.

An appendectomy.

And doing yourself down is often of no less value than making an honourable mention.

This is sometimes done in a calculated way.

Tom Sawyer for example, who boasted that it was a great honour having to paint the fence.

He could sell the right to take part in this worthy enterprise to that crowd of gawping, envious onlookers, if the price was high enough.

Sometimes this is the result of a terrible inner compulsion, to banish (through boasting) the spectre of personal inadequacy that haunts the majority of us, just waiting for a chance to bite into our souls with a row of small celluloid teeth such as you might find on fur wraps.

I remember the case of Nikita Bogoslovsky, one of our most trenchant satirists, who also wrote music.[2] It was I who delivered him the *coup de grâce* or, better still, *le mort qui tue*.*

'Everyone is like an animal of some sort. Some are like bears, others like foxes, some like spiders.

'But Nikita is like a . . . boa.'

This was so close to the mark that he could not even get angry, hurtful though it was.

And I once 'cut' Utyosov with a neat twist.[3]

He once said: 'Eisenstein is a sexual mystic.'

'Better a sexual mystic, than a mystical waiter',[4] I replied (surprising myself with the speed of the retort).

So much for my own wit: I now move on to boast about my 'unrealized proposals'.

* French: 'the deadly taunt'.

These are distinct from 'unrealized productions', that is to say those which were not only conceived and proposed, but even 'given a treatment', to the extent that some pf the ideas were developed.

The following list concerns only those subjects and proposals which, at the very most, occupied us for no more than one or two days in proposal meetings and discussions, before being dropped for good.

Some will anyway inevitably come up again as such things do in the most varied of contexts, but it is amusing trying to assemble the most colourful and unusual of them in one place.

Most of them, as is quite logical, begin at the point when we were leaving for Berlin in 1929 on our way to the USA.

The first proposal was also, perhaps, the most extravagant.

We received a visit from a man who was enormously tall, thin and athletic.

He was the advertising manager of Nestlé, a Swiss firm, and his area of responsibility was condensed milk.

He had watched *The Old and the New* the previous day, and said that never before had he seen such a heartfelt expression of the essence of milk on screen.

The proposal: an advertisement for his company.

The material: a journey round the world.

The theme: whatever you like—even none at all.

The essential condition: to show that the children of Africa, India, Japan, Australia, Greenland and so on drink Nestlé's condensed milk.

We parted company, as I recall, over the size of the ... per diems.

(But the 'difference' naturally ran much deeper: Soviet power had not made me a film director for that sort of thing!)

Our trade headquarters in Paris was on the rue d'Astor. In 1929, there was no film department there.

But there was a sales and distribution office for minerals and diamonds from the Urals.

That department was run by a morose and deadly dull man. Part of his job included dealing with the sale of our films.

He floundered, utterly helplessly, when it came to the commercial side of our films, although I think he took the credit for exposing one of the most malicious and unusual forms of sabotage to affect his department.

The circumstances, roughly, were these.

Superstition has no place in our country—it was dispelled by our materialist—world view and has been banished into the dim and unpleasant past.

But this has nothing to do with the interests of our export trade.

And, if there are peoples and nations who suppose that seven stone elephants in decreasing sizes—even if they come from a society such as ours-can bring them the bloom of bourgeois happiness, then who are we to deny them this? Why stop exporting these *porte-bonheur** bracelets which bring us money? (Particularly in the 1930s, when hard currency was in such short supply that no more than 25 dollars could be taken out of the country for personal purposes, irrespective of the length of the journey. My journey around the world for 28 months on just 25 dollars is a story for another time!)

The seven elephants were carved from malachite, nephrite, chalcedony or topaz.

They were carefully packed.

Then transported worldwide in the unseaworthy vessels of the Soviet Merchant Navy.

But the wretched elephants would not sell.

Why not?

They just did not sell.

* French: 'lucky charm'.

First, the customers in the shops did not want them.

Then the shops stopped stocking them.

And at last the wholesalers stopped ordering them. Perhaps they boycotted them because of their country of origin?

But there was no indication of where they were made! Perhaps they did not bring good luck?

But they were not bought; the efficacy of their miracle working powers was not even tested.

They were just not bought.

At the same time, hundreds of sets of seven elephants made in Holland, Germany (Meissen) and Copenhagen were leaving the shelves . . .

What the devil?

The mountains of carved elephants grew and multiplied. They filled warehouses and stockrooms.

You could have cobbled whole streets with them.

When suddenly light dawned.

The trunks.

It turned out that only those elephants who carried their trunks jauntily aloft brought good luck.

If the trunk dangled sadly, it could not bring happiness or joy.

And the Soviet elephant was sold in all our overseas markets with its trunk stubbornly lowered.

The ill-starred model had a change of image, being refitted with a triumphantly raised trunk. It more than held its own with the competition from Holland, Copenhagen, Meissen and Dresden in the world markets.

The calibre of the fighting elephants may have dwindled since the days of Tamerlane's invasion, but their aggressiveness is undiminished.

One fine day, the man who traded in diamonds made me an official proposal.

I was considered a specialist in historical pictures.

Belgium had been an independent country for one hundred years.

And the Belgian government would have liked to see a commemorative film of its centenary, made by me.

This of course prepared me for the invitation to go to Venezuela and shoot a commemorative film dedicated to the illustrious memory of the South American freedom fighter, Bolivar.[5]

Oddly, in London, Grierson was asked to pass on an invitation from the colonial office that ran the empire.[6]

It was proposed that I film Africa.

The one stipulation being that I showed that English colonial power led to cultural development and prosperity for the blacks!

Grierson was too diplomatic to relay this to me!

I only learnt about it later and regretted that Grierson's tact was greater than his sense of humour: to think of what I could have said in reply to such an idea!

When, much later, I was on the border in Nuevo Laredo, between the two countries of Mexico and America (which refused to re-admit me for six whole weeks), I received an invitation to film a history of the state of Texas, with the undertaking that the local ranch owners would let me have as many horses as need be.

(I have given full details regarding that in a more appropriate place, as a digression in my Paris *Épopée*.)

The first subject proposed to me in Hollywood was the martyrdom of the Jesuit missionaries at the hands of the Red Indians; the last themes were *Jew Süss* and Remarque's *Return* [*Der Weg zurück*].

The talks went no further.

This also happened with *Grand Hotel* and *The Life of Zola*, which Paramount was talking me into while I was still in Paris signing the contract.

And in Paris, I was discreetly approached by an intermediary (one of those jewellers on the rue de la Paix who, like that merchant in the Bible, sold everything to acquire one single stone, a diamond beyond compare,[7] displayed in the window among drapes of dark velvet) with the proposal from Chaliapin that he and I make *Don Quixote*.[8]

'Fyodor Ivanovich is very excited by the idea of working in cinema and would want to try it out with a Russian, at any rate.'

It was Pabst who made the film later, and Fyodor Ivanovich was as unconvincing there as he was once magnificent in this role in the theatre.

When I was in the middle of filming *Que Viva México!* in Mérida, Yucatán, I was sent a proposal by my former Paramount supervisor to go to India and make Kipling's *Kim!*

Poor Mr Bachman had probably never heard of such things as visas or viceroys.

This curious episode reminds me of another.

Our friend Jascha Schatzow lived in Berlin.

As Herr Schatzow, he is a representative for Debrie, the film-camera manufacturers who cover all Europe.

In the autumn of 1929, Schatzow and I debated quite seriously the question of a film for dogs.

He was interested by this, but it was the commercial possibilities of the venture that first appealed to him, bearing in mind that Berliners of both sexes were very fond of their dogs and there was a colossal number of dogs in Berlin.

If one of the most picturesque graveyards in Paris is the one for dogs in Auteuil, then why should Berlin not have its own charmingly appointed dogs' cinema?

This thought occupied me, of course, purely from the point of view of a reflex testing of a series of filmic elements (the degree of suggestiveness, questions of rhythm, 'form', which would all be different from our customary system of thinking and imagery, and so on).

The project of course remained just that, going no further than two conversations: one in Schatzow's amazing billiard room in his house, another in a night club in the west of Berlin.

What could be more extreme?

But even this was not the most unexpected or hilarious thing a filmmaker could be offered.

The crowning glory was proposed by Jean C[octeau] the poet, in Paris, in the spring of 1930.

The proposal was to direct and film. Where? Marseilles itself! And what? 'There is only one sort of film you could make in Marseilles!'

*Ça, c'est le comble!**

Oddly, out of all the offers, this one was the most 'feasible' as it had financial backing. The Vicomte de N. was very keen to sponsor it.[9]

Well, in this case, of course, we did not even reach the discussion stage.

I never even met the Vicomte.

Come to think of it, the Vicomte was deeply preoccupied with another matter. Vicomte de N. was a direct descendant of the famous Marquis de S. On either the female or the male side.

And the Vicomte's villa was litetally crammed with editions dedicated to the illustrious memory of his ancestor, the Marquis.

In fact, the Marquis's memory was not at all illustrious; quite the opposite—it was besmirched.

* French: 'There's the rub'.

And the Vicomte had set himself the task of . . . rehabilitating the illustrious memory of his great and glorious ancestor.

Which explained the countless editions of *Justine* and *Juliette*, *The Philosophy of the Boudoir* and *Nights of Sodom* which filled the drawing rooms and bedrooms of the Vicomte's villa.

Maids, wearing white aprons and starched caps, scurried noiselessly among them (as they do in good houses), no doubt catching a sideways glimpse of a few lines of startling text, printed in the large typeface of plush, contemporary editions.

The subject matter of these lines would later form the subject of excited kitchen talk. And I can picture the smooth-shaven servant with bluish cheeks making a penetrating retort to the cries of the cooks and dishwashers: 'So what? In our village . . .'

And even children, it seems, stuck their noses into them, doubtless staggered by the fantastical woodcuts of the eighteenth-century Dutch pocket editions. 'So what? In our school . . .'

Apropos that, I had a funny experience with one such book on a trip abroad.

At the moment of my departure in 1929, as I stood on the platform, a charming lady, a former opera actress, Rtishcheva, brought me a tiny box: 'for your journey'.

Inside was not 'calico and brocade'[10] but a branch of vine and a golden, overripe Duchesse pear.

A tiny volume was concealed beneath the branch and the juicy, bulging fruit.

On the title page, Rtishcheva had written 'Just think! Pushkin could once have held this little book!'[11]

And on the half-title page, in a French dialect, was *A New Justine, or Virtue Persecuted.*

This was one volume out of eight, the full edition of *Justine* that sold for many years under the counter, costing an average 2,000 roubles the set.

It had illustrations, which were mostly coffee-stained.

The funniest one was where the hero timed his own release to coincide with the explosion of his boat which he had set on fire, which lent his harmless pastime a unique synchronization.

But the most *risqué* one absolutely beggared belief.

Oddly, this unorthodox breviary travelled with me on almost all my travels across America and Europe, at the bottom of various suitcases, but I saw it for only the second time when I was in Stolbtsy —a Soviet customs official had taken it out.

You can imagine how my blood ran cold.

But a miracle occurred: the pages of the book obligingly cleaved to each of the illustrations, concealing them as surely as if they were in envelopes or, like the author, trapped in the Bastille. They thus evaded the official's vigilant eye, as his fingers conscientiously flicked through the little book.

In the descriptions of my adventures in Paris, you will find a digression on the miracle of the 'little saint'—St Theresa of Lisieux.

That is the account of how the 'little saint' obligingly provided us with petrol.[12]

Could I call the event at the border town Stolbtsy the 'miracle of St Justine'?

The atheistic, blasphemous Marquis would have been delighted by such a name!

Jean-Jacques Brousson is of course absolutely worthless, from both a personal and literary point of view.

But his *Anatole France in His Dressing-Gown*, written in the style of Léon Gozlan's *Balzac in Slippers*, is one of the most charming books a reader could hope to find.[13]

I do not agree with the point of the criticism some Frenchman made of this work, although the criticism itself is brilliant in form and style. I quote from memory:

. . . One man was charged with carrying out another's chamberpot each night. Instead, he carefully stored up the contents. Then, after making his own contribution, he published it. That is what Mr Brousson's *Anatole France in His Dressing-Gown* is . . .

Journey to Buenos Aires was much weaker but it played so vital a role in the ups and downs of the graph of my life that I will deal with it quite thoroughly elsewhere.

Less famous of course is the collection of small novellas by Brousson. And, incidentally, they do not deserve special mention.

Only one is amusing, and that is probably a literary retelling of *Boutade* [The Whim] which was once done by the master himself.

(I found the master in Brousson's first work particularly attractive, probably because his nature so strongly resembled that of my own master—Vsevolod Emilevich!)

The hero of this novella is the Marquis: freed from the Bastille and now in his declining years, he vanished into one of the 'Paradises' kept by Madame N. N., and the 'Peyesottes' paid a visit, with their famous ostrich feathers and little *étui de nacre*,* and Mirabeau, famous as the author of *Journal d'un débauché*.[14]

'Teacher! Teach us!' the 'Magdalenes' cried out as one, kneeling—they had been educated by the works of their great and unexpected client.

The master tried to do so.

But fruitlessly.

He was flung out on to the street in disgrace. There was a lot of cerebral anger in this apocrypha, which Brousson had doubtless heard from his master himself.

. . . But nothing could stop the Vicomte and Vicomtesse from working on their ancestor's rehabilitation (*de leur illustre ancêtre*).

---

* French: 'mother-of-pearl' box.

I shall leave the poet, the Vicomte and his wife, half-protected behind their initials.

The famous ancestor has no need of this.

His works, scattered about the villa, speak for themselves. The illustrious ancestor of course is the Marquis de Sade.

It could of course transpire that he is only the spiritual forebear of the Vicomte, and the Vicomte himself has in reality another title.

But I would like to dwell here less on a description of the unrealized 'creative' meeting with the great-nephew than on the question of my long-lived 'creative partnership' with the 'great-uncle' himself.

Incidentally, Mr Gorman's biography[15] wittily exonerates the Marquis, calling him the learned predecessor of Dr Freud, and explaining his novels as the only available form in the eighteenth century for disquisitions into case histories of psychoses and pathological portraits of a particular proclivity!

However, the history of this partnership demands some introductory lines of explanation.

Some enthusiasts bequeathe their skeletons to scientific institutes.

'For science.'

Others—the majority—do so for financial gain: the skeleton is worked to death for a corresponding payment during one's lifetime; the money is spent on living or, more often, in view of the size of the payment, drinking; and after death, the vendor takes the rap for his bones and, instead of a comfortable internment underground, they are fated to stand in a glass case, held together by thin wire clips as an excellent, prepared skeleton.

But underlying both these impulses is a third.

Ex-hi-bi-tio-nism!

Albeit exhibitionism of a most unusual and idiosyncratic variety.

The *ne plus ultra*.

Exhibitionism, to the marrow of one's bones.

Literally.

Come to think of it, there is a greater degree yet.

To set out for inspection, not your 'bone structure' but the ins and outs of your psychical construction.

Not a skeletal but a psychological exhibitionism!

I would ask all that follows to be ascribed also to that.

There is a reason for my favourite joke not appearing in any collections along the lines of 'The Best-Loved Jokes of Famous People', although of course it is the joke that would best typify the luminaries in the constellations of film stars.

Incidentally, this little story concerns male film stars.

A 'star' once took his charming girlfriend out to dinner.

Having spent all dinner talking only about himself, he remembered himself over dessert and, with condescending grace, turned attentively and solicitously to his companion and said, inclining his head:

'I have spent all evening talking about myself.

'Let's talk about you.

'What do you think about me?'

Nobody can interrupt my monologue.

Let me take advantage of that.

An unfair advantage!

I shall move brazenly onwards.

I shall be my own horn, gramophone and record. Incidentally, talking of gramophones, it—the gramophone—has gone through three distinct phases: three completely different social relationships.

First, with its large, fluted horn, blue, pink or green, it travelled in triumph through my childhood years as a treasured novelty of technology.

Then it was branded a banal vulgarity; it was only in the cheapest resorts that records of 'ta-ra-ra boom-dee-ay' hoarsely blared through gramophone horns; spots near Oserki or Pargolovo, which proudly proclaimed themselves Finland, since the train that went there went also to Helsinki, Vyborg, Kelomjakki or Kuokkalu from the Finland Station.

At last, the 'third age' dawned and took everyday life by storm: a portable, the gramophone's younger brother; it had discarded its brightly coloured horn like a mammoth freed from its excess of tusk and become a domestic elephant.

My friends from the older generation even now sometimes get the names mixed up.

And my neighbour in Chistye Prudy, a respectable telecommunications engineer who was later given a medal, was not indignant at the noise of the foxtrots which were brought over together with the Flexatone[16] (the *dernier cri** in fashion in 1926) or the portable from Berlin, but the fact of my passion for the 'vulgar amusement of the gramophone'.

And awesome, exciting, inspiring, frightening but attracting too—after the isms in art (impressionism, expressionism, futurism, Dadaism, etc.), a new pack of quite different isms swept across the land, freed from the shackles of inhibitions and unleashed upon a troubled populace by a professor from Vienna and his zealous colleagues and pupils.

Infantilism, narcissism, sadism, masochism, exhibitionism—these strange words at first passed on in a whisper down the line, later overran the pages of specialist publishers' specialist magazines to enter the more general sphere of medical and psychological literature. Later still, they broke into *belles-lettres* and theatre; replacing the harlequins and columbines of the era of 'reborn theatricality', Hasenclever's[17] *Murder* or *Reunion in Vienna* had psychoanalysts

* French: 'last word'.

running about on stage, and O'Neil's *Strange Interlude* showed us a ponderous, painstaking repeat for the American stage of what had once, long ago, been done wittily, inoffensively and, most of all, with a lightness of touch by Yevreinov's Distorting Mirror Theatre, on the Catherine Canal, in the small piece *What They Think, What They Say.*

Strange though it may seem, this came into fashion much later in cinema, apart from *Secrets of a Soul* [1926] with Werner Krauss. The real 'vogue' in cinema for treating this sort of problem on screen coincided with the Second World War, which brought *Spellbound* [1945] and *The Seventh Veil* [1945] in the mid-40s and *Lady in the Dark* [1944], slightly earlier.

Then, in the wake of universal recognition, came the 'utter rejection' of psychoanalysis, and this 'vogue' abruptly ended.

The gains it had made in methods of treatment had been minimal and science had made still fewer advances in understanding inner, psychic life. But nothing at all had been uncovered that shed any light on its application to art.

In 1932, the Vienna Psychoanalytical Publishing House was closed down, and huge quantities of books on this subject were remaindered.

Words ending in ism began to die out and it soon became unfashionable at tea parties to mention the actual 'complexes' that these terms stood for. They ended up on the scrap heap of vulgarities, somewhere near the fluted pink gramophone horns, corsets from the 1890s, two- and three-seater tandems, and that pastime called 'Diabolo'[18] which everyone raved about until the 1914 War, or skating rinks (where you could smash your kneecaps against asphalt) shortly after the 1905 Revolution and the Russo-Japanese War.

I do not know whether one can (or indeed should) expect a widespread 'renaissance' of the principles and ideas of Freud's school, albeit in a revised and purified form.

That school always did seem somewhat 'transitory'—a 'halt' on the way to an attainment of a much wider and deeper grounding, of which sex would be merely one facet among many.

For all that it is particularly accessible and titillating, it is a very limited facet. And this is not only with respect to the 'right' wing, where the socially progressive cycles of human development are given prominence, but also to the 'left'—the biological stages preceding the happy little 'Paradism' of individual erotic bliss, within the limits assigned to 'the human individual'.[19]

And as regards the actual psychoanalytical 'jargon' of the twenties and the general notions themselves which it signifies, these notions have acquired, through years of use the 'quaintness' that surrounds everything that has vanished in the past, so I do not shrink from using the jargon in the way that old soldiers breezily talk of redoubts and flèches; old sailors of topgallants; and old ladies about the bustles, *accroche-coeurs*,* bugles[†] and whalebone, which they grew up with.

Without wishing to boast, I can say that many millions of viewers have seen *Potemkin*.

The most diverse peoples, from the farthest corners of the globe.

And I expect many felt a catch in their throats during the mourning scene over Vakulinchuk's corpse. But I doubt that even one of those millions saw and remembered a tiny piece of montage in some frames of that scene.

Not actually in that one, but the one when the grief turns into anger and the people's fury bursts out at an angry protest meeting around the ward.

An 'explosion' in art, and particularly a 'pathetic' emotional outburst, is constructed according to the very same formulae as a

* French: 'ringlets'.
† That is, strings of pearls.

detonation of explosives. I once learnt about this in the ensigns' school for engineers in the classes on mines.

There, as here, you need first a build-up of electrical charge (of course the actual means vary, and there is no universal schema!).

Then the constricting framework explodes. And the impact sends the myriad fragments flying.

Oddly, this effect does not take place if you do not interlay, between the build-up and the actual picture of matter flying in all directions, that indispensable 'accentuated' piece which dearly 'signals' the explosion. In a real explosion, this is the role of the detonator cap, just as essential in the rear part ofa rifle cartridge as it is in the packets of gun-wadding strapped to the girder of a railway bridge.

Such pieces are to be found throughout *Potemkin*.

At the start of the 'Steps' scene there is a large caption: the word 'SUDDENLY!' This is followed by the aggressively edited shot of the nodding head, in three different sizes, composed from three short montage-cell pieces.

(This, incidentally, is a close-up of Olga Ivanovna, Grisha Alexandrov's first wife!)

Here, this also gives the impression of a salvo of rifles 'shattering' the silence.

(It was a silent film and this is one of the ways of creating an effect in silent cinema—a way of representing the first salvo that should roar out 'off camera'!)

The emotional outburst of the finale of the 'Steps' sequence is caused by a shell flying from a gun muzzle—the first explosion which acts as detonator for the purposes of one's perception, before the wrought-iron gates and the pillars of the abandoned dacha at Maly Fontan are blown apart: the second and last 'actual' explosion. (Lions stand between them. These images by themselves illustrate the metaphorical role of compositional construction well enough.

Filming the sequence 'the death of Alba' for *The Battleship Potemkin.*

And in this regard they have every right to be included in the article 'On the Structure of Objects' which deals with the composition of *Potemkin.*)[20]

There is a similar accent in the leap from the mourning on the shore to the anger of the sailors who come running to a meeting on the deck of the battleship.

It is a very short section, probably not even perceived as a 'subject' but only as a purely dynamic accent—the unambiguous ictus on the frame which is not there long enough to be discerned and for one to make out what is happening. This is what happens: in that very section, a young lad tears his shirt in a paroxysm of fury.

This section is like a climax, inserted at the right point between the furious student and the fists, already shaking, flying above the sailors' heads. (In the shot list for *Potemkin*, this section is identified in the third part, No. 761).

The anger of the people on shore explodes into the anger of the sailors' meeting on deck and now the red flag is hoisted above the *Potemkin*.

But I am not as interested in the flag as in the section with the torn shirt.

And not as an accent, which is so traditional that it was applied to the rending of the curtain in the temple at the climactic moment of a very ancient tragedy being enacted between the three crosses on Golgotha.[21]

But as an element from my own life.

The point was that, as I said somewhere earlier, sadism for me all comes 'from books'.

I learnt about sadism not from children's games as happens, for example, so charmingly with Dostoyevsky's Netochka Nezvanova, which followed the similar 'first impressions' of David Copperfield, Nicolas Nickleby and other children whom the sentimental Dickens made suffer.

My first impressions of sadism were 'from books'; the first situations to suggest themselves to me came not from life or personal experience but were 'reflected' and 'refracted'.

The inseparable companion of the neurosis linked to the illustrious memory of the Marquis de Sade—Jean-Jacques Rousseau's masochism—is said to date from a whipping he received from a certain mademoiselle when he was at that age when, as the Germans put it, *das lustbetonte Gefühl** was making its appearance felt, and not merely as the sensation of pain.

Jean-Jacques described this feeling with ample ex-hi-bi-tion-ism in his *Confessions*, although he did not even then have at his disposal the whole wealth of nuances that we have.

* German: 'lust-tinged emotion'.

Anyway, *das lustbetonte Gefühl* did not accompany any pain I may have experienced in an analogous situation.

Although, as far as I recall, I was also given hidings as a child.

Admittedly, on only two occasions.

I can hardly recall the first. The main thing I can remember was everything else, apart from the sensation of pain, and the offence which led to the hiding.

I was very young, but my memory has retained all the details of the 'encirclement' very vividly.

First, in 'close-up', were Ozols'—Father's messenger's—green cuffs and buttonholes as he held me by the legs. (I was lying on the bench of my *pupitre**—a recent present.)

I was unused to seeing Ozols doing any sort of work of this nature.

Papa would ensconce himself in an armchair holding a huge register and Ozols would reach up to the top of the wardrobe where the strange rabbit-hutch contraption with the countless pigeon-holes was kept.

The most recent structure of this sort benefiting (or not) from a difference in size, but still providing a full representation of its general character, is the Hotel Moscow, which has completely wrecked the poetry of the Okhotny Ryad of the 'Gribkovs' and the other delicatessens which, during NEP, were still to be found in Moscow, just across from the Iberian Gate and the marvellous Iberia Street (which did a particularly brisk trade in just about anything, from matches and suspenders, to dolls and cocaine).[22]

Each cell of the structure (and there were either twenty-four, thirty-six or forty-eight) held one pair of shiny black boots. Papa would only wear shiny, black boots with square toes.

He did not acknowledge any other sort.

French: 'writing desk'.

And he had a huge collection of them, 'for every occasion'. He even listed them in a register, with any distinguishing features indicated: 'new', 'old', 'a scratch'.

From time to time, he held an inspection and roll call.

Then Ozols would slide up and down, opening wide. The gates of this boot garage. But on that occasion these hands held me.

Somewhere between the corridor and the dining room (the execution was carried out in the dining room), I could hear Salome, the cook, whispering with the maid Minna: they had been admitted too, no doubt to add to my moral humiliation.

The names Salome and Minna are so closely linked in my memory with servants that for many years Lessing's *Minna van Bamhelm* was bound up with eggs and spinach and chicken 'bits' (which was how we used to call that dish made from chicken hearts and stomachs at home).

It was worse with Salome: It took a supreme effort to divorce the name of our lean, miracle-working cook from the play by Wilde and Beardsley's drawings (I read somewhere recently of the hatred the two felt for each other, to the effect that the latter had done the illustrations for *Salome* as parody!).

My second thrashing came a little later, but before my schooldays began and with much less ceremony.

I remember here being half-naked—only my trousers were down.

I remember the 'weapon'—a strap folded three times: normally it went round my little dog's neck when he was taken for walks. He was a little thing, a toy; in those days toy terriers were fashionable.

Mama was the executioner.

And it had absolutely no effect whatsoever.

I laughed cheekily the whole time, although my cheekiness alone deserved punishment.

Stills from the scene of 'the demonstration over Vakulinchuk's body, from *The Battleship Potemkin.*

I had been thoroughly obnoxious to my French (or English) governess on a walk in Strelkovy Park.

It was worse for Eton schoolboys.

The severity with which this privileged school hardens its young gentlemen was quite monstrous in the very recent past.

There were no sheets or mattresses in the dormitories.

Hordes of rats lived under the floorboards.

In 18—, the floors of one building were lifted for repairs.

Underneath, a whole layer of bones was discovered.

Nothing alarming about that.

They were not human. They were the bones of animals and birds; the remains of dinners which rats had dragged under the flooring.

The town squares of Novgorod were made with animal bones; in particular, Veche Square,[23] near the Torgovaya District. But we should bear in mind that this was not in Queen Victoria's time but Alexander Nevsky's—the thirteenth century.

All that remains at Eton of the old arrangement now are the windows of the first class, which have not been glazed since the time of Elizabeth I and have only iron shutters.

I saw this 'system', except using wooden shutters with unglazed windows, in the homes of poor blacks which lined the wide metalled freeway—'Millionaires' Row'—from New York to Florida, or on those parts of it where it cut through the 'black belt' of the Negro states.

But the beams and desks of the building are made from real masts and bowsprits taken from the Spanish Armada which 'Red-Headed Bess' donated to this ancient educational establishment.

By working a penknife in-between the cracks in one of those pillars, one pupil, on the day before the holidays when we visited the school, drew out a small note in genuine Elizabethan handwriting, written on real Elizabethan parchment . . .

And there is a storeroom with canes too.

Although it seems more for form's sake than a practicality, they are still used at Eton.

And below, in the schoolroom, beneath the iron shutters of one of the unglazed windows, stands a small wooden stepladder with three rungs.

The victim kneels on it, bending over obediently.

And, as he does so, the ancient rule dictates: 'There shall be nothing between the birch and the body.'

And in accordance with this same rulebook, after the execution the victim's parents are sent a bill for the administration of 'the school's medicine'.

It would seem that the medicine dispensed here was more effective than that which Mama and Papa tried to administer to me: on the whole, it failed. ·

And my first impressions of cruelty were, as I have said, reflections from books.

However, before the true literary impressions—Oactave Mirbeau's novel (what did I say? and now I do not feel like writing out the full title *The Garden of Torments*, just as I prefer to write the subtitle *Venus in Furs*, and when it comes to the outline of the name von Sacher-Masoch, I have first to overcome certain internal inhibitions) there came cinematic ones.

But a whole new chain of associations linked Octave Mirbeau to the unhappy fate of the French sergeant on the screen.

I remember three which were especially strong.

The first was an article from the 'Diary of Events'.

I think it came from the *Peterburgskaya gazeta* [The Petersburg Gazette] which Papa took. I was regularly able to read Breshko-Breshkovsky's horrifyingly cheap satirical column, before the paper was sent off to Papa's bedroom.[24]

The article was about the savage revenge a group of butchers took on a shop assistant who had either complained to the manager about their abuses or had threatened to do so.

The drunken butchers dragged him into the back room of the empty shop.

They stripped him. Hung him by his legs from a hook in the ceiling.

Then they began to flay him with a double hook, the sort used for hanging carcases up. Skin came off in chunks.

How this 'event' finished for the young man—whether his screams brought the neighbours running and how these 'monsters' were punished—I have no recollection.

Probably because I simply read no further than that . . .

But the man hanging by his legs and the butcher's hook were still indissolubly linked to images' which disturbed me not so much at night as in the daytime.

This picture would suddenly appear before 'my eyes; the text book, novel or saw (I was still doing fretwork at that time) would fall from my hands.

I would stare fixedly and see before me the drunken butchers (particularly brutal was the ringleader), the hanging body and the terrifying hook.

It is interesting to note that I never 'saw' any blood during this.

Chunks of flesh were torn from the body like wax, leaving bloody strips, but they were not saturated with blood.

I expect it was this image that gave rise to my predilection for St Sebastian.

This St Sebastian, the shop assistant from the 'Diary of Events' hanging upside-down, is a frequent visitor to the pages of my works.

St Sebastian often crops up in drawings I do almost automatically.

The butcher, one of the Black Hundreds. Still taken for *1905*.

In my Mexican film I named the peon who was martyred in the fields of agave Sebastian; he died in excruciating agony, after suffering all manner of torture, being buried up to his shoulders and trampled beneath the hooves of the *hacendado's* horses.

In *Ivan the Terrible*, the Tatar prisoners were hung on palings like St Sebastian; they were furthermore pierced by what are clearly stage arrows. (However, this episode also has its own peculiar roots, of which more later.)

But before being realized in the scenes of my own works, images taken from a whole series of external, real, visual impressions augmented my inventions of the shop assistant's harrowing fate.

These images were without number . . . fragments of 'Pinkertons', *The Caves of Leuchtweiss* or the adventures of Nick Carter and Ethel King.[25]

Apart from the news-stands, which sold literature like this on every street corner even in Riga (as was the right of every civilized town in my childhood), there was also a book shop in Riga that had a separate window display for *belles-lettres* of this variety.

The window was horizontal and low down—no higher than a second-year schoolboy of average height, which was far-sighted and expedient!

The *recherché* display of German editions of Pinkertons was changed weekly.

The newspaper salesmen dealt in Russian ones.

The German editions were of a different format and brighter.

The most popular was Nick Carter.

This was at a time when anti-Chinese feeling ran especially high in detective fiction, a reaction to the then famous series of gangland murders in the New York and San Francisco Chinatowns and the all-but-forgotten 'atrocities' of the Boxer Rebellion.

Which was why on the covers almost every week villains with pigtails featured in the various hopeless situations in which Nick found himself.

The covers had a terrifying, magnetic force.

And I remember being unable to take my eyes off those horrors behind the glass, but standing there for ages.

Other covers were worse than the ones with Chinamen.

I remember a shining rainbow-bright cover with a picture of a sarcophagus, filled with molten tin.

Nick Carter was suspended above it, hands and feet tied up in the position of the soldiers about to be put on the rack in Callol's engravings.

On one side was a lady, her dress in disarray, wearing a short skirt (or petticoat?), her bodice undone.

She had one arm stretched out as she took aim.

And the caption read:

'If Nick doesn't tell her what she wants to know, she'll shoot through the rope ...'

The tin bubbled with hospitality, ready for the doomed Nick.

Another cover was even more fantastical.

It showed an underground park full of various implements of torture. Collars were chained to the walls.

Each collar gripped tightly the neck of a young man who was stripped to the waist.

They all had well-groomed hair with a parting.

And their one item of clothing—their trousers—were perfectly creased.

The cover was pale lilac.

There was also a series of pocket-format magazines about Ethel King, an energetic sleuth who went everywhere at great. speed. She was just as popular as Nick Carter.

In one picture she managed to trap the villains near the ant-hill where they buried their victims head down. One was still tied by his feet to a tree trunk.

But the other was already apparently swarming with ants; he was drawing his last breath in one corner of the picture.

Elsewhere, she burst through the ceiling of an operating theatre —this time, holding a machine-gun!

The victim was lying on the table, strapped down by a gang of villains while some of them made precise incisions in his bare, athletic torso.

Small rivulets of red blood snaked out from under their knives.

This scene recalls the half-believable story of Amaro, the one-eyed general who once came to see us as head of the War Office.[26]

The Mexicans are adept at inventing and embroidering on the truth while looking most sincere—they probably even believe what they say!

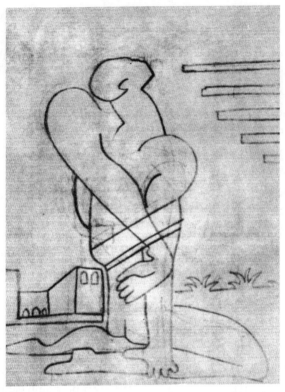

Sebastian. Eisenstein's drawing for *Que Viva México!*

Anyway, General Amaro, who had peon blood, was the model for the boy who witnessed the execution of his own father (at the start of the film *Viva Villa*) and vowed to dedicate his whole life to avenging him and to subject the landlord to the same fate.

In the film, this boy grew up to become the all-powerful and fearsome Pancho Villa.[27]

This actually happened to General Amaro who was promoted to senior command posts during the Civil War and took his revenge on the *hacendado* who had brutally killed his father. They say that, as he swore vengeance, the young Amaro put a metal ring through his ear. He vowed he would not remove it until he had settled the score with the landowner.

Allegedly, after killing the landowner he tore the ring out. There are people who confirm that this scar on General Amaro's ear can still be seen.

There is a character like him in my Mexican film. It was filmed and came out before *Viva Villa*.[28]

In my Mexican film, the boy witnessed the execution of his older comrades at the end.

The future avenger walked away through the fields of maguey, for the present suppressing his pain, hatred and wish for vengeance.

This ending, superficially similar to Chaplin '(but essentially diametrically opposed), was linked to the idea that the revolution in Mexico was still unfinished and that the day of reckoning for the peon's situation—no legal rights, miserable living conditions and inferior status—was still a long way off . . .

Incidentally, the young Felix Olvera, who played this boy, used to arrive in a police car during the last period of the filming.

The village policeman would sit in the shade of the agave, lazily smoking cheap tobacco, his rifle carelessly propped up between his knees and at sunset he would take young Olvera back behind prison bars.

Felix was fascinated by the old fashioned sort of large-bore pistol, a 1910 model, which he used in the film.

Young Felix found the temptation irresistible. One day the pistol vanished.

No one would have noticed anything had the unlucky kid not thought of bragging about the pistol to his sister.

There were live rounds in the gun. That day we were filming close-ups of the landlords' lackeys skirmishing with a group of rebellious peons surrounded in an agave bush.

The bullets thudded into the fleshy body of the maguey, which opened its oily lamina like the arms of a crucifix, torn and shot through, and flowed with blood before the cruel lasso and coarse ropes pulled down the doomed fugitives, led by Sebastian.

Felix Olvera shot his own sister.

And, exactly like the peons in my film who were driven mad by fear, he ran into the limitless expanse of maguey.

A desperate chase ensued.

The landowner's *vaqueros*, raising pillars of dust, were in close pursuit between the bushes.

The old ladies howled for the dead girl.

The girls howled, fearing for the bronzed Felix.

In the slanting rays of sunset, Felix was taken back to the hacienda, roped to the saddle.

Blood streamed from his temple.

Paolino, proudly riding abreast, had knocked him to the ground with a blow from his pistol. His ugly pockmarked mutt, gaptoothed jaws and black sideburns resembled something by Goya.

The wearer of this terrible face, Paolino (the local barber by profession), was a most kindly man but his face, flushed with the excitement of the chase, really looked terrifying in the ruddy rays of the sun.

We did not allow them to shoot Olvera.

But a few days later, when we had 'greased' the *deputado*'s palm, we were able to bring poor Felix out with us each day for filming.

This required a few extra pesos for the policeman accompanying him.

On holidays Olvera was not released to us.

According to an ancient custom, he was treated the same as other prisoners on those days he served at table in the house of the omnipotent local administrator, who was the magnate in this tiny region.

Via the *hacendado*, this *deputadomade* it dear to us in all seriousness that, if it became necessary ('and the papers all talk of the realism of your films, my senors') for anyone to be shot, a couple of prisoners could be provided for that purpose—from the same prison where our friend Olvera later ended up!

The oddest thing was that we could have taken these criminals and coolly bumped them off and this would never have been of the least concern to anyone.

And this brings us back to the story of General Amaro. Filming the festival of flowers on the canals between the floating gardens of Xochimilco (there is now some worry that these gardens are beginning to sink), we dressed, in especially valuable headwear and lace mantillas and coats, a certain dazzling, dark eyed, voluptuously beautiful senorita of not too strict morals.

She was not just any senorita.

She was the one whose name was linked, in a legendary (or perhaps not?) piece of gossip, with General Amaro.

For quite some time she had been Marquise de Pompadour and Madame Dubarry for the all-powerful general.

She then had a secret affair.

The general learnt of this.

But he did not let on.

One fine day in an outburst of simulated expansiveness the general presented his favourite with a newly-built country villa set in luxuriant grounds.

Our heroine moved in.

Life went on as before.

The same infidelities.

The same boredom when they—General Amaro and her unlawful lover—were both occupied of an evening.

Then—a walk in the park.

Aimless walks around the house.

And later—as in *Bluebeard*—a little door.[29]

Of course, there was nothing stopping her from looking within.

It was as though her even discovering the door had not been foreseen, never mind her actually going inside.

The door was shut.

Doors do not remain closed for long.

And the senorita froze in horror: deep in the cellars of her own house, her eyes took in a perfectly equipped . . . operating theatre Gleaming tiles.

A shining tray of surgical instruments.

Chloroform and rubber gloves at the ready. White aprons were near by . . .

What happened next eludes me.

I vaguely remember that the girl fled in panic.

This happened, albeit coincidentally, with perfect timing.

For the general had given the order that boto the girl's arms—left and right—were to be amputated at the shoulder that very night! Every possible precaution was to be taken; the very latest surgical techniques were to be employed; absolutely no pain was to be inflicted.

I could not testify to the truth of this story but, given the general conditions in that wonderful country, the details of poor Felix's fate and the *deputado* who so kindly offered me some 'real' prisoners to shoot, the story has a high degree of credibility . . .

(Interestingly, even the episode with the ants later appeared in *Viva Villa!* when Villa spread honey over Joseph Schildkraut's[30] face—the latter was playing a typically swinish officer from a semi-aristocratic clique in the Mexican military.)

We set out on the deep roadstead off the 'cover town' of San Francisco, on our way towards the real heart of Mexico, away from Ethel King's operating table.

There was a third cover to join those of Ethel King and Nick Carter.

This was one I had at home.

I kept it between the pages of *The Boy's Dum Paper Annual*. And the unhappy butcher's assistant was portrayed here a third way: no longer hanging by his legs, nor chained to the wall by an iron collar, but stretched out on his back by some exotic savages among terrifying carved wood'en fetishes.

The background consisted of impressions of Chinese executions from Wells's *War of the Worlds*, published at that time in *Mir priklyuchenii* [The World of Adventures], a free supplement in *Priroda i lyudi* [Nature and People] magazine which in those years was taken by families whose young sons were thirsty for Alexandre Dumas.

And perhaps also details of Damiens'[31] execution—he had tried to assassinate one of the Louis—reproduced from old engravings in a large book about crime and punishment.

I unearthed this work from one of Papa's bookcases, behind the stylish editions of Gorbunov, Krylov's *Fables* and *Evenings on a Farm near Dikanka*.[32]

This work, together with Dayot's edition of *The History of the Commune*, became one of the most interesting and intriguing.[33]

The retribution Damiens suffered was shown in full detail.

The special system of straps and chains which bound him permanently to a bed.

And the details of how four horses proved insufficient to tear him into four.

And how his sinews were pounded so that the horses could carry out their task.

And the sulphur and tin being poured into his wounds, etc., etc.

But the strongest impression was the white figure stretched between the exotic idols—a young Englishman, the son of a colonist.

Gradually, visual images failed to soothe these piquant impressions which floated before my consciousness.

The piquancy of the impressions began forcing me to recreate these scenes.

Comrades or partners were not to be drawn into this matter.

So the division between object and subject was erased. There was no precise 'allocation' of roles.

And, since I was interested in the sensation of pain, I was obliged to inflict it upon myself.

And, since I was, on the other hand, interested in the sensation of causing pain, I could find no other subject than myself.

Anyway, I remember (not in the most illustrious and iridescent period of my childhood) lying stretched out on the floor with my feet stuck into the fireplace (it was not, it must be said, alight) a mixture of the young Englishman and Callot's engraving showing, '*chauffeurs*'* of the sixteenth century who burnt the heels of their victims to extort money. (I was not yet aware of Callot as Callot and I only knew of his work by chance.)

I never recreated the Hindu's bed of nails, probably because I never had enough nails. I was mad about the 'Nuremberg Maiden'.[34] But I was limited in practice by the fact that two or three logs were put beneath one's spine. Three-sided logs, with the apex uppermost. This was done for a purely realistic purpose, giving an otherwise purely decorative situation a certain amount of real pain.

* The French in this case indicates people who heated things rather than driving them.

Later another application of these three-sided logs attracted me: it was from trunks hewn exactly like those that they used to make the dolls at Troitse-Sergiev Posad (Zagorsk, as it is now called).[35] The 'Hussar', the 'Lady', the 'Nurse', adhering strictly to the costume and everyday style of the 1820s, also observed the rule whereby a figure's profile should end in a thin wedge—the same wedge that lay in later generations beneath the 'young Englishman's' spine.

I remember at other times hanging myself 'à la Nick Carter', on hooks after I had carefully removed the swing which usually hung in the doorway between the dining room and nursery.

And sometimes of course I hung . . . upside down, tied to the nickel-plated knob of the family bed which had passed into my hands and been put in my room!

Funnily enough, my first erotic dream came from a Nick Carter–inspired fantasy.

It was a strange being, whose execution I felt very vividly as someone held its pigtail.

I remember the silhouette of the spine, shoulders and head, as it lay half-turned towards me with its pigtail held high up.

There had been some Chinese performers in the circus at that time; they flew under the big top held by their pigtails and worked as 'catchers' for other members of the troupe.

These flights of course were much more impressive than those on the trapeze and the figure, spreadeagled like a cross of dark blue silk in mid-air and flying round under his almost invisible, black pigtail in the spot light, was a spectacle that held me spellbound.

And I was also at that time fixed on a couplet by Wun-Chi from his *The Geisha*, which also mentioned pigtails:

Chin-Chin
Chinamann
Ist ein a'rmer Tropf.
Jed-jed

Jedermann
*Zupft ihn gem am Zopf!**

But my dreams at night-involving a Chinaman, his pigtail and cruelty—probably came from fragments of the covers of such books as *The Dragons of San Francisco*, where the pigtails on the scalps of enigmatic oriental assassins were wound upwards like rattlesnakes, erect from the end of their bodies!

Any exercises in that genre, no matter of what hue, are usually rapidly developed and broadened from the moment when a child starts school.

Typically, schoolfriends are united by common interests; these shared interests and tastes bring them together and forge the bonds of friendship. This was not so in my case.

From that point of view, school was a hollow, unrewarding place.

That was because I was a horribly exemplary little boy. I studied diligently.

I did not permit myself 'democratic' friendships.

What was more, in that school there was a blatant national ist hatred among the different sections of the population to which the pupils' parents belonged.

I belonged to the 'Colonists'; the Russian civil-servant class, detested equally by the native Latvian population and by the descendants of the first German colonists who had enslaved them.[36]

It should be remembered that Riga had been the residence of Bishop Albert and had been surrounded by knights of the Livonian and Teutonic Orders, whose 'shades from the past' I have been doing battle with on the screen for a good ten years![37]

I did not form a single true friendship in those school rooms.

* Chin-Chin / Chinaman / Is a wretched mug / Sim-simply / Anyone / Can give his tail a tug!

Although, if I try very hard, I can discern a certain 'supposed' friendship, but it was very short-lived: a sentimental disposition towards a schoolmate who was younger and more delicate than I; and to one other—a stronger, older boy who was the best gymnast and a desperate hooligan.

The former was brother to a vast number of sisters, all—like their father—of the same height as he, and who went about in woolly, dark green capes fastened by small chain-like buckles.

His mind was of an abstract, theoretical cast; his complexion was very pallid.

He was an excellent student, particularly in complex branches of mathematics and in such intricate historical problems as, for example, the derivation of the names of the Dnieper's rapids.

The latter was a muscular, dark-haired athlete. A homeless 'guest' who lodged with two or three others on full board with a French master who taught the younger classes, the ginger-haired Mr Gortchen; he was distinguished by his ginger moustache and a faulty pronunciation of the letter y. (He pronounced the French y like the French u. I still remember how the title of a typical lesson from the French textbook would grate on my nerves: 'Le Cygne et la cigogne' [The Swan and the Stork] became 'Le Cugne et la Cugogne'.

He was called Reichert and was a great gymnast.

I not only had no aptitude for this skill; I had a strongly expressed aversion.

I remember, again in my very early childhood, even in my pre-school years, shouting for hours before being compelled (great pressure was brought to bear) to go to gym classes at the Riga *Tumhalle*.*

A bald, bespectacled German-Herr Engels, lame in one leg—practised with us there and later in the *Realschuk* (the gymnasium and the school building shared a yard).

* German: 'grammar school'.

My one clear memory of Herr Engels is that it was he who taught me my first two German palindromes, when I was interested in word play.

I can vividly recall the term Relief Pfeiler, and the phrase:

*Ein Neger mit Gazelle zagt im Regen nie**

Sergei Sergeyevich Prokofiev was very fond of such word play; it is to his staggering memory for such things that I am indebted for a whole range of French examples.

As far as music is concerned, I heard a similar palindrome in a work by Meisel, who wrote the faultless score for *Potemkin* and an entirely appropriate one for *October*.[38]

When he was writing it—and to do so he attended the editing sessions in Moscow—the central heating in the screening-room was being repaired; there was an incredibly loud knocking throughout the building at No. 7 Maly Gnezdikovsky.[39]

I later derided Edmund for writing into the score not only visual effects but also the plumbers' hammering.

The score fully justified my complaints!

And there was the trick with the 'palindromic' music.

The point is that the film begins with frames which half symbolize the overthrow of the autocracy, depicted by the toppling of the memorial to Alexander III next to the Church of Christ the Saviour.

Both church and statue have long since vanished, but for many years the eagles from the throne's plinth lay scattered about the park in front of the Pushkin Museum.

So, in 1927, a *papier mâché* model of the statue was made; it was very funny watching it fall over and disintegrate.

---

* A palindrome in German which translates literally as: 'A Negro with a gazelle never hesitates in the rain.' An English equivalent would be: 'Able was I ere I saw Elba.'

This 'collapse' of the statue was shot 'in reverse' at the same time. The throne, with its armless and legless torso flew up on to its pedestal. Legs and arms, sceptre and orb flew up to join themselves on. Looking dully ahead, the figure of Alexander III sat inviolate on the throne once more.

This was shot for the scene of Kornilov's Petrograd offensive in the autumn of 1917 and these frames showed what all the reactionaries, who associated the general's possible success with the restoration of the monarchy, dreamt about.

The scene went into the film in that form too.

And for that scene Edmund Meisel recorded the music in reverse, the same music that had been played 'normally' at the start.

Visually the scene was a great success. Filming in reverse is lways very diverting and I remember how the first old comic films made good use of this device.

Perhaps I recognized my first, early childhood impressions in this disrespectful treatment of the tsar!

But I do not suppose anyone noticed this musical trick. Relations between Meisel and myself later soured.

Not of course because of that; nor even because he messed up a public screening of *Potemkin* in London in the autumn of '29, when he ran the speed of the projector to suit the music, without my consent, slightly more slowly than it should have been!

This destroyed the dynamism of the rhythmic correlation to such an extent that people laughed at the 'flying lions' for the first time in the film's existence.

The time allowed for the three, different lions to merge into one was crucial: if it took any longer than that, the artifice would be spotted.

The reason for the split was his wife, Frau Elisabeth. She was unable to hide—indeed, in an inexplicable outburst, confessed to her husband—a certain liaison that had existed between her and the director of the film for which he had written the music.

In all other respects, my lame gym teacher ended badly.

I must confess that to my great satisfaction he ended up no more and no less than a quartermaster in the German army and, apart from teaching gym, he had a whole series of secondary commitments in Riga to do with the information service.

At the outbreak of the First World War, Herr Engels was removed from the gym and so on.

There were all the prerequisites for a genuine friendship with Reichert in my dealings with him, if one could go only by the number of times he and I fought so very furiously.

However, it was not easy for friendship to develop since our time together was confined to school hours, talking on the way home, and in doorways.

I was not allowed to invite a 'nasty boy' home, still less take part in the escapades of a group of boys where he was one of the live wires.

These diversions were of the very sort which I was particularly keen on and which he often invited me to join in, on Sunday mornings in spring.

The kids would divide into two gangs, and play at warring bandits each Sunday, going into the countryside as a matter of course; there was a beautiful spot on the shore of Lake Stint, among the luxuriant pine forests of what then was called Kaiserwald.

Sometimes I even went there for picnics with Fraulein and my friends from 'good families'—decorously, sedately, with pies and sandwiches.

This place is now called Meza Park; it is there you will find the most prosperous suburbs of Riga.[40]

The game of bandits consisted of the members of one gang taking those of the other prisoner and 'hanging' them mercilessly.

They were not of course hanged by the neck, but were tied to tree-trunks by ropes passed under their arms.

That was the high point of this game of chase and pursuit, fighting and escaping into clumps of bushes on the lake shore, between the uniform trunks of pines.

You can imagine how I would have loved to play at games like these!

You can imagine that even the merest hint at my playing at such games was *ausgeschlossen** by the strict family regime we had.

It is highly questionable whether this is the best way to bring children up.

Instead of giving instincts free rein and the individual the chance to let off steam, a complex of all sorts of impressions was retained instead of being jettisoned through play or adventure, or being sublimated, without leaving any trace. In the best cases, fleeting memories or impressions—and not only these—settled, or lodged like splinters, or interwove with others. As many years passed they changed their form; they emerged, reworked, in the unexpected shapes, deviations and stylistic peculiarities of an individual outline and genre which led my American hosts to offer, as the first subject for me to tackle in California . . . a biography of those Jesuit missionaries who had died agonizing deaths at the hands of Red Indians. And this in turn led to the fascistic descendants of the old Ku Klux Klan and the precursors of the Silver Shirts, crying out, in Major Pease's phraseology, for the expulsion of this 'sadist' and 'red dog' Eisenstein from the United States. His presence in America was 'more dangerous even than a massed enemy landing'![41]

However . . .

Any delayed reaction that is not immediately discarded with a triumphant 'Ah!' or some similar spontaneity becomes the very thing

* German: 'ruled out'.

which accumulates, builds up and swirls around within us, just waiting for the right external trigger to precipitate a storm, torrent or hailstorm of images, collected by an organizing will into the purposeful invincibility of a consciously created work.

Was there once a glint of cruelty in my games with my friends outside school?

Of all the 'reconstructions' of Nick Carter covers, I can only very vaguely remember just one case.

It was in Bilderlingshof, on the Riga coast; or even further afield, in Bullen, where the parents of my friend, Baron Tusenhausen, had a dacha.[42]

Near the dacha was another, small house whose boilers and pipes gave it the appearance of a wash-house.

The Baron's son moved among its pipes and boilers, 'in my production', stripped to the waist and wearing a cap; I think he had been taken captive by some hard-hearted villain who was forcing him to print counterfeit banknotes.

But the game came to nothing since, once an outline had been created that followed relatively closely one of the above-mentioned lilac covers, I was quite satisfied with the look of the scene itself. I had never gone into the plot, a scene from which was illustrated on the cover, in any depth—indeed I had not read it at all!

This touches on a feature which is, generally speaking, quite a common one of mine.

I form very sharp pictures of what I am reading or thinking about.

This is where a very big store of visual images is created; an acutely visual memory with a lot of 'day dreaming'* training: I transpose my thoughts or memories into film form and run them past my eyes.

* In English in the original.

Even now, as I write, my hand essentially is virtually taking in the outline of the pictures that pass before my eyes in a continuous spool of visual images and events.

These acutely visual images cry out intensely and painfully to be expressed on the page.

Once, I was the only means: the object and subject of such reproductions!

Now I have a good 3,000 man-units assisting me in this; I can raise bridges in the city, deploy squadrons at sea, stampede herds of animals and set things on fire.

But a certain hint of 'generality' remains: very often it is quite enough for me to recreate the general visual image that alarms me—albeit not in every detail—for me to rest, contented.

But this often acts as a 'barrier' too against the other elements of expression, which tannot travel the same intensive path of creativity as the visual side of my opera. Music—particularly Prokofiev's or Wagner's—also counts as 'visual' in this taxonomy (or would it be more accurate to term it 'sensual'?).

There is a reason for the quantity of paper, ink and inspiration I expend on film, searching for a formula to express the relationship between sound and vision![43]

And from another point of view there was a reason. for my total dedication to questions of 'sensual' thought and the sensual bases of form. The sharpest focus of my attention rarely alights on the word 'subtext'. It is obvious and axiomatic that the intensity of my interests in different elements of composition and construction fluctuates.

But I prefer such a 'disequilibrium' to a classically strict equilibrium of elements. The beauty of one area's excessive prominence compensates for flaws and shortcomings elsewhere.

But this does not mean that the 'primacy' of audiovisual elements in my works shows a bias towards form at the expense of content, as any idiot might think at this point.

The audiovisual image is the extreme border of self-disclosure around the fundamental motivating theme and the ideas of the work.

This corresponds to the classics, where none of the connecting links is ignored: in Gogol for example, the subject extends to the actual verbal fabric of the work; or to the metaphorical system of Shakespeare's texts, as any Shakespeare scholar knows.

Here I remember one more summer when, in the decorous setting of Frau Koppitz's guest-house in Edinburg, where I met Maxim Strauch,[44] I tried to 'bring to life' yet another colourless recreation of my schoolfriends' games: this time it was their game of robbers in the Kaiserwald, where I was not allowed to go.

The external trigger was an uncontrolled 'feudal' war with the neighbouring pension, where another crowd of boys was staying; they were led by a sickly but desperate lout with big ears and the auspicious nickname 'The Jumping Jug'.

In fact it was just before this, in the winter, that I saw a turn at the circus which my memory retained in every detail.

I have liked clowns since my nursery days.

I have always been a little shy about this.

Papa also loved the circus, but he went to see the 'highest class of horsemanship', and William Truzzi's 'group of dressage horses'.

I assiduously hid my fascination for clowns and pretended to be madly captivated by the horses!

In 1922 I repaid my debt to myself with interest, 'flooding' my first, independent show, *Wise Man*, with red and white clowns.

Mother Glumova was a red clown.

Glumov was a white clown.

Krutitsky was a white clown.

Mamayev was a white clown.

All the servants were red clowns.

Turusina also red, and so on.

(Mashenka, the strong-woman act, used a powerfully-built girl who was a relative from Riga—Vera Muzykant.[45]

Kurchayev—a 'trio' of hussars in pink tricots and 'lion tamer's' dress coats.

Gorodulin, who was played by Pyriev,[46] took three red clowns!)

So there was one 'imported' clown (most turns at that time were brought in from abroad) who worked as the 'fifth' in a troupe on the horizontal bars and did a very funny trick.

He threw a loop over one bar. Then he let it drop to the ground.

He put it over his head so the back of his neck rested against the rope.

Three clowns: Gorodulin, the fascist (Ivan Pyriev), Joffre, the warmongering general (Alexander Antonov), and Mamayev, the white émigré (Maxim Strauch) in Eisenstein's play *Enough Simplicity for Every Wise Man*. The First Workers' Theatre, Proletkult, 1923.

Then, with his shoulders resting on the sand, he raised his legs, slightly bending them at the knees (close to the so-called 'grouping' position in acrobatics). Then he took hold of the free end of the rope with both hands and lifted himself, hand over hand, into the air.

When he reached the bar he stretched out to grab hold of it which meant letting go of the free end of the rope, so . . . he plummeted like a stone, landing on his back in the sand.

I found the 'technique' of his elevation fascinating; the descent less so.

Later, I simplified the 'technique'. I sat in the loop and, moving my hands up the free end of the rope, I reached the branches of the tree which I had thrown the loop over.

I also remember the way the game was played, vaguely.

Playing bandits, Riga 1910.

There was an 'execution' in it. This entailed lifting the 'condemned' into the tree in the sitting position, but it is not worth dwelling on the details of all this. I think the whole idea came from Justifying' one's 'ascent' into a tree—it was the first attempt at an external 'projection' of the situation. I can only recall that one governess, after watching our game for some time, shook her head reprovingly, saying:

'That really is a very savage game, children.'

Gradually, moving into work in art, I began to notice that it had one great advantage over other types of 'play'.

Art gave me the chance of giving a much fuller and more logical version of my tormenting dreams.

Part of them was projected externally, independently, as a simple, 'purely artistic' need.

Another part was 'camouflaged' by allegory.

And a third part was physically and spontaneously 'hurled out',

The *Lustbetontheit** of a great many details goes back to my very earliest experiments in direction.

I learnt about the mechanisms of 'sublimation' at some depth from books; but for some reason I hardly applied them to my introspections.

What precipitated that was a shudderingly distasteful impression from the first picture by Abram Matveyevich Room, *Chasing the Moonshine*.[47]

It was a nauseating scene: some ragged workers were devouring tomatoes like pigs, covering themselves and each other with juice.

This is of course one of the least appetizing approaches by which one may return to the childish state.

Children make awful messes of themselves when they eat, but at that level of development it only serves to endear . . .

* German: 'tinge of lust'.

The series 'Our Gang'[48] showed countless close-ups of black women stuffing their faces with watermelons!

Once this behaviour is removed from its appropriate context and transposed into an adult setting, the effect is revolting.

One of its commonest manifestations, beloved of so many amateurs, is of course the custard pies which the heroes (and other actors) of classical American slapstick* (of the older generation— Ben Turpin, early Chaplin, 'Fatty' Arbuckle, etc.) threw in one another's faces.

Here, speed is everything and the parallel 'leading' impression' is a fight, or some comic situation, etc.

In Cambridge, I was introduced to Peter Leonidovich Kapitsa.[49]

He was then a member of Trinity and wore a black gown.

He showed me his laboratory, of which I understood nothing of course except for two things.

First, that there was an electric generator capable of lighting up something like half of London, and that all that energy was directed at an area no more than a few millimetres across.

This machine had something to do with the early attempt at splitting particles of matter, I think.

But the machine and matter are not important here.

What is relevant is one idea of the nature of time which Kapitsa explained to me.

About the shortness of time, as it happens—which minimizes the effects of unbelievably high temperatures which inevitably accompany such a colossal efflux of energy.

The effect of this energy was contained in so brief a moment that only its 'fundamental' effect could be realized—the effect that interested the scientist as he experimented; and any byproducts, such

* In English in the original.

as for example a massive temperature increase, did not have any time to take effect.

I may not have described it with complete accuracy, but I grasped the actual principle precisely in that way: neither the researcher's solemnity as I sat at high table* with the professors and the Master, beneath the high Gothic vaulting of the naves which vanished into the gloom, nor the antiphonic prayers, sung in Latin by two voices before the food was served, nor all the other marvels and charming details of my three days in a Cambridge college could erase it from my memory.

I think that 'timing'* (which comics in American cinema consider the highest virtue in their art) is applicable even here.

This antiphony, the general setting and atmosphere of the whole scene remained so powerful that after many years it could still 'surface', first on the screen of my memories and then in the screen images of *Ivan the Terrible*: in the antiphonic reading of the psalter and the report of the boyars' treachery with the overlying voices of Pimen and Malyuta in the scene with Ivan and Anastasia's coffin.

Switching the structure of the childhood experience on and off, via associations linked with the 'oral zone', happens so quickly that there is no time for 'staleness', 'stagnating' in a mire of psychological detail; the viewer's perception is not allowed *zu schwelgen*†—which is how the Germans neatly define a complex of all manner of emotional sensations, in which every pleasurable physiological taste may manifest itself.

It is naturally important to strike a 'balance' and such a dramatic description is only appropriate of course in cases where the artist is completely enslaved by the unique 'behind-the-scenes' motif.

---

* In English in the original.
† German: 'to wallow'

The other extreme—the complete absence, ignoring or 'repression' of any 'behind-the-scenes' motifs-condemns any scene, episode or detail to sterility. The artist will go fatally off the boil.

The only essential is to keep it simmering; if it goes over, you will be bound to scald yourself.

On the other hand, keep it as hot as you can.

As we saw, this element must not be at all limited by images from the narrowly sensual range—that is, tinted by eroticism or infantilism—no matter how much they have been watered down.

If the artist's interlocking with that impression is shown too strongly, that impression will endeavour to 'throw itself into' what the artist is doing, and will prevail, whatever it is.

Which results in the artist falling into an inorganic stylization; that is, forcibly stretching the material so that it fits another 'true' motif.

I have met with a whole series of such failures in my life. Situations from the Bible are fundamental. In the minds of impressionable young boys forced to study the Old Testament in their childhood, they remain very distinct images.

The rhetorical manner of Rzheshevsky's writing and the situation surrounding *Bezhin Meadow* were bound to stir up legion similar images and impressions.[50]

They worked their way into the picture in such a thick stream, led, what is more, by the theme of 'father and son' which informs my entire opus, that they completely 'crushed' the objective theme: namely the struggle to establish the collective-farm system. They also buried the theme; subject and stylistics in a welter of purely subjective 'behind-the-scenes' subject matter.

Figures and situations were here 'ossified' in biblical stylization: Abraham, Isaac, Rustum and Sohrab all came together in one character on screen; and the long-legged adult who overturned the icon stand developed into an echo of the blind strong-man from Gaza.*

And the social value of the film was wholly lost in the alleyways of 'private' subject matter and the complex of the author's impressions.

Such a mishandling affected, if not the whole, then certainly at least one of the episodes of *October*.

This was the bestial slaughter of the young worker by ladies' umbrellas on the 3–5 July 1917. I have very vivid childhood impressions of the Paris Commune. A splendid album fell into my hands when I was going through Papa's library; I saw reproductions by the great Daumier, and photographs of the smashed columns at Place Vendome.

To this day I cannot understand what such a seditious work was doing in my father's collection; his devotion to 'Church, Tsar and Fatherland' was genuine.

But a fact is a fact.

I read up on the Paris Commune very early on (presented in the most impressive form—pictures, sharply underlined caricatures and portraits of the age). Moreover, it brought with it an early and quite detailed knowledge of the Great French Revolution.

I can remember very clearly wearing a cream suit with chevrons—patterns of silvery-white lace-and white shoes, standing near a fir tree radiant with candles and silver and gold tinsel—*Engelshaar*†—as those thin strips of gold and silver foil were called. They cascaded in spirals down the tree, crossing over the garlands of sparkling beads or rings of gold paper.

The foot of the tree was hammered home into a grooved piece of iron painted white, and decorated with cotton wool that had been covered with naphthalene (which regularly caused fires).

* That is, Samson.
† German: literally 'angel's hair'.

As the candles burnt down they dropped readily into the cotton wool and the dehydrated fir tree instantly became the 'burning bush'!

There were toys around the tree. It was apparently a Christmas tree.

Before going to 'see the tree' at the Wenzels' house—they had a monopoly of that evening since it coincided with the wife's, Yevgenia Modestovna's, birthday—I had been 'admitted into' the dining room, which was where the presents were.

There were some masks. And toy soldiers.

And a circus, comprising a clown, a chair and a donkey. It was called a 'Humpty-Dumpty circus',* distinguished by all the artistes having jointed limbs, so being able to adopt any attitude and combinations of movements.

The original set could be augmented annually: a ring-master, a trainer in tails, an elephant, lion, tiger and horses—all could be bought for it later.

There would also be sure to be one of Wolf's one-volume editions of Pushkin, Lermontov or Gogol.

I also had one of those each year, beginning, I think, with Pushkin.

I remember how many complications there were the next morning when I stumbled upon the poem 'On a Stormy Autumn Evening' when I could not think what 'the fruit of love corrupted', which the young woman was tenderly carrying in her arms, could be.

But no clown, mask, no cannon or swords could distract the curly-haired boy from two French volumes in their traditional yellow covers.

These were Mignet's *Histoire de La révolution française.*

* In English in the original.

One phrase, *le tocsin sonna** became for me the most irresistible call to revolt and was deeply etched upon my memory probably on that evening.

A few years later, romantic pictures of the history I had devoured came to the surface in a romanticized form. In 1913 *Priroda i lyudi* magazine started bringing its subscribers volumes of the complete works of Dumas; the historical scenes of Mignet were fantastically coloured by *Ange Pitou*, *The Queen's Necklace* and the full series of *Joseph Balsamo*.

Of the episodes on the Commune, I remember Louise Michel and the '*pétroleuses*' with special clarity and affection.[51] There were also the terrible events at the Versailles concentration camp† where women blinded the imprisoned Communards with their: umbrellas.

However, my interest in the Great French Revolution goes back even further.

At the age of eight (in 1907) I was taken to Paris (after the 1905 revolution it was too dangerous to go to the dacha).

I have only vague memories of Paris and those recollections are what you might expect of a child.

Dark wallpaper and the huge feather pillows in the du Helder Hotel on Rue du Helder!

Lift shafts, probably tbe first I had ever seen.

Napoleon's grave.

Red-trousered *pioupious*‡ in the barracks around it.

The bitter taste of hot mulled wine which spoilt my impressions of the Bois de Boulogne (I had dysentery and was given the drink for 'medicinal purposes').

---

* French: 'the alarm sounded'.

† E uses this term in Russian: *kontslager'*.

‡ French: 'infantryman' (usually a conscript).

The heavy grey dresses and white headwear of the waitresses at father's favourite restaurant.

Méliès's films, described elsewhere.

The Jardin des Plantes.

And the black pinafores with sleeves and hoods, which the little girls wore for playing hoopla, in the Tuileries Gardens.

The terrible anger I felt at not being told when we were inside Notre Dame—I raved about the gargoyles I had seen in photographs of this cathedral!

And, of course, above all else, more than anything and more powerful than anything, was the Musée Grévin.

My impressions of the Musée Grévin are even now as fresh as ever.

The triumphant carrying out of the Pope on his throne beneath the ostrich feather fans, the whole scene represented by scores of life-size wax figures which filled the central hall.

Sadayakko, sitting life-size among the Japanese fans and countless little tableaux set out on either side.[52]

In another scene Abd-el-Karim was surrendering to the French.[53]

There were dark passages in which a subterranean archway would suddenly appear out of the darkness on either side, giving a view of early Christians caught at their various activities in the catacombs.

Some were praying.

Over there, a baptism: you could see the silvery water, frozen in mid-air between the hand holding the cup and the new convert.

In the distance, a panoramic view of the circus.

And in the foreground, terrifying Roman soldiers manhandled some Christians who were huddling in a frightened group around the priest.

And here they lay lacerated beneath the lion's paw, near the iron grille.

We were met on the steps up by Demosthenes holding a lamp; Demosthenes fruitlessly searching for someone.

Higher up, we passed through a Napoleonic epic, set up as a reception at Malmaison.

There was even Josephine, the exotic Roustum, and Bonaparte himself, dazzling in his coat and stars, and glittering Parisian society.[54]

Standing by a pillar, near the cord which divided the splendour of Napoleon from the humdrum present, stood a grey-haired, moustachioed Frenchman who was tightly holding on to a small black dog.

He could not tear himself away from the spectacle.

We passed him once.

Twice.

The old man was gazing at Josephine's elegant gesture as she handed someone a golden tea cup.

He could not take his eyes off her.

But this old man was by no means a fanatic of the illustrious age of Napoleon. He was one of the wax figures meant to fool the visitors, scattered here and there around the tableaux and seated on benches.

My cousin Modest, claming he was 'just checking', tugged the plait of a living Frenchwoman . . .

But the section on the 'Terror' was the most impressive of all: it was somewhere above the early Christian 'catacombs', with the clear intention of providing a 'context' in which to view both the tableaux.

Bill Mauldin set up a more successful 'context' for the catacombs.

In one of his Jtlarvellous drawings devoted to the American *poilus** on the Italian front in the Second World War, he showed

* French: literally 'hairy men' but the nickname for the common soldier.

two soldiers in Rome, hopelessly seeking a hotel bed: all were filled with the officer and service corps.

A local stood near by.

'He says we kin git a room in th' Catacombs. They used to keep Christians in 'em.' (Bill Mauldin, *Up Front*, p. 164.)* [55]

In the 'Terror' section, there was even a small, unhappy Louis XVII standing by a drunken cobbler.

And Marie Antoinette in the Conciergerie.

And Louis XVI in a chamber being pursued by the patriots.

And in an earlier tableau 'the Austrian woman' (*l'Autrichienne* = *l'autre chienne*†—one of the first puns I really liked!) swooned as she looked out of the window to see a procession bearing aloft a pike with the head of the Princesse de Lamballe.

I moved on from the fates of individuals in the revolution, as seen in the Musée Grévin, to the life of the masses, as seen in Mignet. But at the same time, to something much greater: to the first notions of historical events conditioned by social injustice an lawlessness.

And the huge white wigs, the figure of Samson and the aristocrats' jackets, the picturesque '*tricoteuses*' or Théroigne de Méricourt,[56] the swish of the guillotine's triangular blade and even the visual impression of probably the first 'double exposure' which I also saw on the screen in time immemorial—Cagliostro showing Marie Antoinette's ascent to the guillotine in a carafe of water—for all the brightness of the impressions, nothing could displace the image of the hellish society of pre-revolutionary, eighteenth-century France.

One scene of the Paris Commune I cannot forget is the one where the ladies blinded the Communards imprisoned in the camp at Versailles.

* E's reference.

† French: 'the Austrian woman = the other bitch'.

The image of these umbrellas gave me no rest until I had included it, 'contrary to reason', in the scene where the young worker was killed, in the July Days of 1917.

In this way I delivered myself of a persistent image, but I overburdened my canvas, quite pointlessly, with a scene whose tone and essence was quite inappropriate for 1917!

Had I had more time for the editing, I would probably have cut that scene much more as it was rather a 'case history of the author's illness' than part of the history of events that make a great epoch!

However, I think that the actual umbrellas here were a 'secondary' image.

They tore the poor lad's shirt before executing him.

After the execution, the young man's perforated torso lay on the granite steps, half submerged in the Neva.

And the ladies wielding umbrellas were not such a far cry from Ethel King with her machine-gun, stooping over the 'martyrs' in exactly the same way, albeit with a different assignment ahead of her.

The paths along which the images converge are strange, unexpected and whimsical.

However . . .

The two halves of the boy's torn shirt lying on the granite steps near the sphinxes of the Egyptian Bridge (which was, in the Petrograd of 1917, opened) bring us back to the start of the article —to the young man who tore his shirt in shot 761 of *Potemkin*.

I tried to argue as convincingly as possible that this was not a mere detail but a *leitmotif*.

If we compare the momentary 'sublimated' appositeness of a few parts of *Potemkin* with the 'long drawn-out' episode in *October*, we find further confirmation of how one's *idées fixes* should, or should not, be treated.

What failed in *October* was of the same order as that episode in *Chasing the Moonshine*; and the explosive accent in *Potemkin* belongs to the ranks of 'purified' images.

'Brazenly' shown in their entirety, but at the same time framed by a brutal system of forms of expression and, further, inset into a piquant situation where they would act on the situation and not vice-versa! These images defined the very powerful and effective 'Peons' Golgotha'—the execution of the three dayworkers in the landlords episode in *Que Viva México*!

The system of plastic images, in which the idiosyncratic 'three bronze youths' played out the tragedy among fields of cruel maguey, was highly praised: references were made to El Greco and Zurbarán.[57]

But what pleased me more was that the stress was not on the similarity, the influence or my recreation of it, but the sense of 'kinship' with the tragic 'spirit' which informed the imagery and the scene.

But here is an example of a sizeable, if not an absolute, fiasco caused by these very images.

The production 'became tongue-tied'.

It did not say all it had to.

It did not say everything.

It failed to put the finishing touches to the system of living bodies for a similar scene in the first reel of *Ivan the Terrible*.

The siege of Kazan.

Kurbsky led the captured Tatars to the front of the palisade.

The half-naked prisoners were roped to posts and palings.

'Shout: "Kazan, surrender!"'

Kurbsky commanded them.

The Tatars were silent.

The iron gauntlet smote them.

The Tatars remained silent.

But two or three gave in.

Their piercing, piteous cry:

'Kazan, surrender!'

'Better you should die at our hands, than at the hands of the uncircumcised infidels!' The mullah cried from the walls of the city.

And a hail-storm of arrows hissed down on the prisoners, throwing them against the walls.

The rush of arrows brought Ivan running out.

He was wearing black armour and was seething with anger. There was a sun on his black armour.

And a moon on Kurbsky's silver armour.

(Who has seen this film and taken the hin t that Kurbsky's glory was only a reflection?)

'This is pointless cruelty—stupidity!' Ivan shouts.

And speaking barely intelligibly, he set out his view that cruelty was only admissible when expediency dictated.

Ivan Vasilievich actually did say that once.

But he did so in quite different circumstances, in a letter to the Emperor Rudolf relating to the St Bartholomew's Night Massacre,[58] which he thought was not expedient for so trifling a reason as religious differences . . .

(I think that Ivan saw deeper springs motivating this 'woeful event' and, keeping his own counsel, he disguised his disapproval of the event as 'religious tolerance' although in his own policies the great lord himself stuck to this very same principle whenever doing so might strengthen his multinational, extensive and mixed empire.)

The first part of the scene followed historical traditions.

I found it a very rewarding backdrop for the sharp clash of characters and 'intelligent cruelty' with 'senseless cruelty'.

Seen from the purely human angle, Kurbsky's accusations of Ivan's cruelty on the pages of his letters and history, are abhorrent hypocrisy.

Ivan's actions were born of brutal necessity at a brutal time, during the forging of the autocracy.

Prince Kurbsky's *Life in Volhynia* showed the true character of this 'merciful mercenary' whenever he was guaranteed impunity and absolved from responsibility.

Then Prince Andrei's life was crowned by the episode with the creditors, whom the prince ordered be buried in a pit with leeches. By the time the royal emissaries arrived, they could only obtain a thick gore from it.

This scene is even more rewarding from the purely visual point of view:

The clash between Ivan and prince Kurbsky at Kazan. Eisenstein's drawing for *Ivan the Terrible, Part One*. Alma-Ata, 17 March 1942.

HOW I LEARNT TO DRAW

(A CHAPTER ABOUT MY DANCING LESSONS) [1]

In the first place, I never learnt how to draw.

But this is how and why I draw.

Was there anyone in Moscow who had riot heard of Karl Ivanovich Kogan, the wizard and magician of stomatology and osteology?

Anyone who did not take their worn-out teeth to him? Anyone who did not strut about with excellent new jaws made by his hands?

Take Karl lvanovich.

Make him much thinner.

If this makes his nose too short, stretch it a bit.

Give him a pronounced stoop so that his Madam Situpon, as we said in Riga, sticks out.

Let him wear a railway engineer's frock-coat.

Let him have a wife on one arm—she had the highest hairdo in Riga.

You have just drawn Mrosimov, the greying railway engineer.

I am indebted to Afrosimov for instilling in me the compulsive need and inclination for drawing.

Like all society ladies, Mama was 'at home' on Thursdays.

That aside, Mama and Papa organized monster receptions on their birthdays.

Then all twelve leaves of the round dinner table would be pulled out.

It was as long as the dining room.

It groaned beneath the opulent dinner.

It now stands in my home in Potylikha, circular again, as it was on the day of Creation, in the room I call my library. It was in point of fact a library until my books, bursting their allotted banks, flooded every room and my entire flat was turned into a bookcase!

. . . Near the large table there would be a smaller one, for savouries.

We would have supper after cards and light piano music. The society was select.

The guest of honour would be the governor. His Excellency Zvegintsov.

He would preside on Mama's right.

With Papa at the opposite end of the table.

Sometimes, tables were moved into the dining room and set in a horseshoe.

I have forgotten where Papa sat on those occasions, but I do recall that by that time I sat at the table too, on the inside of the horseshoe and straight opposite Mother.

Before that time, I was only wheeled up to the table, nodding off, barely awake.

Even earlier, I would be put to bed before the guests began to arrive.

And I saw only the table, set for dinner, gleaming with silver and crystal.

The maid, Minna, and Ozols, Papa's messenger, would fuss about the table. Ozols wore full dress on such occasions.

First of all, I was only shown the table.

Then I would be regaled with treats from the savouries table.

I loved pickled mushroom. Fresh caviar. I was less keen on salmon. And I did not see the point of oysters.

After Mama and Papa were divorced such receptions ceased: 'The house had fallen.'

Furthermore, Papa's business affairs looked very uncertain. There was nothing to entertain with, either.

Mama had taken the furniture, which had been her dowry. I was quite unconcerned—even happy—about all of this. The unbearable domestic quarrels, which took place mostly at night, ceased.

And I had a whale of a time on my bicycle, racing up and down the empty dining room and drawing room.

There was even some sense of triumph.

Father, who was a fearsome man, was very strict with me.

I was simply not allowed into the drawing room, for instance and, since an arch led from there into the dining room, a cordon of chairs was put across the archway. I would crawl along those chairs, peeping into the promised land of the drawing-room.

Later I cycled boldly across this room which now resembled a *Niemandsland** after the couches, chairs, tables, lamps and mountains of *Nippsachen*† had been removed (chiefly porcelain from Copenhagen, whose milky-blue colouring, washed-out grey pattern and streamlined forms delighted lovers of elegance in those happy years).

. . . But the future desert now teemed with people.

The drawing-room was full. So were Mama's boudoir and Papa's study.

At any moment they would all surge into the dining room for dinner.

But for the time being they sat at the card tables.

I was at that age when I was allowed to meet the guests, but not to sit at table.

I walked among the guests memorizing them.

* German: 'no-man's land'.
† German: 'knick-knacks'.

There was the governor. A head showing good breeding, an aquiline gaze beneath thick eyebrows.

But in all other respects he was what we call a *Tischriese*—a giant at the table.

A giant only as far as the waist, if you begin from the top.

His legs did not match—they were too short.

Just like Lev Tolstoy.

Just like Karl Marx too.

Dollfuss, the late Austrian chancellor, was a mere dwarf.[2]

He was delightfully called Milli-Metternich, and word had it that they were issuing new stamps in Austria with a ... life-size portrait of the chancellor.

The governor's magnificent head was set magnificently, slightly askew, on magnificently broad shoulders.

Just as pelicans in Mexico hold their heads slightly askew when they dive out of the sky like an arrow for fish in the amber bay of Acapulco.

Actual Privy Councillor Zvegintsov's gaze is aquiline.

Coal-black eyes set beneath grey brows.

He should have soared above the fields of conflict.

At any rate, above the heads of his subordinates and those in his charge.

But this would not have been feasible, even if those in his charge and his subordinates were to bow down almost to the very ground.

As I said, the governor was very short.

I only remember the ladies who were young, for some reason.

The vice-governor's daughter Mademoiselle Bologovskaya. And that is probably because she Nadezhda [hope]—was always called by the French translation of her name—Esperance Bologovskaya.

With bicycle, Riga, 1911.

Eisenstein dancing with the ballerina Sara Mildred Strauss.
New York, 1932. (Photograph: Grigori Alexandrov)

This is like the Spanish, where such widespread names as Incarnacion, Felicidad or Soledad have retained their meaning.

When Dolores Ibarruri[3] celebrated her fiftieth birthday (in 1945) my greetings card made that point: I said, 'For your next fifty years, may you have a new name: not Dolores, but Victoria Gloria Felicidad.'

As well as Espérance—for some reason, I distinctly remember Mulya Wenzel all in blue, and her sister Tata, all in pink.

My friend Vadim's third sister, Zhuka Wenzel, was too young to be allowed to come.

How did it come about that of that whole galaxy, constellation, I remember only the Wenzels, dressed in the colours of lampshades?

This was not mere chance, it transpires.

In my memory, the sisters (according to all the rules of 'agglutination') have merged with the lampshades. There was no great difference between the lampshades and the ballgowns worn in those years.

The same puffs, frills and flounces.

Suddenly the Wenzel sisters are no longer the Wenzel sisters; they are the Amelang isters.

Two youngish sisters, in their Sunday best. It is virtually impossible to distinguish their dresses from lampshades.

But Papa's drawing-room, full of people, is no longer Papa's drawing-room but a quite different one.

It is empty. Only a dazzlingly polished and horribly empty expanse of parquet.

Convulsed with spasms of fear, I was about to have to dance a waltz across this empty parquet . . .

I was even younger.

And this was my first dancing class.

Little boys and girls, we sat on little chairs and stared at the terrifying parquet.

This huge drawing room was in the house of another rail way engineer: Daragan, the head of the Riga-Oryol Railway.

This is where we learnt how to dance.

The drawing-room carpets were rolled back and the palms moved up against the windows.

A few years later, the grey-haired Mr Daragan, looking like a saint or a monk in an icon, left Riga.

He was succeeded by the father of another childhood friend, Andrei Melentevich Markov: Melenti Fedoseyevich Markov, who had an official residence in Petersburg, in the building of the Nicholas station itself.

Andrei's father's face was terribly pitted and wrinkled; he wore his hair *en brosse*.

And oddly pale eyes were set against a dark complexion.

And in Andrei's rooms in the mezzanine, near the archway of the left-hand exit from the station, was a colossal electric model railway.

A toy locomotive ran on rails crossing bridges.

There were working signal posts and points.

A landscape of sand surrounded it.

And rivers made from blue paper lay under shiny pieces of glass to add to the effect.

At a certain age, Andrei and I would play here for hours on end.

He was fascinated by the train's workings and operations.

I was fascinated more by some ridiculous toy character—I always made him miss his train and run after it between the rails, and get mixed up between the points.

Not far off, real locomotives whistled and even, occasionally, you could hear the station bell.

The toy railway was synchronized with the noises of real trains and that made the game more life-like.

When we were older, during the war, that same Andrei tried, utterly hopelessly, to teach me cards. And he took me, as his guest (Melenti Fedoseyevich was dead by that time) into the firstclass waiting-room of the Nicholas station, and showed me what a prostitute looked like.

The cheapest 'priestesses of love' had made this waiting room (the station is now called October) their headquarters. They sat there in the buffet making one cup of tea last a whole evening.

Not all evening, come to think of it, but until a client arrived, at least . . .

This is not the case in Mexico.

The girl sits out, in front of a small booth on the street. Her pimp sits in a bar opposite.

The pimp drinks beer.

As many glasses as the girl has customers.

So he does not lose count, he makes a pile of the beer-mats. One beer mat for each glass.

In Petersburg the pimps stroll up and down on Ligovka.

However, I am still petrified, confronted by the parquet flooring in Daragan's house.

And I was particularly petrified because of these sisters—the Amelang ladies.

They were significantly older than me.

They were English.

I think they were twins.

And only differed in the colour of their dresses.

They partnered the older boys.

I had dreamy Nina and voluptuous Olga, the Daragan daughters.

Antrago, the high official. Drawing from a childhood notebook.

But I was in love—utterly, madly—with the unattainable Amelang sisters.

With both at once.

Since they were twins . . .

My dancing classes had no effect on me at all.

. . . However, we left Mama's guests when they were about to sit down to a game of cards.

We shall rejoin our guests.

Especially as Mr Mrosimov is seated at one of the tables.

Now Maria Vasilievna Verkhovskaya[4] sat at one table, her silk dress rustling. She had the best snub nose in Riga and her painted eyebrows were as thick as your finger.

I dashed across the drawing room.

Because Mr Mrosimov, using a finely sharpened white chalk wrapped in pale yellow paper with tiny stars upon the dark blue cloth of the card table as he waited for a game . . . was drawing for me!

He drew wild animals.

Dogs. Deer. Cats.

I remember particularly well what delighted me the most: a fat, bow-legged frog.

The white outline stood out against the dark blue cloth.

The 'technique' does not allow for, shading, or the illusion of solidity.

Only an outline.

But never mind that this was a line drawing.

Here, before the eyes of the delighted beholder, this outline took form and started moving.

As it moved, the unseen outline of the object traced a magical path, making it appear on the dark blue cloth.

The line was the track left by the movement.

Years later I still remember this acute sense of line as dynamic movement; a process; a path.

Many years later it made me record in my heart the wise saying of Wang Pi from the third century BC: 'What is a line? A line speaks of movement.'[5]

At the Institute of Civil Engineering I came to love Descartes' seemingly arid analytical geometry: it spoke of the movement of a line, expressed by the mysterious formula of an equation.

I devoted many years to my enthusiasm for *mise-en-scène*–to those lines of an actor's path 'through time'.

The dynamics of line and the dynamics of 'movement', rather than 'repose', remain my abiding passion, whether in lines or in a system of phenomena and their transition from one into the other.

This might explain my tendency towards, and sympathy for, disciplines that announce dynamics, movement and process as their underlying principles.

And on the other hand, I have always liked Disney and his heroes, from Mickey Mouse to Willie the Whale.

Because of their moving figures—again animals and again linear. The best examples had neither shading nor depth (similar to early Chinese and Japanese art) and were made up of outlines that really did move!

The moving lines of my childhood, outlining the shape and form of animals, animated the real lines of the cartoon drawing with real movement.

And perhaps, because of these same childhood impressions, my drawing on the blackboard with chalk in my lectures always gives me the same savour and enjoyment; the sketches fascinate and delight my students and in the process I try to instill in them a perception of line as movement, as dynamic process.

That is probably why it is precisely the purely linear drawing that is my favourite; that is the variety I use to the virtual exclusion of all others, or most of the time.

Dots of colour and shade (in sketches, designed to be shown on' screen) are scattered between them almost as a record of the intended effects.

In letters to his brother, Van Gogh recorded, on the preliminary sketches, the names of the pigments where he was going to use them.

But it was not Van Gogh who dominated my thinking at that time. Incidentally, surely it was the linear drawing of his brushstrokes and their clearly-defined outline on the canvas that first aroused my sympathies towards him?

At that point, I had not seen or heard of Van Gogh.

In those early days, it was Olaf Gulbransson's sharp, unadorned outline that had such a beneficial influence.[6]

And the mountains of graphic rubbish, dross like that arid PEM[7] in *Vechernyeye vremya* [Evening Times] and the album War and PEM which drew so much attention to itself during the First World War which were full of boring Wilhelms who captivated me for absolutely no reason.

In fact, at this time I began to find Moor's lubok prints fascinating.[8]

By now there is some sense of shading and outline, and very often a solid block of colour fills in the surfaces indicated by this outline.

In this period I did a great deal of drawing and that very badly, muddying the original, true source of the inspiration with a multitude of inferior images and a 'Wanderer'[9] fascination with subjects instead of an 'ascetic' quest for forms (which occupied me later, to the detriment of the former, during my 'artistic' period).

For some reason, I did not study drawing.

And when I had to draw plaster figures, teapots and Dante's mask it came out all wrong . . .

And it now turns out that recollections of my first dancing classes, even though they sneaked in here after the Amelang sisters, are much more relevant than they might appear.

Actually, not so much the classes themselves as my complete ineptitude for learning.

I still cannot manage a waltz, although I was able to pull off a foxtrot with great panache, albeit a jerky, black version in Harlem; and only recently my leaping about caused the heart attack that has laid me low these past months.[10]

So what is this all about?

Where's the link?

Drawing and dancing are branches of the same tree, of course; they are just two varieties of the same impulse.

Much later, after an initial break from drawing and a subsequent fresh start,[11] after the 'lost and newly-regained paradise' of drawing (which I experienced in Mexico), I was awarded my first (and last) press review far my skill in drawing.

I also have a one-off review of a performance . . . as an actor.

It makes me desperately proud.

Just think! It did not only say that 'the whole cast (myself included) grossly hammed it', but also that 'they all [and I was moreover the amateur producer] turned into circus clowns'!

This was at the end of 1919 and referred to the amateur show that was put on by the engineers, technicians, and accountants. from the army engineering corps, when we were stationed in Velikie Luki.

The notice appeared in Velikie Luki's local newspaper. The notice my drawings received came fifteen years later and in the *New York Times*.

And this is how it happened and why.

In Mexico, as I said, I began to draw again.

This time in the proper, linear way.

This was influenced less by Diego Rivera[12] who drew with a heavy, broken stroke, or my much-loved 'mathematical' line, which was suitable for the whole diversity of expression which it achieves by the mere variation of its continuous outlines.

In my early films I was also fascinated by the mathematically pure course of montage thought and less by the 'thick' stroke of the accentuated shot.

Fascination with the shot, strange (in fact, quite logical and natural—remember Engels' 'Attention is drawn first of all to *movement* and only afterwards to *what* is moving')[13] though it may be, came later.

'Before and after exams'. Drawing in a letter to his mother.

It was in Mexico that my drawing underwent an internal catharsis, striving for mathematical abstraction and purity of line.

The effect was considerably enhanced when this abstract, 'intellectualized' line was used for drawing especially sensual relationships between human figures, usually in especially complicated and random situations!

Bardeche and Brasillach believed that a particularly strongly expressed sensualism, coupled with an aptitude for the most removed abstraction, is the basic hallmark of my work; I find this both highly flattering and most apt (see *Histoire du Cinema*).[14]

The influence here, I repeat, is less Diego Rivera, although he too assimilated (in a way, and to an extent) this synthesis of all the varieties of Mexican primitivism: from Chichen-Itzá bas reliefs, via primitive toys and painted implements, to the incomparable pages of illustrations by José Guadelupe Posada for street songs.[15]

Here the influence was those primitives which I spent fourteen months greedily palpating with my hands, eyes and the soles of my feet.

And perhaps, even more, the actual, astonishing, linear structure of the stunning purity of the Mexican landscape; the square, white, peon's dress; the round outline of his straw hat; or the felt ones of the *dorados*.

Anyway, I drew a great deal in Mexico.

On my travels through New York, I met the proprietor of the Baker Gallery (Baker himself, I think).

He took quite an interest in the drawings and asked me if I would leave them with him.

Their subject matter was quite fantastical, such as the 'cycles' of Salome, drinking through a straw from the lips of John the Baptist's severed head.

In two colours—I used two crayons.

A 'suite' on the theme of the 'bullfight'. This subject merged with that of St Sebastian in widely varied combinations.

The martyrdom of first the matador, then the bull.

There was even a drawing of a . . . crucified bull, pierced with arrows like St Sebastian.

Do not blame me for any of this.

It was Mexico: in one element of the Resurrection festival they mix the blood of Christ from the morning mass in the cathedral, with the streams of bulls' blood in the afternoon *corrida* in the city's arena. The tickets for the bullfight are decorated with the likeness of the Madonna of Guadelupe, whose four hundredth anniversary is observed not only by the many thousands of pilgrims and scores of South American cardinals in their crimson robes, but even by the splendid *corridas*, 'to the glory of the Mother of God' (*'de La madre de Dios'*).

Anyway, the drawings aroused Mr Baker's (or was it Mr Brown's?) curiosity.

But when the ill-starred, emasculated version of my film, *Que Viva México*! came out in the cinemas, transformed by some one's grubby hands into the pitiful gibberish of *Thunder over México* the 'enterprising Yankees', as our evening paper would call them, exhibited these drawings in a small side-foyer of a theatre.

Which was how an article about my drawin.gs came to appear in a newspaper.

And one picture was actually sold.

And I received. . . . $15 in payment.

I strongly suspect that Mrs Isaacs[16] bought it, because later I saw a drawing from the 'bullfight' series in the *Theatre Arts Magazine* (before it dropped *Magazine* from the title).

If I ever find that unique, yellowed review of me as draughtsman among the heap of cinema praise that has been printed, I shall nail it to this spot.

But I remember the chief point it made, and that is what is relevant here.

It was the reference to the lightness of touch: the figures were put on to paper 'as if they were dancing'.

Drawing and dancing, which take their root from the same impulse, here converged.

And the line of my drawing was seen as the trace of a dance.

Here, I think, is also the key to the 'secret' of my double failure in drawing and dancing.

The plaster casts I drew for the entrance examination to the Institute of Civil Engineering, and in my first year there, were even more repugnant than the things I scribbled in the *Realschule*.

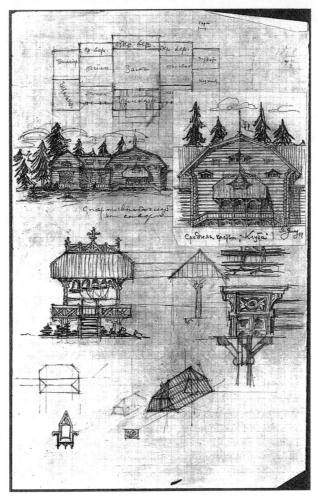

A sports club in the north. Eisenstein's student project.

I recall with a shudder that stuffed eagle which clawed at me for months at Herr Nie Hinder's drawing class like the eagle that attacked the bound Prometheus.

Incidentally, the theme of Prometheus and the eagle is one that always returns to my pen or pencil whenever I start filling a series of pages with drawings (for which hotel writing-paper is especially suitable).

(Somewhere I mentioned that it was a matter of principle for Maurice Dekobra to use hotel paper for writing his novels, preferably in Pullmans or other sleeping-cars).[17]

One day I shall have to analyse the 'thematic' course of my drawings .

But there are more holes here than cheese.

The most revealing and shamelessly frank drawings are torn into tiny shreds almost straight away, which is a pity: they were drawn almost automatically. But how obscene they were!!

Those stubborn, blunt, deathly plastercasts were not at all to my taste!

Perhaps that is because a finished drawing is supposed to have volume, shading, half-tones and reflected light, whereas there is a strict taboo on drawing a graphic skeleton, the line of ribs.

But even more because in drawing from plaster there is an unbreakable, iron law; like the strict set of *pas* in the dance in my childhood and youth—*pas de patineur,* with the arms folded across the chest; *pas d'Espagne,* where one is supposed to 'feel Spanish'. That was the cry of another dancing master at school: Mr Kaulins, a Lithuanian, with his small, dyed beard and moustache, and who wore a dress coat with padded shoulders and satin breeches with black stockings and shoes. Yes, yes, yes—imagine it!

1914. I remember the date well because it was from the windows of his dancing class that I saw my first patriotic torch-light procession, with cheering, shouting and a portrait of the tsar.

We also danced the Kikapu, Hiawatha (on the basis of *Hacke—Spitze—eins—zwei—drei!*)* and the inevitable Hungarian *csardás*.

Now I know for sure what inhibited me then—it was the dry, rigid formulae and canons both of movements in dance, and of drawing.

And I grasped this in 1921, when I began to learn the foxtrot with Valentin Parnakh, a frail man with a ready smile whom I had invited to our Moscow Proletkult studio to teach it to our actors.[18]

They were also taught the 'technique of comic narrative'; Vladimir Khenkin was moved to tears by my invitation to teach so 'academic' a course.[19]

Acrobatics—techniques of stage flight *y compris*†—was taken by Pyotr Kronidovich Rudenko,[20] who ran the incomparable 'Trio Georges'; when I was still a child he held me enthralled as he flew, in his golden yellow *tricot*, under the big top of the Salamonsky Circus on Pauluccistrasse in Riga.

Pauluccistrasse. Pauluccistrasse.

I would not say it was memorable.

I was born on Nicholas Street.

But . . . my parents spent their honeymoon in Papa's former bachelor flat.

On Pauluccistrasse, next to the Salamonsky Circus (or was it Truzzi? In Petersburg it was the Ciniselli. Where, then, was the Salamonsky?).

At my foxtrot lessons, I understood something very important: unlike the dances of my youth, with the strictly prescribed pattern and sequence of movements, this was a 'free dance', governed only by the regularity of rhythm, which could be used as a peg from which to hang any free, improvised movement.

* German: 'heel—toe—one—two—three'.
† French: 'included'.

A photograph Eisenstein presented to his mother, with the inscription on the back: 'To my kind, dear mother from her hairy son, in honour of the [the play] *Can You Hear Me, Moscow?* Moscow, 20 December 1923.'

That was more like it!

I discovered again the free run of a line which so enthralled me; a line, subordinate only to the internal law of rhythm, through the free run of the hand.

To hell with the stiff, fragile plaster—all that was good for was setting broken bones.

This was also the reason why I could not cope with tapdancing. I went over it, repeatedly and conscientiously—but hopelessly —under the guidance of the inimitable Leonid Leonidovich Obolensky—a man of great charm, then still a music-hall dancer, yet to direct the notorious film *Bricks,* and 'involved' with Anna Sten; and yet to become my unfailing assistant at my directing courses at the VGIK (he began at GTK in 1928).[21] He certainly never imagined he would . . . become a monk in Romania, which was where he landed up after escaping from a German concentration camp (he was caught when he tried to jump on to a lorry when our troops were retreating from Smolensk in 1941!).

Only my complete incompetence at penetrating the secret of tap-dancing stops me from reminiscing about how I knocked off a tap-dance as I queued up with the other red-blooded males awaiting admittance to Madame Bruno's bedroom, in a production of *The Magnanimous Cuckold.*

. . . Producers were very free in those years!

I even introduced into a production of *Wise Man* a detail worthy of Aristophanes or Rabelais—something even better than what you might find in an Atellan mime[22]—when I obliged Madame Mamayeva to mount the 'mast of death'—a tightrope which stuck out from under General Krutitsky's waist and stretched as far as the balcony of the ballroom of the Morozov villa on the Vozdvizhenka. That was where the mad plays of 'my' Moscow Proletkult theatre were performed.

Many years later—quite recently, in fact—that room was the scene of a banquet, given in joint honour of Priestley, who had just arrived; the anniversary of *The British Ally*; and the departure of the British military mission.[23]

Good grief! I sat at a table with these honoured guests on the very spot where once had stood our small, moveable platforms; my actors would perform before them, on around carpet sewn with a broad red stripe which was a sort of circus barrier.

And I am sitting on the very spot where the metal cable stretched up from a hook in the stalls, diagonally across the auditorium and finished in the wall of the balcony at the other end of the room.

With an orange parasol to help him balance and wearing a top hat and tails, Grisha Alexandrov ascended the cable in time to the music.

Without a safety net.

It happened once that the upper part of the cable was. smeared with engine oil.

(It had dripped from the small pulley which Mishka Eskin held on to as he followed him back down the cable. Mishka died, after he had left our company. He lost both his legs when on the road with the 'Blue Blouse' troupe, which was a terrible end for an acrobat—especially for so brilliant an acrobat and clown as Mishkal)[24] Grisha, sweating, was going all out and becoming winded. He was wearing thin buckskin shoes, which held the big toe apart for him to grip the cable, but nevertheless he kept sliding inexorably backwards.

Zyama Kitayev—our pianist—began the music from the beginning.

Grisha's feet were sliding.

He could not make it.

Finally, someone worked out what the matter was and held out a walking stick from the balcony.

This time Grisha landed safely on the balcony!

It seems like yesterday.

That only yesterday I was running through the cellars of the Morozov villa, through the blue-tiled kitchen, blocking my ears as I tried not to think about Verka Yanukova who was at that moment flying up the wire, or Sasha Antonov (Krutitsky) who was not entirely sober that evening.[25]

A deathly hush.

Everyone up above had frozen during this deadly trick. Then the roar of applause, which reached the kitchen, muffled.

That was for Verka—Verochka!—she had completed herturn, and had cried out 'Voilà!' in triumph.

But how long ago that really was!

. . . I tried finding the lighter patch on the parquet under the table: that was where the hook had been for the wire.

I realized just how long ago it was when the General with steely grey temples, the head of the departing British legation who was my neighbour, brought the conversation round to . . . how he educated his children.

'I brought my sons up,' (and one of them, a colossus wearing a funny British Army coat, was dancing nearby on the same parquet flooring where Parnakh once gave me lessons) 'to understand that when it's an uphill slog, he will be glad even of a dry crust of bread.'

Hell, was I really so old that I had to endure such talk, at the very spot moreover where I once taught—and utterly differently— a whole crowd of young enthusiasts who ascended wire cables that stretched up as far as the balcony from the very spot where we were sitting, not finding it an uphill slog, as that puritanical motto has it; there, they turned somersaults on the matting; they made love here at ,night when the carpets were tolled back, under the drying posters for the sets; for one of my plays they even led a . . . camel into this very room, bringing it all the way across Moscow from the zoo.

It carried Yudif Samoilovna Glizer, the honoured artist still doing great things, in one of her first roles—certainly her first grotesque role.[26]

. . . My attempt at eurhythmics was even worse than at tap-dancing.

At eurhythmics—I would call this idle pastime taught by out-moded adherents of Dalcroze's[27] flawed system 'metrics'—I simply and invariably 'came round', at both the entrance and final exams (happy memories!) in Meyerhold's director's studios on Novinsky Boulevard.

Just as well then that I was found to have other qualities which saved me from ending up in the gutter after each examination.

But who will believe this, after someone wrote in America (vis-à-vis *Potemkin*) that I opened the eyes of the world to rhythm in cinema (and rhythm really was and is one of the most powerful devices in my films)?

But who would believe, if he had not seen it for himself, that the miraculous master of rhythm Prokofiev hopelessly missed the beat when dancing (again, dances!) in the drawing room and mercilessly trampled on his partner's toes!

All this talking—or rather writing—has been leading to this: that there is deep within me a long-standing conflict between the free course of the *all'improviso*, flowing line of drawing or the free run of dance, subject only to the laws of the inner pulse of the organic rhythm of purpose (on one hand); and the restrictions and blind-spots of the canon and rigid formula (on the other).

Actually, it is not entirely appropriate or fair to mention formulae here.

The charm of a formula is that, while laying down a general rule, it allows, within the free current which filters through it, 'special' interpretations, special cases and coefficients.

And that is the charm of learning about the functions of theories of limits and differentials.

This touches upon one of the fundamental, pervasive themes, which is also the formula (when taken that way) running through almost all the basic stages of my theoretical searchings, where it always repeats this primordial pairing, and the conflict between its components.

Only the 'special' interpretations change, depending on the nature of the problem.

It may be an expressive movement or the principle of the form's structure.

And this is not a matter of chance.

For this conflict contains the all-pervasive conflict of relationships between opposites, on which everything that is old, like the world, moves and rests.

Such as the ancient Chinese symbols, the yin and the yang, which I so love.

My work progresses like that too.

By a whimsical, arbitrary flood in my pictures.

And with attempts at stemming this flood later, with the metronome's dry beat, 'to make it regular'.

But even here I am always on the look out for flexibility of method rather than an iron law; my favourite theme and field of research was and remains the initial 'protoplasmic' element in my works and productions, and the role it played in the structure and realization of the form of phenomena.

This flood overwhelms my theoretical writings, when I submit to it with myriad digressions from the key theme, and banishing it from my pages makes them dry as dust, like the plaster casts in the drawing class, or like the spasms of paralysis when I met the Amelang sisters at Daragan's or Kaulins' dancing lessons.

It was in order to stem this primeval flood that I began writing these reminiscences with the sole (perhaps, but certainly the chief) purpose of giving myself complete freedom to wallow in the twists and turns of all manner of associations which might crop up during these accounts!

But the corrections and editing of what should be sent to the printers lies nearby, shamefully, criminally and degradingly, like an inanimate plaster cast; all because I do not at all feel like 'tempering' what poured out in wild torrents on to my notebooks, bursting its banks as it did so!

I also derive pleasure from writing this because now I am released from the categories of time and space. I do not have to be consistent in the way I narrate events, nor in the way I order them.

I am also free from their synthesizing brother: strict logicality, which carries the principle of consistency over into the field of judgment and disciplined thought.

And again, what can be more diverting than sheer, brazen narcissism, for what are these pages if not an endless array of mirrors for me to see myself in and at any age I like, at that?

Perhaps that is why I have taken such pains always to give the date and place in this mockery of the logic of time, where the scene of action is changing constantly and there is no neat logic of direction or purpose!

Freed from all three at once!

What could be better?

Surely this is nothing short of heaven, a slice from that happiest stage of our life, even better than carefree childhood: that blessed time when, gently rocked in our sleep, we lay curled up, protected and safe' from aggression, in the warm womb of our mothers!

If only I posed more than I do.

If only I had thought of writing this work in the style of a detective novel.

This is how I would have begun.

It was a wet day in July 1946 in the resort village of Kratovo on the Kazan railway line.

I was sitting, reading a relatively new detective story about Len Wyatt's adventures as he battled against black marketeers and Nazi spies.

The twists and turns of the chase were not so gripping as to divert my attention from the stylistic niceties of such a book as this one by Nicholas Brady—although I doubt if the author himself would make any claims on this score.[2]

But writers of such books either naturally incorporate good examples of genuine 'slang'* or they improvise expressive turns of phrase and coin new words in this style.

Coining slang expressions and turns of phrase is a collective process, at once anonymous and popular, as all other forms of folklore were once anonymous, collective, popular and widespread.

Each individual witticism adds its anonymous weight to the common cause, but the expression that has the most resonance is the one that will continue to enjoy common currency in speech for a long time.

If an image (and expressions are always figurative) resonates with the deepest layers of one's perceptions (and this can only happen to an image when the idiom itself naturally and organically

* In English in the original.

derives its source from the same layers of its 'creator'), then image and idiom have every chance of remaining current and giving great pleasure to the usual audiences and those who take a keen interest in expressions of contemporary popular and poetic comage.

A broad cross-section of Soviet writers and literati—the intelligentsia—has long been of the opinion that it is good form to admire folklore.

I must confess that I always found this admiration somewhat bewildering.

A small number of zealots apart, it always seemed rather insincere, even a pose, not a genuine understanding. Rather a borrowed admiration with a 'lit-crit' variety of *comme il faut*.

Perhaps this is not entirely fair; maybe this is nothing more than a reflection of my own attitude to this 'fashion'.

I was never terribly keen on images from the *Kalevala*,[3] even though people tried to introduce me to it.

Even after Pushkin had reworked them, neither Bulgarian epics nor the 'Songs of the Western Slavs' ever attracted me.[4]

I must confess that this perplexed me.

Nevertheless it is doubtless from here that the people's soul and spirit take their roots.

Turning to these primary sources had proved fruitful and fertile on so many occasions throughout the history of the arts: like it or not, I had to ponder the question of why my soul remained stubbornly 'unmoved' by the unquantifiable abundance of images from folklore, which was held in such high regard everywhere and was indeed the subject of a great number of books published by Academia when admiration for these works of popular narrative had reached its apogee.

There were of course exceptions as well: *The Lay of Prince Igor*[5] is something I have cherished since my schooldays.

The Miracles of the Mother of God, a medieval folk tale, is a cycle containing some of my favourite stories.

I have loved the *Nibelung* since childhood, before Fritz Lang's films spoilt it for me.[6]

Wagner put things to rights later, but he could not restore my admiration for this Germanicized epic: I found a new admiration for the Nordic *Edda*, the ancient Yggdrasil[7] and the whole wonderful cosmogony in the 'characters' of the extreme Scandinavian North.

I admired more the nameless primitive peoples in Frazer's *The Golden Bough*; so, to a lesser extent, those of Veselovsky, for he turned them into his 'lesser brethren', making them smaller and less colourful than did Sir Joshua.[8]

And in fact, their folklore is like them: be it Bushman, Polynesian, Australian, North American or Mexican; barely noticeable, it is not accorded half the respect shown to more popular folklores that have images people drool over.

But it is these aspects that are much more fascinating; they convey vividly the sense of figurative thought as it is in the process of emerging. You can witness in them ideas that are still in their formative stages; and you can virtually assist in the dynamic of the formation of concepts, while the actual images of the works are sensed as a staging-post in the development of intellect and thought.

More popular—more popular precisely because they are!—more marketable patterns of folklore—even, for example, Dobrynya Nikitich in comparison with Svyatogor![9]—no longer seem a creative lava just boiling over. It is as though the lava has cooled; its intricate patterns have set into a solid mass, formed not forming, and therefore so readily appropriated wholesale as simple forms of inspiration.

And this takes us straight to that unrestrained excitement—fervid turmoil—as I yield to what I find fascinating, when it fascinates me genuinely, profoundly and actively.

It simply never occurred to me systematically to suppose that this was an offshoot of folklore, even though that was how it enthralled and fascinated me.

At a time when the average Soviet intellectual had been exploiting all his 'connections' to be able later to boast of having the complete set of the Academia volumes even though he would never utter one word of popular slang, I very quietly drew volume after volume into my network of books, each of which was full of Paris argot, London cockney and later American slang.

Although the academic interest in French argot forced the publication of a wide range of relevant dictionaries and research a very long time ago, it was much later that fully comprehensive books on slang (I do not mean the highly specialized works that went out of print a long time ago) began coming out (in copious supply, too).

Landmarks like Mencken's *The American Language,* in 1919; (the *Supplement,* in 1945); a *Dictionary of Slang and Unconventional English,* in 1937; and the almost exhaustive *Thesaurus of Slang* only in 1943.

But the first copies of my collection were on the shelves much earlier. *Dictionnaire de la langue veneis,* dated 1921.

And Aristide Bruant's dictionaries (*L'Argot . . . ,* 1901).[10]

But before I had access to specialized dictionaries and research papers, I had instead a solitary volume by Balzac.

Une Instruction criminelle[11] was part of the *The Splendors and Miseries of Courtesans* series, one of my favourite Balzac novels, including the Corantin and Vautrin cycles. (I suppose that *Cousin Bette* was the best of the others; I tried on several occasions to dramatize it for the stage. I even have somewhere a fairly detailed, overall plan laying out the dramatic and stage solutions.)

This 'Instruction' fell somehow into my hands ages ago and by itself, too. It was not among the other novels (I think it was even before the Revolution).

Then, later, like Isis gathering up the scattered limbs of Osiris,[12] I collected the other novels in the series to gain a full picture of Rubempre, Rastignac, Vautrin, Coralie and Esther.

Perhaps it is the subjett matter that makes this novel impressive; taken on its own, with no reference to what comes before or after, the pages devoted to prison slang stand out especially vividly.

Balzac of course delighted in this language for the same sense of living, dynamic emergence.

We should not forget his fascination with etymology (a vice I have long been guilty of!), nor that he wrote a charming passage on that very subject in *Louis Lamben*. He mentions the pleasure to be had from travelling backwards through the history of words, to the roots from which they were formed or evolved.

But it was not Balzac who introduced me to argot.

Nor *Les Mystères de Paris*, which I was lucky enough to acquire in Riga (before 1914) in an edition partly illustrated with 'woodcuts' of drawings by Daumier.

I remember the window of Kumpel's bookshop: it was on a small street. Inside was the book, opened at a page showing the young tramp and a hooligan, Tortillard, the associate of La Chouette and the Schoolteacher. These were some of the illustrations by one of Balzac's namesakes—also an Honoré!* It is more than likely that this alone led me to buy this charming masterpiece by Eugène Sue!

Chance does not even come into it, if you bear in mind that Balzac himself wrote *Splendors and Miseries* while he was influenced by Eugène Sue's work, which was then very popular.

Balzac envied his success and tried consciously to imitate him and the influence one had on the other is self-evident in this novel; incidentally, this is in its closing sections which, highbrow critics

---

* That is, Honoré Daumier (1808–79).

maintained, contribute least to Balzac's reputation as a classic. (*Tant pis** for his reputation!)

This wonderful 'display'† of colloquialisms and turns of phrase, vibrant with life, was taken from the fleshpots, prisons and alleyways of Paris—all those *tapis-franc, gouailleuses, chourineurs*‡—but that was not my first acquaintance with the colourful lowlifers of the French capital, nor their vivid manner of speech.

The first slang phrase I heard which struck a chord were the words: *Les cognes sont là.*

They were written on a note which was flung down in Victor Hugo's novel *Les Misérables. Cognes* are policemen.

This terse note serves a complex, dual purpose: it is first the image of what somebody (I have since forgotten who!) was able to write down.

And then it suddenly starts to function as the 'idea' of its content.

Flung at the right moment (by whom?) into an opening in the wall, it saves Jean Valjean from a very tricky situation: two villains were about to satisfy their curiosity with regard to his identity, aided by a heated iron bar . . .

I read *Les Misérables* with utter delight.

My mother sent it to me after she had left us, I think, as I was leaving the second class and entering the third.

The books broke through the exam fever and I managed a completely fantastic tour de force: during a month of revision I not only passed all my exams; I also devoured a vast, multivolume novel!

L'Abbé Myriel and his candelabras; the noble Javert who vanished at the point of his greatest triumph; the strong arm of the

---

* French: 'so much the worse'.
† In English in the original.
‡ French slang: 'low dives', 'drinking dens' and 'cut-throats', respectively.

escaped 'hard convict' who helped little Cosette carry the bucket of water; 'Monsieur Madeleine' who put his shoulder under the haycart that had toppled on to the old man, and lifted it off him; the wanderings through the labyrinthine Paris sewers—all these cut a swathe through arithmetic problems, history and geography textbooks, scripture and Russian during that memorable and, of course, in its way unique school revision period.

The first word that staggered me was '*la veuve*',* applied to the guillotine.

I am not sure I grasped the unparalleled precision and 'generality' of this periphrasis at first. It was so merciless a depiction of the perpetual hunger of a woman abandoned.

It would be hard to find a more vivid name for it: the space at the bottom, for the condemned man's head, was like a mouth always hungrily agape.

Perhaps I found this allegory delightful at first because of the more superficial interpretation: simply, widowhood.

But I doubt if that would have been for long.

And of course the most interesting thing is that it was subconscious, intuitive: a long time before the real sense of the image became clear.

I expect it was this that made me react so strongly, many years later, to Sadger's conception of a similar derivation for all linguistic formations that had their origins in erotic/symbolic images and to accept it unquestioningly for some time![13]

I found this in the work of Hanns Sachs and Rank, *The Meaning of Psychoanalysis in Science and Spirit.*

I think this book was the first I found that applied psychoanalysis to culture and art. Hitherto, my basic knowledge of psychoanalysis was derived from 'Leonardo da Vinci and a Memory of His

* French: literally 'the window'.

Childhood', and in its application, to the 'early erotic awakening of a child!'[14]

I actually met Hanns Sachs—that marvellous, bespectacled, wise old salamander and his terrifying African mask—a 'symbol of complexes' which hung above his small low patients' couch—in Berlin many years later. We became great friends. He gave me a most interesting book about psychoanalysis, *Versuch einer Genitaltheorie* [Essay in Genital Theory] by Ferenczi, which explained a great deal of things (admittedly *post factum*) which I had come across on my obsessive quest to penetrate the secrets of ecstasy.[15]

But Sachs and our meeting come in their own time . . .

The text of the note in *Les Miserables*—*les cognes sont la*—has a dual meaning, as I have said. It is purely an outline (proof that someone was able to write) and also it conveys a message.

Curiously, the very nucleus of 'argot' word creation is contained in that phrase, or more accurately, in that dual use and interpretation of it.

But, more than that, this is like a formula for what seems the undisputed 'backbone'* of any detective story. More than that again, it is the universal, real, invariable and sole plot of all detective fiction from any age, country or nationality.

Chesterton came close to one general single theme informing all manner of detective fiction.[16]

But he did not touch on it more precisely than with a 'winged phrase'. What was really invariable and eternal appeared to him in the inviolability of Catholic dogma which distracted him from examining systematically what he dropped on the way with the ease of paradox.

The solution to the material basis 'of the mystery story' eluded him.

* In English in the original.

Blinkered by the mysteries of his attraction solely to the Catholic Church, he could hardly examine this matter, either condescendingly or impartially.

Chesterton progressed from his detective Father Brown to non-detecting fathers—church pastors.

Father Knox (?) or O'Connor has left us with a description of Chesterton, on the threshold of the church where he was converted, which has a charming symbol and surprising internal sense.

When he was asked if he had a two-penny catechism (the cheapest edition, probably, as a symbol of meekness), Chesterton searched his pockets feverishly to see whether his customary absent-mindedness had got the better of him again.

And the first thing he took out and hastily shoved back into the depths of his pocket was also worth two pennies, but it was a detective story, not a catechism.

The detective novel is built entirely upon a double meaning.

And if all the varieties of peripeteias in the whole, worldwide epic of detective literature (and what makes this folklore less than universal in its sweep—what makes it inferior to the *Odyssey,* the *Divine Comedy,* or the Bible?!) are reduced. to their central core, this core is always and invariably a double reading of the evidence: a false one and the true one.

The former is superficial, the second penetrates to the essence.

Or, to use more specialist terminology, the first is spontaneous perception; the second, a mediated response.

Or, to go into the mechanics of both ideas, the first is a 'physiognomical' interpretation, perceived in images; and the second is an 'understood' interpretation revealed conceptually.

But this double interpretation applies not only to different methods.

It also represents different stages, different levels of perception and understanding of phenomena in general.

It is precisely those two stages through which developing mankind passes: every individual's assimilation of nature, through poetry, emotions and images, shifts towards a mastery of it by science, understanding and learning.

So that he can master nature and communicate with it at the highest summits of his relationship with the universe, through a synthesis of the link between science and poetics.

In this sense, any novel about a secret ('mystery')* is a work of mystery, treating of the eternal and immutable 'drama' of the emergence of an individual's consciousness; and everyone goes through that drama, irrespective of race, class or nation.

And this of course is the basic reality behind my constant fascination with detective fiction.

Its appeal to that most delicate of processes in the emergence of a personality is invariable, immediate and direct. The individual progressively moves from thinking in images and emotions to the maturity of consciousness; and the synthesis of both in the most sophisticated patterns found in the inner life of creative and artistic people!

And we can see a similar regularity of structure in world folklore and detective fiction as in works by individual, highly gifted artists (and sometimes artists of genius); a universal regularity, which permeates the principle of the whole or any detail to equal degree; and to take it further, the structure of language also (*vide* Shakespeare).[17]

'Argot' and 'slang' are not only for *couleur locale*, for establishing a framework within which the 1,001 variations of the universal, two-part theme will develop through a double interpretation of the evidence. Every last sequin of the literary apparel which clothes the theme and ideas—its verbal fabric—is coloured with them.

* In English in the original.

'Argot' and 'slang', like the highest manifestations of poetry, show abstract concept and idea again returning to the primary, sensual charm of an image spontaneously created and expressed.

And when we read the commonplace in what has now become an unusual exposition but which was once uniquely accessible and possible (in terms of method) we travel anew that same path, as we move towards perception and understanding, that we travelled as individuals and as the smallest parts of humanity as a whole; that same path, from thinking in terms of feelings, images and myths, to a really conscious understanding. Moreover, the actual slang image becomes alive and *irrésistible* when its word formation is derived from no less original mechanisms; and the structure of its imagery hints at the stages of emergence a human individual himself physically passes through, reflecting the stages of his transition in the early layers of the thought process, just as later, with the first shoots of social organization and, further, social systems, the individual starts to mould and form his own consciousness, basing it on a reflection of these social systems which now have peculiarities of structure and progressively developing social relations.

Which finally brings us back to that amazing quotation from the book by Nicholas Brady.

It would not be true to say that this quotation gave rise to all the ideas I have mentioned above.

They are very, very, very much older than that.

But the penetrating piquancy of the quotation seemed to resonate not merely in the depths of my brain or spinal cord, but deeper still—in the lymphatic vascular system which has preserved within us the stages corresponding to one-celled life forms and primary protoplasm.

Where in hell's name could a man have taken the image for this idiom from?

Len Wyatt, the detective, says: ' . . . I'm going to have a cold bath, and then start working. But before I make a start, I'm going to wrap myself round a warm breakfast. See you anon . . .'*

This is the very way in which a single-celled amoeba, a ball of living protoplasm, swallows any enemy it may meet, any edible object it may encounter, any breakfast coming its way!

When I come up against imagistic constructions of this kind I feel a jolt like an electric shock.

A responsive reaction is triggered deep within me—beyond the convolutions of the brain, somewhere in the tissue—by the very structures which are my contemporaries from the time when I was an individual on the evolutionary ladder, no more than a child; an embryo, a ball of albuminous protoplasm or a fertile drop, which is all that I once had been.

It is said that a sense of time is instilled beyond all conscious pathways and is connected to the most subtle, structural bases of our tissue—simultaneously the object and the subject of the phenomenon of time in an organic phenomenon of physical developrrient and growth—which only later, later, a great deal later, is able to divide the actual process up as it feels it. Then, on the basis not only of the subjective phenomenon, but also of that same phenomenon in the world around us, a sense of time gradually becomes an idea of the movement of a process, in order that, a great deal later, it may be abstracted into a concept of time separate from the process of movement!

I am often struck by such 'basic thrills'†: by the most unexpected images and scenes in the most unforeseen works and their unexpected peculiarities, but the ones which remain unequalled and unforgettable.

---

* p. 119, *Coupons for Death*, by Nicholas Brady, Robert Hale Ltd, London, 1944. [E's note in English in the original]

† In English in the original.

I remember two brilliantly lucid examples, from Jacques Deval's play *L'Age de Juliette*. (I saw it quite by chance, and it was utterly delightful.) (His *Mol'ba o zhizni* [Prayer about Life] was on in Moscow; the title was a Russian mistranslation from the French: *Prière pour les vivants* [Prayer for the Living].)[18]

I remember the sign that hung above the inn for the torch-bearers opposite the entrance to the Père Lachaise Cemetery in Paris: it read 'Au Repos des Vivants'.*

What is particularly salient here is that the play's heroes—who were very young, but about to commit suicide because their parents did not consent to their marriage—lost their innocence, after the boy took a bath when the girl had done so.

Or that after their temporary exit, while electricians were repairing the radio, the audience discovers their relationship has grown deeper when the two go into the next room wearing each other's bath robes—one white, one grey.

But . . .

But I won't repeat myself. I just want to set out an account of this scene as it was, with all the supplementary details, as I did in far-off Alma-Ata, when I was an evacuee, one bitter, gloomy and miserable winter evening. Or when *Ivan* was yet to go into production, or when it ran into difficulties at the production stage, or opposition and squabbling about the way it was being produced.

It would be unreasonable, on the strength of a brief retelling of the plot, to expect the reader's perception to be as entranced by these two fleeting details or rather, two psychological nuances—one in the characters' behaviour and the other in the way the audience is informed of this behaviour-as mine was: I did read the play in its entirety.

I touched on these details at the beginning.

* French: 'For the Repose of the Living'.

The bathroom scene.

And the scene where the bath robes are swapped, after the electricians have been on.

Why was it precisely these episodes, these details, that held my attention and were so strangely—alogically—emotionally—attractive?

I should have to presuppose remote sources of ideas very deep within me and even more, a social and biological existence that had apparently sprung up in new, ultra-contemporary forms: a couple of bath robes, one white, the other grey, instead of bearskins; and the gleaming tiled bathroom at the Ritz, instead of secret paths and hidden places in tropical forests.

Or so it seems.

Both in the process of the lovers' sensual excitement on stage and even more so when the audience is keying itself up for the young lovers' celebration of their love, Deval makes both the actors and audience think back to the sexual communion of living beings in its oldest form, to touch upon the forms of sexual communion dating from a pre-human age, beyond the limits of one's own human level, human appearance and the forms of these forebears. And among them is the oldest one of all.

Miletta—Deval's touching young heroine—cannot restrain herself from succumbing to the temptation of turning on the gleaming taps in the dazzling bathroom in the Ritz.

And indeed, before departing this life for ever, why not allow oneself one bite of a luxury that rich people enjoy daily?

Offstage you can hear first the noise of gushing hot water as the bath runs. Then, the joyous splashing and laughter of Miletta, as she capers beneath the stream.

The noise she makes stops her campanion from writing a farewell note to both their families.

But it does not stop him too from delighting in the elemental hot water, as it covers the dazzling white tiles.

. . . Hot water which Miletta leapt out of; before putting on a white bath robe to run on stage.

Now he comes on stage too.

His bath robe is grey.

A small, theatrical quid pro quo.

The radio has broken.

Two electricians come on.

To mend it.

The young people go offstage for a while.

To the bedroom.

The radio is being mended.

The electricians depart.

Miletta comes on, and this time she is wearing the grey bath robe.

And he the white.

What is it?

A cynical device, worthy of a farce?

A smutty trick to tell the audience that during that time the actors had disrobed; then succumbed to the heat of fresh passions; then, once these had. been quenched, forgotten in their haste whose was whose?

Or was it something else: to use this detail—the exchange—to exert influence on whole 'layers'* of early sensual notions, connected with what had happened; an evocation of a whole complex, via the generations who once consecrated and later romanticized this high point of man's biological existence?

* In English in the original.

Shooting *Bezhin Meadow* (the second version). Crimea, 1936. (Photograph: Mikhail Gomorov)

All the action unfolds with the utmost purity, romance, romanticization.

And this detail, supplying the unstated, appears as one of the most subtle and transparent pieces of writing in this play, woven entirely from the wholly mysterious charm of first love and its transition from slumbering emotions to a glorious celebration of love, which the two young beings are introduced to for the first time.

Of course, the detail of the bath robes is for information.

Of course, the slightest false step in the production, or by the actors, and the detail might miss that lyrical note which rang out so clearly—the mother-of-pearl tenderness of the action.

I doubt, of course, that Deval ever thought that the outward sign he used to show it, the form he chose to reveal what had happened, could fix in the subconscious the most profound stream of ideas, beliefs, rites and interpretations that have enshrouded marriage throughout all history.

He was probably not aware—did not even suspect—what he was creating when he invested the wedding rite of his young heroes in the outer apparel of the most ancient of customs.

Just opening Frazer's *The Golden Bough*—Part Two, devoted to Adonis, Attis and Osiris—one can see a long list of examples showing how the exchange of clothing between bride and groom became an obligatory ritual tradition of the wedding ceremony, even among radically different peoples. This list is in the notes, regarding the bride's wedding robes which were worn at some ceremonies by male priests.

Not only the bride and groom exchanged clothing; in some cases, their parents did also.

And the increasing number of participants in such an exchange of clothing, perhaps originating precisely from that point, from that very wedding ritual, led to cross-dressing en masse at saturnalia and in whatever forms they have survived—Feasts of Fools, etc. (see Willson Disher, *Clowns and Pantomimes*, London, 1925).

So we can see that there was a firm basis of fact underlying the young lovers' strange, chance, marriage 'rite' in Deval's play; it dated from ancient times and the present too, temporarily lagging behind at a level of immaturity—the initial stage of future cultural development.

The colossal wealth of factual detail Frazer amassed is equalled by the modesty of his commentary on it.

He goes no further than to suppose that this is some means of keeping out the evil eye and hostile spirits. If this explains, to some extent at least, some of the cases (elsewhere) when, in order to avoid the vengeance of a dead man's soul or a beast, the warrior male hides dressed in women's clothing, that explanation is not valid where the exchange takes place when both the 'persecuted' people are still alive and have simply changed places!

I think this ritual is in fact very closely allied to all those superstitions about the original androgynous being who divides into two discrete aspects—male and female—whose conjugal coupling celebrates a new recreation of the original, initial, single hermaphroditic origin. This situation recreates this point of departure: they are both in communion with this superhuman essence, becoming, at the moment of the ritual, like the original deity; in all cults, this deity unites both male and female origins.

But the worlds which stir beneath the preceding scene are just as deep set: I am referring to that scene where the water brings them close together for the first time. The warm bath, which the young lovers take, the one after the other.

'Have you seen goldfish mating?'

I have not.

The reader may be more fortunate.

But I do not ask the reader this rhetorically; I had once been asked this in all seriousness.

The question came from a strange man with a shaggy ginger beard and a shock of red hair on top. Between these conflagrations, which gazed at each other like the two worlds of the Arcana, there shone a pair of glasses; and behind them his large, penetrating brown eyes looked out with a surprisingly fixed gaze.

That apart, this man was a sapper by calling; he held the position of second-in-command of military construction. I served under him in the Civil War in Velikie Luki as well as in other remarkable towns and' small villages of our vast country.

His hair was of an intense colour, despite his age; he would wear army shirts and quilted trousers, a dull brown belt, calf-length boots cut wide, and he was very well disposed towards me.

He was called Krayevich and was a noted eccentric.

He was extremely well informed.

And about the oddest things. He was an excellent sapper and knew a lot. But he was famous above all for knowing how literally all animals 'do it'.

His short, hirsute figure, which looked like a Konenkov[19] wood sculpture, was wont to stop, fix you with a steady gaze from behind thick lenses and ask abruptly:

'But do you know how . . . ?'

The first half of the phrase was always the same.

Only the species changed, in the second half.

We had kangaroos, camels, giraffes, crocodiles, tortoises and so on and so forth. The list was endless.

Once the question was about goldfish.

And so from the lips—lips surrounded by the luxuriant fiery growth of Krayevich's beard—I learnt how goldfish mated. I had never thought about it previously, so it was with considerable astonishment that I heard that there is minimal contact between the two—that it is purely adventitious and takes place solely between their secretions (nothing to do with the word 'secret') in the water and between the two dramatis persona—or *pisces,* in this case!

We discussed the pros and cons of sexual communion that way and then parted until the next time; but the strange happiness that is the lot of goldfish was stored away in the deepest recesses of my memory to be recalled when needed, once the right association had been made.

How could I forget Engineer Krayevich, disguised as Neptune and surrounded by darting goldfish, when I read that description of the scene from *L'Age de Juliette?*

True, that scene came fifteen years later; I was even better informed in that area then, though not from any urge to know about each and every variety, but from curiosity about general tendencies and the very definite, evolutionary directions that later forms took.

I was curious about the evolutionary changes that the most vital act of any creature underwent.

It was to know more about this (Dr Ferenczi's book *Versuch einer Genitaltheorie*, published in 1924, seemed interesting both from an historical perspective and assessed on its own merits) that I made the acquaintance of our universal forebear, who exists at the lowest level of animal life, and is little more than a vegetable. It looks like a fish, and scientists maintain that it is the official ancestor, the first rung, the beginning of the fascinating truth of evolution that Darwin had deduced.

The founder of all future species which developed by evolution has a beautiful Latin name: *Amphyoxus lanceolatus*.

So even if we are not the direct descendants of goldfish, we

do at least share the same forebear with the elegant Latin name.

This last would not be at all important, except that we can trace this path (not the social or biological path, but the evolutionary one) back to the ancestor whose mating ritual was identical with the amazing *vita sexualis** of goldfish.

Which made me realize that the element in the two young beings' lovemaking in the Ritz Hotel that excited me without my understanding why, was chosen intuitively and was successful in all respects.

As opposed to Wedekind's fairly crude *Spring Awakening* [*Fühlings Erwachen*], Deval described this awakening with charming nuances that strike distant chords which reverberate deep within our instinct. And the awakening of emotions involves worlds which are dormant within us—sublimated forms of the emergence of our instincts, as well as of our behaviour, *modus vivendi*, rituals . . .

---

* Latin: 'sex life'.

I don't suppose I can say exactly when I was jolted in that direction—or what by; but whatever it was, that impulse broadened and developed In my personal practice and in my analysis of other people's works, finally to become what I term the *Grundproblem** of all my conceptions. I set it down, extremely briefly, but with all the detail to be expected of fundamental theories, in 1935, at the conference of the 'great' Soviet cinema.[20]

I can remember one such case very distinctly; it may even he what led me to this.

I had to familiarize myself with how our organs evolved—with the sense organs first of all.

My unfailing adviser, friend and consultant in all such matters— Alexander Romanovich Luria—suggested that I got to grips with a short book by Goldschmidt called *Ascarides*.[21] In a very poetic and populist style (but without compromising the scientific thoroughness), a fascinating picture emerged showing the peripeteias in the emergence of the perfected apparatus of our organism, from the earliest stages and on the lowest rungs of development.

I remember very clearly a passage describing the still-water hydra which grows new tentacles to replace broken ones.

Clarification was provided by the image of Hercules who wrestled with the Hydra (capital *h*), in Greek mythology—not this small, defenceless, still-water creature.

But some other early, amazing event was described in images analogous with a marionette, each of whose limbs acquired a life of its own and darted this way and that before being brought in to a whole.

I saw this standard trick—the dancing skeleton, whose arms and legs are flung first wide apart, and then brought close together —in Moscow at that very time. It was during a performance by a

* German: 'basic problem', a term frequently used by E.

wonderful touring puppet company from Vienna, in the premises of the old Music Hall (next to the Tchaikovsky Concert Hall on Mayakovsky Square). That was also the venue where, so many years later, I admired the mastery that gave the puppets a life of their own: stage pieces by 'the magician of the pear orchard', Mei Lan-Fan.[22]

The stout Austrian with his wife and daughter, lit fantastically from below, were seated on a low bench and leaning over the theatre of miniatures' backdrop and hidden by the harlequin of the small mirror of the toy stage.[23] They rhythmically moved their dancing hands which held the wooden crosses, the four ends of which were connected by threads to the puppets' arms, legs and joints. In the capable hands of the Viennese family, they were fantastically alive and limber.

I saw them sideways on, an oblique view from behind the wings.

I saw two rows; living people and dancing figures, spots of light on both and shadows of two sizes—the humans also entering the puppets' dance—conducting sheer Hoffmannesque phantasmagoria amid the sets of the real stage and the toy theatre, piled up on real platforms.

I saw a similar small theatre (but stationary) in an Antwerp cellar in one of the darkest, most crooked alleyways near the port.

The black hulks of depots and houses all around, the pennants of schooners framed by narrow streets. The glimmer of the moon.

And the tiny 'den' with the empty, tiny apron of the stage, in the depths of a small, dim hall.

There was no performance that evening.

And the next day was to be my last there.

But then the owner of the toy theatre kindly showed me the equipment by candlelight.

The puppets were larger here: they were almost as high as my knees.

And they were crudely fashioned from lumber, their moustaches carved with a few strokes and their cheeks coarsely painted.

But perhaps as they danced in the flickering shadows cast by the candle this incompleteness, roughness made them even more unreal and fantastic than the exquisite workmanship of the Viennese collection, coarse though that was in comparison with Teschner's ultra-aesthetic (and utterly enchanting) puppet troupe.[24]

But to go back to the Ascarides and the actual book on this small and charming vermiform ancestor of all our great-great-great-grandmothers.

It is possible that I will get the details hopelessly wrong—I have not picked the book up in twenty years!

But I remember clearly the idea—a kind of 'inversion': of course the funny picture of the skeleton flying apart and the warlike image of Hercules doing battle with the Hydra, were far from chance analogies, thoughtfully provided by Viennese puppeteers and the Greeks respectively for Herr Goldschmidt to use to illustrate a point.

Both Hercules and the small marionette of a skeleton, with its limbs so horrifyingly independent, are little more than the realization of 'memories', reminiscences of those early biological and physiological peripeteias and adventures which our revolting species once experienced on its way towards the perfection of today's shape and forms!

And hence the conclusion that self-expression lies at the very heart of works that are genuinely exciting in the types of both subject and forms, within which the subject and even the theme are simply the first stage of the crystallizing creative 'urge'. Sometimes even they are omitted (*vide* the group of works that have no subject; or a work which is an adaptation of someone else's, with a pre-existing subject).

Any freely selected subject or even one that has been foisted upon me (in either case the interpreter will have to adapt it) is relevant to my vision, understanding and perception—from the inclination to take that very one, right up to breaking the 'received subject' down.

Here it would do no harm to dwell on the high proportion of my works (especially the successful ones) which were 'made to order' with respect to the theme; and in the historical films (that is, in almost all of them!) I was 'blinkered' by the actual events, even though I was at some distance from what really happened!

It would be true to say that I distorted history considerably, with regard to its 'image and likeness', its flavour and the sense of haphazard; but if I sometimes missed the letter I tried at least to catch the spirit; and I immersed myself enough in history for this.

Further, I always tried to pin the situation and the image of an historical event and fact on to the scheme of the primary sensual situation as each element of the form grew and flowed from the language of form—the inexhaustible wealth of means of expression: seams of sensual thought which only inspiration can dislodge, inducing an active trembling of the whole body from head to toe; from the topmost layers of consciousness down to the deepest bases of primary, past, sensual and pre-sensual thought, where the actual terms 'thought', 'memory' and even . . . 'feeling' have almost no place.

But that is precisely what the sighting-point, which my volitional work is aimed at, is like. And it will strike home, with enough all-encompassing inspiration!

P. S. Later, in another 'volute' of these spiralling creative impulses, I will introduce this idea even into the relationship between 'creative associations' born of vivid impressions and the role they play in the imagination (not 'primary' at this point, or 'original'; but even apparently random although I should add an N. B. that the most persistent of those random impressions will of course be those closely connected to the 'deepest layers'* of 'originality').

This will appear in the first edition of my lectures at VGIK ('A Soldier Returns from the Front').[25] While I was devising them, I made a note of the associations and memories which came to life when one link or other had been forged; and by the end I could formulate these associations which arose *post factum*, apparently (and probably actually) comprising the total sum of what my desired plan needs if it is to be realized.

In one example of the so-called *torito* (one of my photographs from Mexico) I was able 'to disentangle'* almost all the elements of previous associations, which were inevitably included in the elements of a natural setting.

To round the whole subject of folklore off, let me say that its value and attraction—from the Bushman to Father Brown and from images from the Bible to the images of Chicago 'slang'—was that it introduced me to early vivid and dynamic ways of grasping the world and the universe with an image that helps us to understand them both, taken together, which is a halfway point to recreating the world.

---

* In English in the original.

INVERSIONS[1]

Sometimes, I sum people up well with words.

Especially when I am being malicious.

Comrade E was holidaying with me in Barvikha. I thought he looked like a pink skeleton wearing a lounge suit.

People who know Comrade E can back me up on the 'sensual accuracy' of this description.

Analysing this formula is well worth the effort.

The interesting—realistic—'core' of this apparently non sensical image is of a skeleton worn on the outside.

But this is an entirely natural state of affairs, in the case of . . . shrimps, crabs and lobsters.

With crustacea, the outer surface acts as the skeleton; their plates and casings house the soft tissue!

'Crab-like' features are a very popular metaphor for people. 'Crab's eyes' are almost a commonplace.

Why should 'crab's skeleton' be less so?

The 'denouement' of course came much later.

And led of course to the . . . *Grundproblem.*

The actual description derived from Comrade E's customary bared grin, his smooth, shaven head and his glasses, which exaggerated his eye sockets considerably.

Also, Comrade E's complexion was an intense pink, like a piglet.

The first thing I saw was the outline of the skull: its structure could easily be discerned behind the flat features of his face. But what about the pink colouring?

This skull must be made pink.

The pink hue of the skull makes the pink not alive and healthy, but painted and ridiculous.

But a skull pushing through the surface of the skin is an ominous image. No doubt there is an ominous element to Comrade E, especially for those whose articles and plays he cut 'like a censor'! But there is much to be respected in this ominous picture.

But the image must be grotesque.

A skeleton encapsulating a naked body is again a pretty ghastly image.

The 'lounge suit' at once clothes him, makes him normal, taking him out of the symbolic abstraction; and then deflates the whole combination once more.

Furthermore the ominous overtones of a skeleton as a symbol of death are here cancelled out: it is being worn above a jacket, and so is itself no more than an overcoat or a macintosh.

The lounge suit also hints at the 'fullness' of the figure.

The terrifying body with its pink, grinning skull, becomes a joke as you look lower down.

Let us now consider the three 'sources' of the image.

One we have already touched upon.

This sits somewhere in our own ideas physically. With the primary principle of 'ambivalence', which, 'setting' into uncoupled extremes and opposites (a long time before becoming in their apogee the conception of a unity of opposites) it 'recalls' its past ambivalent unity through the device and form of . . . an inversion . . . (which is also funny as a level of development already experienced!)

The dynamic of an ominously living process turns into immobility.

The extreme 'images'—the skull and the face—fragment, and are now put together mechanically and also by the 'deflated' action of dressing.

The pink skull, 'worn over the face', is little more than a farcical device, a crude mask.

Too real!

The fantastic shift is achieved by the shift from the skull face to the whole skeleton-body.

The 'skeleton' is worn over the body.

In some parts this is not entirely feasible technically and it is slightly awkward.

What would happen to the skeleton's arms and legs?

Would you have to sew stripes on to the sleeves and trousers?

The torso can, however, be shoved inside the ribcage which surrounds it, one size larger.(just as galoshes need to be slightly larger than one's shoes.)

It is harder with the pelvis . . .

So, all in all, the expansion of the skeleton, as we see it, stretches the simile.

The 'change of places' between the skeleton and the person's outward appearance is part of that same family of inversions which makes the horse ride the knight in fairy tales. Swift, in his *Gulliver's Travels,* employed this switching of horse and rider, but on a much higher and more sophisticated level.

This is what the broad, general human premises for such an image would have been.

But I myself have two more to add, of a purely personal nature.

One concerns a very subtly worked, figurative canvas of living faces, skulls and cardboard masks, representing skulls, developing from a very remote plan as both 'inversion' and . . . 'double inversion'.

The second premise touches an even deeper past. It is connected not to some figurative association, but to a purely dynamic, figurative interpretation that emerged from a verbal characterization of the process which makes expressive movements happen.

This was something I thought very deeply about in Moscow in the '20s; the play of masks, faces and skulls came in Mexico in the '30s.

That line written above about 'a skull pushing through the skin' served as a vivid reminder not only of my ideas regarding the principles of expressive movement as a whole, but also of those brief moments of spontaneous practice, where I sketched out the principles in order to understand how mimicry worked.

Another anecdote.

An illustrated one, at that. A Gavarni lithograph, from his series 'Les Enfants terribles'.

An extremely perplexed subject sits, his eyes fixed on the viewer.

A 'little darling' has climbed on to the arm of the chair.

'Ooh, look what's happening to you. Your head is growing through your hair!'

The dear little boy is looking at . . . a bald patch.

A simple 'inversion'?

Assuredly.

Head and hair have changed place and functions.

But that is not all!

Strange though it may seem, the skull, the layers of skin and the hair really are linked to one another in expressive movement in the most diverse and dynamic relationships.

The link which really exists in nature is applied to a situation which is externally close to but not dependent on that link. That is one of the causes of the comic effect here.

At the same time, there is the sense of some sort of essential correctness in the 'dynamic' picture of the process, as well as the obvious fallacy of applying this process to the given conditions.

(To take an example: if a very tall man stands in cold water, the cold will take at least a fortnight to reach his nose.)

The body, the layers of skin and the follicles are of course linked to one another in expressive movement.

Even the ancients thought that an animal 'bristled' to make itself look larger.

A more scientific point of view would reject this as excessive anthropomorphism and would explain it by saying that when an animal prepares for battle it takes in a large quantity of oxygen which always makes the body expand.

This makes the skin tauten, which in turn pulls each hair into an erect position.

But the hair will do this in precisely the reverse case: when the volume of the body beneath the skin is constant, but the skin's surface rapidly shrinks.

This happens on the head, for example, where of course the volume of the skull cannot change. However, the skin contracts convulsively.

It is well known that people instinctively shrink when they experience terror.

Obviously, as far as the head is concerned, this can only affect the scalp.

Which is what happens.

Like the hands, feet and knees, the scalp is 'pulled' towards the 'centre' of the body as a whole, to protect and hug the chest.

The head performs a similar action.

It buries itself in the tucked-up knees and the person hides, crouching, in a position of total defensiveness which comes naturally, and in which he spent nine heavenly months utterly relaxed in his mother's womb before emerging into this hostile, unfriendly world which for some reason is thought to be God's own!

But our organism, in the process of expressive movement, is marked by a surprising ability (in some cases) to react as a whole, with one motive.

Stills from the epilogue for *Que Viva Mexico!*

And conversely, with several motives.

And chief among them are motives which oppose one an other.

More accurately, make us react in two contradictory ways to one and the same motive.

And to realize such opposites, the different parts of the organism react in different ways.

Some of them take one line of action.

Others a different one.

In movement, this is no more than the realization of a contradictory reaction, which is inevitable for a consciousness that responds spontaneously and with mediated reactions in equal measure.

Thus our system is divided, more often than not, into two camps, each trying to realize a contrary plan of action.

Here a basic division occurs between the 'centre' and the 'periphery'. The system's broadly understood—'centre' is linked to a simpler, internal, spontaneous response.

Then, the 'periphery'—the extremities and the mimetic surface of the face—is fundamentally linked to the motor execution mediated by the responsive function which makes the movement . . .

But the 'boundary' between these spheres is by no means fixed.

As one or the other component grows stronger, it seizes more and more elements of the motor system and of the body as a whole, in order to realize its planned movement.

Finally one becomes completely dominant, 'breaking through' into real action and out of that 'struggle between motives', which characterizes directly opposing interpretations.

Furthermore, if all groups of muscles are in all cases locked, one should also take into account which muscle of each group is affected first or wholly by innervation, as a result of the impulse to move.

Which is why 'shrinking' in terror, for example, is associated with the opposite image: arms raised upwards and to the side, neck outstretched and eyes wide open.

Assuming that the skin (the extreme periphery) undergoes a rapid contraction, or the whole body rapidly folds in on itself, then there is the same tension of the skin that makes one's hair stand on end.

A division which goes as far as the very limit of the body the skin—is rare enough and has more to do with the class of phenomena which we ascribe 'to ourselves' as purely physiological, a part of our expressive conditions: tears are forced out; our skin is covered with goosepimples or perspiration and we shiver violently.

Meanwhile, according to how they are realized, all these phenomena are subordinated to those actual formulae, but they are played out at such a peripherally 'remote' spot that they are physically localized at some extreme boundary of our flesh to be registered somewhere beyond the region of a distinct sensual interpretation, not as an 'emotion' this time, but a 'physical condition'.

Exactly the same thing applies to the other extreme, where for example bouts of diarrhoea induced by fear, or 'premature birth' have nothing to do with expressive processes and everything to do with purely physiological phenomena.

The study of 'surface' phenomena is interesting for its links with the distant past; the original, expressive manifestation is the relationship of reciprocal tensions between the inside and outside of amoebae: pseudopodia, where part of the protoplasm alternately protrudes and retracts, as tendency overcomes tendency; endoplasm beats ectoplasm.

And as always, extremes meet.

At the highest level of expressiveness, there is almost the purest reproduction of this first plan (which at its highest level can be sung as a chorus).

Which brings us back to the relationship between the whole and its thinnest of coverings. Except that the endoplasm here is the head, as the foremost unit of the body as a whole, and the ectoplasm is the mimetic covering, what we call the face, made up of skin and muscle.

The millimetric seismograph of the face's features which mimetically echo the microscopic vacillations in the struggle between the motives or impulses (and essentially the wearer consequently reacts in opposing ways), is a piece of apparatus that is infinitely refined and perfected, yet it operates according to the same fundamental plan as the pseudopodium.

And it seems no longer wild, strange or absurd to define the principles of mimetic expressiveness as the relationship between facial contractions, as the head tries (precisely tries, rather than succeeds) to push through the surface of the face. Or as the surface of the face tries to run freely over the skull's immobile surface.

When we stand agape in astonishment, what is that if not a spontaneous reaction before the face lights up with comprehension?

A face pinched with grief is a skull, which with the body slides through the thin surface of the face.

And a face bursting with smugness, sleek (that is, the skin tautened) is like a self-satisfied, well-developed chest, ready with the ribcage to pop the buttons of the coat from inside; to blow away the face, the first to carry the impulse of the body and skull!

I can well remember the day when I was doing practical work on expressive movement and a friend and I had a breakthrough— the realization of the dynamic of expressive movement came with the verbal formula: 'the skull pushes through the face'.

I have two very close friends.

To me they are virtually two Ajaxes.

I cannot think of one without also thinking of the other. Actually they were both Aristides, not Ajaxes.

Their surnames sounded similar as well: Bruant and Briand.[2]

One reigned in Montmartre.

The high priest of bars like 'Le Chat Noir' and '[Au] Lapin Agile'.

This second Montmartre bar was a play on words, in honour of the artist who painted the, sign: *l'a peint A. Gill.*[*3]

Just think of Hugo's *Le Pot aux roses* [French: 'The Pot of Roses'], which became *le poteau rose* [French: 'the rose thorn']; or his *Tu ora* [Latin: 'You pray'] which became *trou aux rats* [French: 'rat-hole'], which was where Esmerelda found sanctuary when she fell into the hands of the mad old woman.

Or again, that Catholic and reactionary, King Charles X—*le pieux monarque* [French: 'the pious monarch'] whom Travies turned into *le pieu monarque* [French: 'the blockhead monarch'].

My greatest, truest affection was for the former; his soft black hat and red scarf came to stand for all the charm and romance of Paris in the early decades of the century.

The Paris of street songs and argot.

Cafe concerts and Yvette Guilbert, Toulouse-Lautrec and Xanrof.

It was some time before I gathered where this strange, apparently abbreviated name was taken from. Its owner wrote songs for Yvette; they were particularly ironic or enchanting.

I think it was Emile Bayard's notes about the Latin Quarter that solved the riddle for me.[4]

A young versifier, Fourneau, was looking for a pseudonym.

He was expecting an inheritance from Uncle, but this would not be possible if he were to be identified as the author of frivolous ballads.

Translating Fourneau (*fourneau* means 'stove') into Latin gives *fornax*—but that would be transparently obvious.

* French: 'painted by A. Gill', but something similar to *Lapin Agile*.

The women in the vanguard, pouring into Winter Palace. Stills from a scene in *October*.

But if you then write it back to front—now that's more like it. From Fourneau to Fornax, and thence Xanrof. But anyone who likes Xanrof will have found this out for himself as I did; and those who do not know or care for him will be pretty much indifferent to all this . . .

I love the other Aristide for just one thing he did.

I mention it on every possible occasion.

And I think that this is the best place to mention it.

Briand was famous in his later years as a fervent campaigner for a United States of Europe. It is not that dubious idea that I find attractive, however, but how this idea was born. It struck him, as the saying goes, like a 'winged phrase'.

At some meeting or other he threw out this formula as no more than a rhetorical device contrasting Europe with the United States of America.

The Women defending the Winter Palace and the Bolshevik envoys.

It was only later—significantly so—that he began to contemplate what this 'winged phrase' implied—

Of course, when he hurled out these words he could not have been thinking of anything specific; this chance (or maybe not so chance; more a tendency his subconscious encapsulated in a slogan) phrase preceded the formulation and it magically caught on, welding disparate elements of his plan into a programme. That can happen, even in politics.

But good heavens, I am an artist as well.

Not only a researcher.

And the (seemingly) wild, paradoxical (in form) formula will lodge in me without fail, somewhere; even if only as an image ('the skull pushed through the face').

This is bound to appear as a dynamically spontaneous picture.

Not as a figurative description, but as a living image, in which the skull really does come to the surface. The face emerges through the skull. And the face is like a certain image of the skull and the skull like a certain independent face . . .

One, living on top of the other. One hidden beneath the other. One living an independent life through the other.

And one repeating the physical outline of the process via the interplay of face and skull, changing masks.

Masks!

Of course.

Now I can see the masks—now the mask of a skull on a living face, now the mask of a living face on a skull—materializing in this way.

And I have only to surround myself with real masks for that old forgotten secondary paradoxical formula to come into its own in all the fullness of its figurative form and, in that form, to pick out the formula for the new essence, theme or idea which leaps out of the climactic chords of the whole artistic concept, the whole system of images, the whole picture of the whole film.

The Day of the Dead in Mexico!

I have written elsewhere about precisely how the image of the Day of the Dead took me to Mexico.

That is not the part of the subject that interests me here. If it was the Day of the Dead that prompted me first to go to Mexico, then it is natural enough that my last word on that country—the ending of the film—should be expressed in images from that same Day of the Dead. The more so as the theme of life and death, expressed ultimately by a living face and a skull, is the key, basic theme which informs the whole film.

The theme of life, death and immortality.

In the crucible of new ideas which were born of the Revolution and followed the ruthless purging of old ideas and beliefs, there appeared a new conception even of victory over death, the conquering of death; immortality.

We are mortal, biologically.

Only our social deeds make us immortal; the small contribution we make to social progress, the short distance we run before passing on the baton to the next generation.

This is now a bookish platitude.

Once, people worked out for the first time ever that twice two is four. Many centuries later, the age of relativity gave an innocent problem like that any answer it liked. And this was a new, crucial step towards the threshold of the new, atomic age.

And although we are old enough to remember the time before the October Revolution, we were also sufficiently young when it came to assimilate the ideas that came in its wake.

Now such ideas can be applied to an infinitely wider field than that one-sixth of the world's land mass where they are more than words!

Uncle Sam's recent need for human beings to fly his planes and perish on the battlefield resulted In this new creed of immortality consistently being preached from American screens.

A Guy Named Joe [1943] showed dying, dead, smashed-up pilots sitting behind the trainees; pooling their experience paid for with their lives, they led wave after wave of young pilots into the skies.

That says it all.

American inventiveness and skill at extracting from situations a range of possibilities—from lyricism to farce, from low comedy to tragedy—divide the situations into an endless succession of scenes.

But the tenor of the subject rests with the 'General in the Sky' who assigned the smashed-up pilots to the recruits.

And the idea that the hands of each trainee would be guided by the thousands who perished before him attains the height of pathos.

Although Lionel Barrymore uttered this speech in his usual, querulous way, and Spencer Tracy as Joe, a dead pilot, listened with his eyes screwed up sceptically as he was commissioned to return to earth and guide the young pilot unseen.

But there is a fundamental difference too. Our idea of immortality is not as a beyond-the-grave cooperation between young and old! We see it as a cause which generations fight and die for.

And that aim is man's freedom, which we supposed our allies were also fighting for.

It was only after the gun smoke had dispersed that we realized that the same words can have completely different meanings in different parts of the world.

Our ideal is to fight for Revolution, to live it, in the name of true freedom; the Allies fought for something quite different.

Time and time again our understanding of immortality was emphatically defined as immortality in the struggle for the revolutionary ideal of freedom.

The bookish platitude for many, for our generation—I say again—was the emergence of a new awareness of life and reality.

But then, as often happens, it is not only a reflection of facts that is repeated in a work's emergence, but also the dynamic of the process; this majestic and magnificent highway leading to a new life, new thoughts and ideas—this very thought—not a formula but a bright and living image—blossomed into the chief subject to emerge from the chaos of countless intersections of episodes and facts, rituals and customs, anecdotes and situations in which the course of life and death intertwine one with another in Mexico as nowhere else, either in tragic images of death, trampling life underfoot, or in rich images celebrating life's triumph over death, or in the fulfilment of one's allotted span, or in the immensity of an eternal future, engendered by the coming generations that will grow up out of the spilt blood of the dying present.

The interplay of life and death, as they struggle for the upper hand.

The film starts with the cult of death in ancient Aztec and Mayan civilizations, among the stillness of the ancient stones. And it finishes with the contemptuous *vacilada,* a specific form of Mexican irony which makes the very image of death appear ludicrous, so much liveliness does it generate.

And in, between comes the peon, dying beneath the hooves of the *hacendado's* horses; and the Catholic monk, in the blasphemy of self-denial and asceticism as he turns his back on the rich pageant of life in the tropics. And the bull, shedding his blood in the arena to the greater glory of the Madonna; and the country, torn by fratricidal strife and awash with blood, all to the accompaniment of Vatican-inspired shouts of *'Viva Cristo Rey!'*, not *'Viva el Hombre Rey!'*,* which is what should have been shouted out in a thunderous roar.

All this comes together in the finale.

The ironic, distorting mirror of the Day of the Dead; the phantom of everlasting death to whom the ancients humbly bowed down in the prologue.

But it is no longer in the form of Aztec and Mayan marble or granite skulls, nor the terrifying image of the Mother of Gods, wearing a necklace of human skulls, nor even the sacrificial stone of Chichen-Itza, where the rocks are carved to look like skulls—

No!

Here, a cardboard mask of death dances a rumba, which changes into a funeral march among the carousels, fairground stalls and

* Spanish: 'Long live Christ the King!' and 'Long live Man the King!'

markets to be found on the avenues, squares and boulevards of every town and village, however large or small.

The carousels and Ferris wheels spin.

Some people are dancing a wild rumba.

Skull masks are going in all directions.

There is one, under a peon's straw sombrero;

and there is one under the gold-embroidered sombrero of a charro.

There is one with a lady's hat pinned on top.

There, a topper.

There, a tricorn.

There is one above a workman's overalls; a mechanic, at driver, a smith, a miner.

The carnival is in full swing!

At its climax, masks are flung upwards.

There is one frame filled with cardboard skulls. A gale of laughter blows them away and instead of a white wall of skulls, a bronze wall of peons doubled up with mirth is revealed.

Another frame—also showing explosive laughter—shows a pale mask of cardboard death giving way to the merriment of a day-worker, a mechanic and a driver locked in friendly embrace.

Bronzed, laughing faces.

Eyes glittering like coals; white teeth.

Another group of masks. And wearing the same costumes that they wear throughout the film.

This is what the man who exchanged shots with the *hacendado* was wearing.

This is what he was wearing when he died after being caught.

This is what he wore when he toiled in the fields, or in the cement works.

But the masks spill over into this group of true 'positive heroes' who, in the film, confirm the authority of life; the masks are wearing the clothes of those who, throughout the film, are identified with violence and the enslavement of life (death).

It is they who wear the *hacendados'* suits as they ride their horses over the buried peons.

It is they who wear the shawl and hat that belong to the landowner's daughter.

The same grinning cardboard masks bob between the wing collars, above the stars and ribbons on their dinner jackets and beneath their top hats.

And the general silhouette hints at the president who reviews the firemen's and ... police parade in the film.

The general's plumage and tricorn hang above another cardboard skull, this time one with a ... moustache. He elegantly escorts a skull half hidden by a lace fan and wearing a fluttering mantilla, holding castanets.

And he raises his hands to the sky and turns on the spot, mimicking the gestures of the Papal Nuncio and the Archbishop of Mexico on the day of the Madonna de Guadalupe (which is also in the picture). He is an oddity, dressed in his full episcopal regalia; and his gold tiara burns in the sky above that same dull, motionless, cardboard face of death.

This carnival is not derived from Saint-Saens' *'Danse macabre'*, nor Holbein's 'Dance of Death'.

It comes straight from the heart of Mexican folklore: on this day, traders' street stalls are covered with skulls wearing helmets, top hats, caps, sombreros, matadors' berets and bishops' mitres. It comes straight out of the paintings by Mexico's most populist artist José Guadalupe Posada, known as *calaveras*.[5]

On the Day of the Dead, newspapers and special broad sheets are full of pictures on the same subject.

They are all regarded as dead. But if one should only speak well of the dead, then carnival death demands malicious, heartless, venomous epigrams for each quasi-corpse, to tear off the veneer he sports in life.

And so, in the whirlwind of my screen carnival, after the peon, the mechanic, the driver and the miner have taken off their masks, so too, with a lighthearted flourish, do the dancing *hacendado*, the maiden, the matriarch, the general and the bishop.

And what lies beneath?

Whereas the first case revealed living, bronzed faces, creased with mirth, here one and the same face was exposed.

But it was not a face.

But the yellow bone of a real skull.

Those living people who progressed carrying the seeds of creativity and life beneath the cardboard image of death, had living faces.

Those who carried the seeds of death wore a cardboard grimace to conceal what was even more frightening—the grimace of a real skull.

Historically condemned to death, it carries its emblem on its own shoulders.

This dead face, wrapped in the shreds of an overcoat, or with epaulettes, dinner-jacket and medals, or with surplice and cross, seemingly utters a ghastly warning to those wearing such clothes in the film: it was written above the skull lying at the foot of the crucifix, and addressed to the passer-by:

'I was as you are; you will be as I am.'

Passer-by!

You will not find this description in any versions of the film.

They were mutilated and edited by other people even though all the material was ours and indeed had been filmed by us, during our stay in Mexico, the land of miracles. By thoughtless splicing of the material and selling off negative stock for different films, they effectively destroyed the concept and ruined its coherence. Many months' hard work was simply wrecked.

And perhaps I can detect the hand of the Mexican goddess of death in all this, wearing the masks of the obtuse vandals, of the dull-witted American film buyers, taking her revenge for my over-familiar poke in the ribs?

'The Day of the Dead' went out as a separate, independent 'short' without achieving its purpose: to be a tragic and ironic finale to a great poem about Life, Death, and Immortality; I chose Mexico as the material, but the conception was never realized on the screen.

Irony helped me overcome the death of my own child, in whom I had invested so much love, labour and inspiration.

But Comrade E's pink skull has a direct ancestor!

One of José Guadalupe's *calaveras* has two skulls, both black.

As a black living in Harlem might picture black angels in his heaven, so the Mexican imagines that blacks have black skeletons!

Long live coloured skeletons.

COLOUR[1]

Colour. Pure. Bright. Vibrant. Ringing.

When did I come to love it? Where?

Perhaps it was in Vologda.

More accurately, in the Vologda guberniya.

In the little hamlet of Vozhega, to be precise.

I was flung there by Civil War.

Dazzling snow.

Women stood on the snow.

They wore short dun-coloured fur coats with a braid.

And felt boots.

Between the fur and the boots, I could see a strip of a sarafan.

Woollen. Striped.

Relentlessly bright vertical stripes.

Lilac, orange, red and green.

With a strip of white between.

Another one.

Deep blue, yellow, violet and crimson.

Worn through, faded and moth-eaten.

A pillow on a wicker chair.

A tablecloth, spread out.

A quarter of a century later and I can still see their patterns just as clearly.

The stripes of the Mexicans' ponchos, equally relentless, intertwine with them.

The inexhaustible heat of the tropics burns within them, while crystals of white frost scintillate in the background.

Voluptuous pink interweaves with pale blue. The yellow mingles with green. White separates brown zigzags from deep indigo.

Perhaps the once pure colours of icons were a prelude to the savage joy of the pure colours on the Vologda sarafans.

Perhaps the penetrating choir of pink flamingoes, standing out against the pale blue backdrop of the Gulf of Mexico, picked up the refrain where Van Gogh's canvases in the Hague Museum left off with their whirlwind of colour produced in Arles by the great madman with the missing ear.

Anyway: the green square of the tablecloth in the lemon room flooded with light, the dark-blue teapot among red cups, the golden buddha against the azure walls or the books in their orange and black binding on the green and gold brocade of the round table.

I always surround myself with such spots of colour. The spines of my books, gold next to purple, draw an ever tighter loop around my rooms like the vertical stripes on a Vologda sarafan.

Dark blue, white, white, orange.

Red, light blue, orange.

Red, light blue, green.

Red, red, white again.

Black. Gold . . .

I find it dull when there is no yellow pencil next to the blue one to set it off; no red and green striped pillow lying on the blue couch; when the multicoloured dressing gown fails to dazzle, when there are no yellow stripes running up the curtains, crossing blue stripes or intersected by crimson ones . . .

And I like it when a bright ribbon of Philippine embroidery meanders across an Uzbek wall hanging. Or a Mongolian stitchwork design sprawls across the dull crimson background of a wall that so advantageously sets off the whiteness of the cardboard emblems of the Day of the Dead, and the Moorish masks black. with bloody wounds. These unexpectedly mutate into the semi-ritual dances of the Mexican Indians, which symbolize for them now not the Moorish conquest of Spain, but their own enslavement by the Spanish hordes under Cortes.

GOGOL'S MASTERY[1]

You could see it from a distance.

And from beneath.

It looked like a gate leading into the sky.

Beyond was the massive vault of the heavens.

Before us stretched the narrow, steep-sided thoroughfare. Going uphill.

Out of the hollow.

Along the flat.

Out of the gulley to the heavenly gates.

But this was not Tibet.

We were not climbing up the sacred mountains, where thousands of steps lead thousands of hesitant pilgrims to merge with the heavens.

Nor was this the pyramids of the ancient Aztecs, heathen temples which wily priests had turned into Catholic cathedrals, fountains of grace which granted the wishes of those who had come to pray.

It was outside Moscow, of all places. A country estate.

It is now a holiday home.

Uzkoye.

It must have been 1932 or '33. Winter was ending.

There were two of us sharing a room.

It was strange. My roommate this time was no learned stomatologist or a phytopathologist commissioned to draw the bookworm out of the depths of the Leningrad book depositories, nor even simply a specialist in ancient Greek vases.

Until you have enough medals and honours to qualify you for a single room, you can count on a short month's holiday to bring you into close contact with someone like that . . .

This time I shared a room with the editor of a publishing house.

We did not get on particularly well.

For my platonically dry dreams and sighs about my next small book on problems of cinema immediately materialized into the rectangular yoke of a contract which it took me years of bad conscience and inventiveness to wriggle out of, without having to return the advance.

But I heard from him a fair amount of praise for the other clientele who were foundering in the tentacles of this tenacious book-producing octopus.

A most curious person ended up in its snares.

Bugayev, the writer, took on a new lease of creative life—one last flourish—before he died.

He wrote as Andrei Bely.[2]

Bely was then writing a book on Gogol.

He was going to read extracts from it in the office of the editorial director.

For a small, select circle.

I saw and heard this remarkable old man for the first time, a few weeks later, in the corner room of the editorial office.

He was wearing a professorial hat.

Very fine, silvery hair formed a halo under it.

There was a waxen hue to his pallid features. The wrinkles in his face were of a dull silvery colour, as on an early firearm.

His eyes shone with a rare radiance.

Most biographies look like an ill-considered assortment of facts.

Often haphazard.

Each title seems a flash in the chaos.

They are linked together with biographical details.

But these facts are threaded together without logic.

The writer Andrei Bely on the day before the evening given in his honour at the Polytechnic Museum, Moscow, in 1932.

So the first thing we heard was the element of Gogol's images which seemed arbitrarily to interweave and generally to slip and slide at random through the ins and outs of the author's life.

There is Taras.

And there, Dovgochkhun.

There is Chichikov; and there are Selifan and Petrushka.[3]

There is the bright colouring of *Evenings*.

And here is the quite different key of *Dead Souls*.

And Bugayev suddenly brought this whirlwind (or swarm, as Gogol himself would have said) to a stop.

Forget Taras.

Forget the sorcerer from 'The Terrible Vengeance'.

From this point on the line takes another direction.

From Taras to Dovgochkhun.

From Dovgochkhun (less surprisingly) to Peter Petrovich Petukh.[4]

And from the sorcerer to Petro Mikhali in 'The Portrait' and from him to Kostanzhoglo in *Dead Souls*.

Bely's brilliant commentary—part bold hypothesis, part indisputable fact and part unexpected quotation—shows the link in its different phases; its modification, rethinking and development into a motif with a new point of departure, the original motif blossoming out into the succeeding one: the historic-heroic motif fades into the mediocrity of the petty landowning class (from Taras to Ivan Nikiforovich), and what was fantastically frightening with its sheer foreignness, finishes by threatening the old patriarchal and patriotic order with imported industrialism (from Kudesnik to Kostanzhoglo).

And the troika—Selifan, Chichikov and Petrushka—are not just a driver, servant and master in a carriage to which three horses have been harnessed. They are also in their own right a threesome; and as a threesome, a certain complete unit; and Petrushka is not just Petrushka, but the entire unappealing essence of Pavel Ivanovich; that part of him which he hides so diligently behind the thinnest veneer and fragrance and beneath the false bottom of his notorious box . . .

And then, all of a sudden, Bely hurled a whole series of tables, statistics and figures at us.

What?!

The percentage of different colours which Gogol used at different stages of his work.

The seemingly chaotic assembly of characters in Gogol may be arranged in order of seniority, according to the degree to which the key feature is developed, according to the movement in characterization towards an even deeper interpretation. And what unexpectedly seems a suddenly self-willed kaleidoscope of colours running through the short stories and novellas, the poems and evenings, the plays and sketches, can also be drawn up in neat ranks showing increases and decreases, surges and abatements, flourishing and fading.

Bugayev's laborious work on every shade of the spectrum, every piece of biographical data, his burrowing between the covers of every work in a considered way, examining every detail, reaffirms his conviction, crucially and conclusively, with the two zeros and oblique stroke of a percentage sign . . .

Quite marvellous.

A marvel of industry and attention.

A marvel of care and respect.

A marvel of insight and poetic affinity with the writer's soul.

Later, as in a dream or a whirl of vision,

I shyly approached the magician.

It transpired that he had known of me for some time, through my films.

I asked him why, in the magnificent roll call of authors (Gogol and Blok, Gogol and Bely, Gogol and Mayakovsky) there was no entry: Gogol and Joyce. For a long time I had been struck by the similarity in writing styles between the Ukrainian who became one of the greatest Russian writers and the Irishman who became the pride of English literature.

Bely was not familiar with Joyce's work.

Having linked Gogol with futurism, why not link him with . . . cinema?

Although he had brilliantly pointed out the 'cut'—everything that happened while Ivan Ivanovich was pushing through the doorway.[5]

We will return to this conversation later.

But for the moment . . .

Bely's brilliantly scathing attack on the Moscow Art Theatre production of *Dead Souls*[6] was launched with Gogol's inimitable palette in his hands. That production was senselessly and unforgivably colour-blind and shortsighted, but the main thing was that it was not dramatic; or more accurately, that it ran counter to the drama of colour and characterization through colour (which in Gogol are quite inseparable from subject and content) which were here treated obtusely and without meaning.

A Bely evening at the Polytechnic Museum.

I was in the chair . . .[7]

That marvellous evening with Bely at my flat on Chistye Prudy.

Much later in some sort of blur.

A dissolve sequence.

The tragic death of Boris Bugayev, better known by his pseudonym Andrei Bely . . .

The sole memento of those marvellous few months of vivid impressions 'inside Gogol' is the eye-catching yellow binding of *Gogol's Mastery*, published by OGIZ/GIKhL in 1934.[8]

The yellow binding burns on the table like the cover of the Goncourts' *Germinie Lacerteux* in van Gogh's portrait of Doctor Gachet.

Bely's book, yellow as the sun, frames his invaluable observations.

Here they are measured off according to the creative phases.

Into tables and diagrams.

In distinct images and patterns.

By the juxtaposition of quotations which merge into one another like adjacent hues on the spectrum. Or which ring out, a clash of complementary colours.

Gogol's elemental colour courses through them, illuminating the columns and tinting the images.

Yesterday it was different from today.

And tomorrow it will be different again.

First came light.

Light condensed into colour.

Light remained an underlay for colour.

Writing with light underlies writing with colour in the first phase, let us recall: mosaic and stained glass preceded and gave rise to Giotto, the father of modern painting; and the history of painting in Gogol's prose, from the glass landscape in the excerpt from *The Drowned Woman* right up to the description of Plyushkin's room, is analagous to the history of painting, from the mosaic of Ravenna, through Giotto, to Rembrandt. (p. 135)

This becomes even clearer under closer scrutiny.

... The tendency of painting in its first stage.

The colour spectrum of *Evenings*, *Taras Bulba* and *Vii* is motley and bright with few compound colours, like 'translucent white', 'dark brown', 'fiery violet' and so on. Red is 'red' and it is dominant (eighty-four references in the tally); 'red as fire' (ten times); 'as blood' (seven times), scarlet (seven times), crimson (four times); ruby (once); 'as a buoy', 'as a poppy', 'as a bullfinch' (its chest). Typical combinations are of gold and red, red and dark blue, red and. green, red and black. In *Vii* the floor is carpeted with red nankeen; scarlet velvet covers the body in the coffin; golden tassels and fringes reach the floor, and the candles have green tracery (red ... gold ... green) ...

The next most frequent colour is gold, with only thirty-seven references (11.6%); then come black and dark blue (11 % and 10.7%).

The same thing applies to the people in *The Terrible Vengeance*.

... Gogol studied painting. His manner of dressing out the scenes in *The Terrible Vengeance* in colour shows the synthesis of hues in the first phase of his works: red predominates (26%); after red, only black and dark blue manage more than 10% (10.6% and 11.5%). The same proportion is observed in *The Terrible Vengeance*, where there are nineteen mentions of red for eight of black and blue. Mentions of red include 1) spots on clothes 2) flashes like red fireworks. These areas are also mixed with dark blue and green. The sorcerer is cloaked in red; red is the colour of the boiling blood whose roar fills his ears and makes him reach for his sword. On the sorcerer, the red is a patch over a black hole; the black is beneath the red; the red jacket races through the black forests, cutting the moonbeams in two in the black boat, appears from under the black mountains as it slowly makes its way towards the black castle ...

... Each of the three main characters is accompanied by his own colour: Danil's colour is gold and dark blue; Katerina's is light blue, pink and silver; the sorcerer is black and red. Red Molyaka prophecies his appearance: a silver willow weeps sorrowfully for Katerina.

Subject matter and colour have been firmly bonded together ... (p. 73)

Bely put this particularly well when he wrote about Katerina, depicted in light blue and pink; and the reflected light of Danil's dark blue (and gold) as he approaches her and the red (and black) ofthe sorcerer . . .

As Gogol's works progress, the spectrum continues to shift.

Especially noticeable is what happens to the red.

From the exuberance of *Evenings on a Farm near Dikanka* to the tragic second volume of *Dead Souls*.

26.6%, 12.5%, 10.3%, 6.4% (p. 121).

The figures speak for themselves.

But here is Bely speaking for them too:

> . . . The coloration of the second and third phase.
>
> The spectrum reacts: with a diminishing number of red bits, beginning with *Ivan Fyodorovich Shponka and his Aunt*, *How Ivan Ivanovich Quarrelled with Ivan Nikiforovich*, *Old World Landowners* and ending with the comedies, the percentage of red drops: from 26.6% to 12.5%; and it falls lower still in both volumes of *Dead Souls*; 10.3% to 6.4%; in the second volume there are fewer than a quarter of the references to red in *Evenings*; dark blue falls from 10.7% to 6.1 % and from 6.1 % to 4.9% (in the first volume of *Dead Souls*). Gold falls too, from 11.6% to 8.9%, from 8.9% to 2.8%; silver drops from 7.1 to 3.2 and 2.8 . . .
>
> . . . The shift in vocabulary is matched by a shift in the spectrum too: as the colours glimmer and die, the effect becomes chiaroscuro. In Part One of *Dead Souls*, white, black and grey are foremost. Colours are cast in shadow . . . bluish-grey, like Manilov's wallpaper.
>
> . . . At times a lot is shrouded: 'with beauty-spots', 'flies landed on it', 'the sun . . . was shining and . . . flies . . . turned towards it', 'a swarm of flies, borne on a light breeze',

'airborne squadrons of flies . . . scattered . . . pieces', 'an inkwell with a number of flies', in Korobochka's room 'countless flies', a glass 'with three flies' and hence, associations with flies: 'flies, not people', 'they died like flies', 'smaller than a fly', and so on.

Corresponding to these specks of black are white parts of women who are chiefly wearing white make-up, but are ironically described as 'shining'. Chartokutsky's wife is shown having white parts (her linen and blouse are white); the governor's daughter in *Dead Souls* is petite and white; the ladies wear dresses. 'white as swans', and bootees white 'as smoke' with stockings white 'as snow' . . . there are other white toilet appurtenances. . . 22% white in the first volume, and 17% in the second.

White lies beneath the specks of black.

There is plenty of *blanc et noir* here . . .

From the bright flashes of red and blue in a golden setting to black/grey/white, and finally pure *blanc et noir*.

This spectrum in Gogol's works was to etch itself into my memory for a long time.

THREE LETTERS ABOUT COLOUR[1]

I began writing these 'memoirs' while I was still bedridden, in the Kremlin hospital, and with only one real reason, of course:

I wanted to prove to myself that I had after all had a life . . .

Then I hastily began to justify my writing by saying that it was an exercise for perfecting my literary style; that, more important, it was a training ground for 'writing easily'—cultivating the skill of spontaneously transferring every idea, every feeling, every image that might occur to me on to the page. This would save time on whatever intervening processes there might be, by pouring it out on to paper then and there.

Another motive prompted me from behind the scenes, which was to give myself a free rein and 'throw out' on to the page the whole gamut of associations which spill out uncontrollably at the least provocation and sometimes apropos nothing at all.

Anyway, I gave myself absolutely free rein for several months.

So far—up to today—I can observe the following:

I have acquired a certain facility for writing, and have achieved total irresponsibility with regard to what I am writing, and on a good day I can manage up to thirty-four pages of manuscript (this is in the region of one printer's sheet) at one sitting.

But then again . . . I have completely ruined my style of 'serious writing', highbrow journalism.

My style has not got any lighter; fatally, I am now launching into unrestrained expatiations in all directions, digressing from what is germane to the article.

I had conceived three letters about colour (as an appendix to *Nonindifferent Nature*) before my illness.

Three Letters about Colour.

The Attack on the Cypresses—an exposé of the principled approach to the question of colour. *Andante héroïque.* *The Springs oj Happiness—scherzo* on the theme of *les tribulations*, during the practical realization of these lofty intentions.

And the third article—*The Letter That Was Not Sent*—consisted of a letter to Tynyanov that I really did not send.

After it had been written, news reached me that this great writer had died an agonizing death in hospital (was it in Orenburg?) during the evacuation.[2]

I used to sit and write under the apple-trees at a sanatorium in the hills near Alma-Ata. It was not snowy blossom that weighed down the branches in the spring, but real snow. I spent a winter there, reading Part Three of Tynyanov's *Pushkin*, published in *Znamya* [The Banner].

I learnt the details of his last days only recently, from someone who had been in the same ward.

He was unable to lie down; he sat hunched up, his knees up against his chest, suffering unbelievable agony.

The last time we met was in the Central Executive Committee building; I drove him from there in 1939 after we had both been given awards by Mikhail Ivanovich Kalinin himself, who died only a few days later.[3]

Tynyanov could hardly walk; I all but carried him to the car and he told me that my *Mexico* was really an outstanding film. They tried to cure his monstrous illness in Paris, where his doctor told him about the film with great enthusiasm.

And if the doctors in Paris say a work is good, then it really does deserve praise.

Doctors are the greatest connoisseurs, the sternest art critics there. I know that they are particularly fastidious collectors.

Darius Milhaud did not take me to galleries to see the best of French painting; we went to dentists' waiting-rooms. They are the most discriminating collectors of paintings.

LEFT. Yuri Tynyanov, writer and literary expert. (Photograph: N. Nappelbaum).
RIGHT. Alexander Sergeyevich Pushkin. (Engraving by N. Yutkin, from the
portrait by Orest Kiprensky)

... A terrible detail:

Tynyanov hunched up on his bed, holding a huge red lobster
claw.

The hospital had been hit by an acute food shortage.

They fed the patients with a consignment of huge lobster from
the Far East, which fate delivered up to the city ...

I am not going to digress here on the subject of lobsters.

I shall avoid mentioning my first encounter with them, in my
childhood, in Houlgate, on the Brittany coast; there were mountains
of them—dead, with their muddy orange stomachs uppermost—on
the rocks of the bays (*sur les falaises*). At low tide the sea would
retreat so far into the distance as to be only a thin dark green strip
on the horizon.

I shall not talk about them here, for any reminiscing about them is sure to lead me to my seven-year-old friend Jeanne. I was eight when I was in Trouville and little Jeanne only knew me in my bathing costume.

Once it happened that I met her after lunch, properly dressed (we met each day in the morning when we would sit side by side shrimping).

Little Jeanne walked past Without recognizing the spruce little boy—her friend she splashed around with in rock pools each morning.

Remembering Jeanne brings me to the big wave.

The vast, towering, headlong waves of the Atlantic, which the broad sweep of the ocean hurls on to the beach as the tide rushes in; a shattering rampart of water thundering on to the emptying shore.

Woe betide the lingerer, lost in thought, who forgets about the tide!

Where a minute before lay the smooth surface of the beach, pools of warm water here and there with a starfish wallowing at the bottom or a family of shrimps, now a gigantic, ominous green-blue wall of salt water rears up.

A short pale figure in a light knitted costume is still splashing about among the shrimps, and the treacherous glaucous swell of the ocean is already swinging round in a broad arc. In a few minutes, the foam-flecked crests of giant ridges will crash together with a roar.

If it were not for someone's strong, firm grasp and athletic dash, carrying me to the safety of a distant strip of sand which lay beyond the reach of the sea, then young Jeanne would never again have met her young friend, nor would this pale little boy have grown up to be sitting here now, drawing an idle pencil across a pad of white paper, swallowed up by a sea of memories.

. . . Tynyanov had died and the letter was not sent.

The letter concerned my wish to do the life of Push kin in colour.

Pushkin, strange to say (for me, not him!), the lover.

On the basis of Tynyanov's theory, which is expounded in *A Nameless Love.*[4]

The fascinating history of the poet's secret love for Karamzin's wife is told here in a much more inspired way and much more acutely, than in the last part of the novel, where he seems to be in a great hurry to finish, frightened that he will not live to see it completed.

The letter was also full of ideas about the colour capacity of film.

The letter was in draft form.

And this gives me now the right to work it up into a more detailed exposition of the way colour was conceived in the film, made in colour.

But I seem to have spoilt my writing style irretrievably: two introductory lines for what became an independent, extensive 'page of memoirs' (instead of the second article 'The Springs of Happiness') itself expanded into an entire fragment of a memoir, with shrimps, lobsters, little Jeanne and the Atlantic Ocean.

And they were only meant as an introductory piece to explain the origin of the pages that follow.

What began as 'a few words' of introduction to the 'second letter about colour' turned into everything except what they were meant to be; and now, instead of an *Anhang** for *Nonindifferent Nature*, they lie in a heap of *freie Einfiille*† with the pompous title *Memoirs*!

They do indeed deal mostly with how, through various associations, key images and impressions and recollections of earlier works, I came to resolve the banquet scene in *Ivan* in the way I did.

* German: 'appendix'.
† German: 'free ideas'.

THE SPRINGS OF HAPPINESS[1]

Sanin by Artsybashev,

> *The Wrath of Dionysus* by Nagrodskaya,
>
> The novels of Lappo-Danilevskaya
>
> and of course Verbitskaya's *The Springs of Happiness.*[2]
>
> This is a whole epoch in literature.

An epoch which clearly demonstrated the loss of whatever stability there had been in those echelons of the intelligentsia that had failed to latch on to the Revolutionary movement.

We were still too young to read all that when the books came out.

We learnt about them second-hand, from the arguments of grown-ups, from fragments of the polemics linked to their publication, but more from their titles and the authors' surnames.

How long ago it was!

How much has changed: our country has changed its character; the face of Europe has been altered; the whole world has changed over these decades.

How strange it is when chance turns up a photograph of Madame Lappo-Danilevskaya, among the other denizens of the Stage Veterans' Club. I remember her when she was part of the troupe of actors working for the Political Administration of the Western Front in 1920. I myself was working as set-designer in Minsk, just after its liberation.

It comes as a shock to realize that the author of *The Springs of Happiness* had a son who can be seen almost daily—on the stage of the Moscow Art Theatre, acting in *Anna Karenina,* or Gorky's *Enemies.*[3]

This is almost as strange as the thought that Matisse, that old museum piece, is still alive.

Or that Edvard Munch—the father of expressionism—died only two years ago, in 1944.[4] That movement reached its height and we saw it do so; it passed into oblivion long ago (and we saw it do that, too), supplanted by Constructivism and Surrealism which succeeded it and which have also left the stage.

Yevreinov's 'theatre for oneself'[5] emerged from the turbid whirlpool of these pre-Revolutionary, pre-war years.

It was one of his three small volumes that had model scripts for plays for this theatre which had no audience, critics or auditorium.

I remember one such script.

It is called *The Trying on of Deaths*.

The reader is invited to experience the delightful sensations Petronius felt as he died, his veins cut—a small incision of the auxiliary blood-vessels in his arm in a warm bath—monitored by a concealed accomp (a doctor) and to the strains of a distant harp.

It is supposed that the first impressions of death from odours is of banks upon banks of flowers . . . etc. . . . . etc.

The title *The Springs of Happiness* has been explained by contemporaries thus: this is a story about wells or sources of happiness.

The title *Dead Souls* can be read in two ways: as a literal reference to the serfs on the register who have since died and whom Mr Chichikov wishes to deal in; or metaphorically, concerning the moribund souls of his clientèle—the representatives of the Russian landowning classes.

Springs of Happiness has a meaning quite different, hidden from the 'wells' idea.

And it is quite cynical: it corresponds fully, in the sphere of love, with the above-mentioned entertainment at the Yevreinov Theatre, *The Trying on of Deaths*.

The 'Springs of Happiness' were a kind of lottery when I was a child.

Every charity fete had one, next to the hoop-la where you had to throw a ring around a stick to win the prize that was hung around it; or the game where you had to throw little balls into coloured bags which were hanging up with sweets and lollipops inside.

The 'Springs of Happiness' consisted of a box standing on a table.

A box, locked up.

Next to the box were twelve keys.

Only one of the twelve would spring the lock.

To 'fit' a key cost one rouble.[6]

When the box opened, its contents would be the prize-ten roubles, I think.

Sometimes, it worked first time.

Sometimes, at the second or third attempt.

And sometimes, it took twelve keys and the player lost. Mme Verbitskaya subjected her heroine to such ordeals andquests in the sphere of love.

The title *The Springs of Happiness* is more than just appropriate. But as far as I recall, the heroine did not come off any the worse.

The Springs of Happiness is not only a method of searching for love. *The Springs of Happiness* is in many respects the method of searching in art.

In those murky periods of its development, when new possibilities that have not been recognized or assimilated suddenly appear; new methods of expression, new means of influence.

Where should we search for our approach? How can we find the right paths? Where should one look for the key that could spring the little box open, revealing wonderful new secrets and possibilities?

The box could of course simply be smashed open. 'Vandalistic art' aptly describes the thorough-going wrecking of cinema, with regard to what happened to music and dialogue in the talkies.

It is happening again with the practice of colour, which has ransacked oleography rather than painting.

The other way is by fitting the keys to the locks.

For one may have a very distinct idea of one's desires; a very precise set of equations which the unknown—x—must satisfy: new possibilities and a very precise idea of the formulae in which the solutions must be expressed.

But the step from abstract ideas, tangibly exact and close, to their realization in practice, is sometimes barred by the unbridgeable difficulties of trying to assimilate the peculiarities of the new area of creativity.

In my *Attack on the Cypresses*, I tried to formulate the principles which we brought to bear in our assault on the question of colour in cinema.

The real 'Springs of Happiness' should concern some of those right (but more often wrong) keys we used to attack the Pandora's box of colour film.

I am not sure whether I can say that it was good fortune, or even only chance fortune that led to my first work in colour.

But there was definitely a chain of chance events.

This chain led to the work itself.

And the same chain and the conjunction of the unexpected with chance determined the course I was to take in solving the actual problems of colour.

Colour in cinema had long been a preoccupation of mine. For so long, in fact, that I regard my entire output in black-and-white to have been in colour too.

In colour, but confined to a limited spectrum of monochrome shades.

But work in colour proper occupied me for a fairly long time too. At least, since the time when I thought that the technical problems had been conclusively solved.

Different pioneers have tackled it differently.

Some worked on mastering the technical possibilities, fascinated by the work on perfecting the new technical phenomenon.

Sound had attracted such vigorous research also—when sound was still not considered an independent element in its own right, to be arbitrarily married to the visual element.

There were the same enthusiasts for mastering colour, which needed a lamp of unprecedented brightness, an optical cube and three films of different tones all running through the same projector, so that one could see on the screen the not particularly fine confetti of different colours (no hues) and tones (no halftones): reality distorted beyond recognition.

I have had nothing to do with pioneers and enthusiasts of this sort. I am not interested in quests for making a soprano sound as good on film as in reality (in the early days of sound, she was quite indistinguishable from a tenor with a sore throat).

I think that before the present quest should begin, screen technology should be of a standard able to guarantee accurate replay of a piano and life-like violin music. So much time and effort has already been spent on this.

Only when that has been established can one start on worthwhile research into audiovisual counterpoint, the *sine qua non* of audiovisual cinema.

It is just the same with colour.

The first, almost incoherent projections of colour film (*Giordano Bruno*), just like my first colour film to be worked out in detail (*Pushkin*), were 'archived' as soon as it became clear that the technology was still in its infancy; that not one formal solution could guarantee success.

And the recurrent theme of *Ivan the Terrible* is the very one that runs the entire gamut of colour in the overwhelming first two-thirds and is quite accessible to black-and-white cinema. Traditional black, grey and white has the richest variety of textures, from the metallic gleam of the brocade, with its varying quality and style, through the material and cloth, to the soft play of furs, which includes the whole range of shades, from sable and fox to wolf and bear; brown when it is worn, and white for carpets and bedcoverings.

I saw the first models of colour film a very long time ago. Méliès's magical touch.

It was an underwater kingdom, where bright yellow knights in armour hid in the jaws of green whales and light blue and pink sorceresses were born from the foam of the sea.

Soon afterwards films began appearing with natural colouring. I have allready forgotten the system and technique used, but they came out in Riga, in about 1910 or 1912.

True, it was in just one cinema—in the Wermann Park, with the portentous name *Kino-Kultura*. This did not stop it from showing, after these short colour films of an 'educational' nature, weekly episodes in the *Fantômas* and *Vampire* series.

The films were short and had an overall pink cast and showed white sails of yachts skimming across an azure sea; fruits of different shapes and sizes and flowers which were to be picked by girls with a blaze of ginger hair—or it may be flaxen—and people working the fields in the spring.

My first personal attempts at using colour were: a handpainted red flag in *Potemkin* and the less well-known montage made from short sections in the scenes surrounding the separator and the 'bull's wedding' in *The Old and the New*.

The question of using colour concretely in film production arose in 1939. In connection with the completion of work on the film *Fergana Canal*, after 'my Tamerlane was amputated', as I used to say at the time.[7]

I conceived the film about the Fergana canal as a triptych about the struggle for water.

Central Asia in a blaze of flowers, thanks to the amazing irrigation system constructed all those centuries ago.

In Tamerlane's fratricidal conflicts and expeditions, man's control over water is destroyed. Sand overruns all.

The poverty of the sandy wastes under the tsars. The fight for one more cup of water from the waterways, where once there had been a perfect irrigation system.

And finally, the miracle of the first collective feat—building the collective farms in Uzbekistan: the Fergana Canal which was an unprecedented project in terms of scale and brought wealth and prosperity to socialist Central Asia.

For reasons not revealed to me, the shooting of the first panel of the triptych was cancelled the very day before we were due to begin work.

The composition of the entire work hung helplessly suspended in mid-air.

The whole plan was dropped very soon afterwards.

I had taken over the production of *Die Walküre* at the Bolshoi Theatre;[8] I devoted the whole conception of the last piece, *Feuerzauber*,* to searching for ways of combining the elements of Wagner's score with a changing play of coloured light on the stage.

Despite the extremely limited technical resources and the far from perfect lighting and the lighting equipment of the Bolshoi's stage, which drastically reduced the range of colours available to us for the fire, we nevertheless achieved an extremely convincing rendering in colour of 'Wotan's Farewell'.

Perhaps it was from this point, the random cessation of work on *Fergana*, that the series of regular co.incidences began, that led in practice to working with colour.

* German: 'Magic Fire'.

With only a limited spectrum of colours to play idly from the flies above the stage of the Bolshoi, on to the *Feuerzauber* of Wagner's *Die Walküre*, no more than two tonal qualities were possible.

Allow me to set all the tints of this Magic Fire into play and alternate the purple-crimson and blue lights which are all the colours you have under your control at the console.

It is as well also that before this, in the scene of 'Wotan's Farewell', you have managed to retrieve for the colour-change square lights as large as the whole of the backstage.

Here it is, metallic bronze to begin with.

Now it fluidly changes into silver.

And now, with the embrace in the music, it suddenly changes into the deepest, lyrical blue . . .

Wagner's score is not too rich in its coloration, but it flares up, burns, bathed in light, organically and in the spirit of movement within the music.

In the Magic Fire, Loge's theme runs like a thread of blue through the purple of fire, the underlying element.

Now that theme melts in the fire.

Now it seems to have smothered the fire.

The scene with Wotan and Brünnhilde, from Richard Wagner's opera *Die Walküre*, in Eisenstein's production. The Bolshoi Theatre, Moscow, 1940.

The perspiring and begrimed face of the electrician looks up, tired and plaintive, from beneath the lid of the lighting box. Only he is able to match the knife-switches and rheostats to the movements of the assistant director's finger as it twitches in time to the score, synchronously with the frenzied orchestra, now wailing, now seething, now roaring, how mellifluous as it reaches the finale of the last act of the second opera in the Ring cycle.

One way or another, I take the first practical steps in chromophonic—a synthesis of sound and colour-counterpoint, on the stage of the Bolshoi, for myself.

I must also mention my other 'firsts' in my work which for some reason have always so uncannily linked me to this building.

It was here that a fragment of my first, independent work as director was shown. It was some anniversary connected to the theatres of the 'Left', in 1923.⁹

It was here that for the first time I was on a poster, identified as the 'director' and 'producer'.

And here for the first time, before a flabbergasted spectator from the edge of the pit, came the whistle and roar of the percussion band that answered my hoot of the football siren as I leapt out of my red velvet seat and a young actress of my then Proletkult theatre performed in her dazzling yellow costume the first circus trick in the whole history of the Bolshoi Theatre, ascending a six-metre-long pole . . . the mast of death!

And it was here, two years later, that the white rectangle of a cinema screen was unrolled: again for the first time. Making its own evocative entrance, it cast those ancient, deep-rooted and rigid traditions to the four winds.

The waves of the Black Sea, the surge of the revolt and the firing on the Odessa Steps burst out of that projection box, somewhere near the old 'royal' box; they lashed the screen, hit the audience and the prow of the victorious battleship broke into the auditorium, the red pennant fluttering above.

The premiere of *Potemkin* took place on the anniversary of 1905, within these very walls.[10]

In 1940, silver horses rose up into the lighting rig above the stage, as if soaring into the clouds.

There was no dazzling sunlight to hasten the joyous song of love into the audience; instead a yellow spotlight shone from behind a curtain, saturating the auditorium with light.

And the wind machines beneath the stage always failed to blow—they never once fanned the tongues of fire, which hung limply in the blue and scarlet light, looking more like streamers above a butcher's shop than the play of fire which was supposed to protect Brünnhilde's sleep, until Siegfried came to wake her . . .

The chromophonic combination of streams of music and light. The play of the beams of light.

The magic, when links are found . . .

That is not so much, but what I derived of infinite emotional value from this work, with its burning aspirations, inspired strivings and tragic achievement, was condemned by insuperable technical difficulties to crawl where it should have burst into the heavens . . .

But where, among the warlike maidens' unruly steeds leaping into the heavens, lay the chief object of our quest—the life story of Alexander Sergeyevich Pushkin?

Right in the middle.

I had still not finished arranging *Die Walküre* by May 1940. It went on until the autumn.

And I devoted the summer to Alexander Sergeyevich.

I reached the point where I felt I knew my hero well enough to call him by his first names.

That is how historians speak of great figures in the past.

I remember some historians discussing the screenplay of *Alexander Nevsky* and debating the various theories about how he was poisoned when he was being entertained by the Khan.

'In my view,' one of them said, 'it was perfectly simple. Alexander Yaroslavich simply had tuberculosis. Nor should you forget that he had had a difficult journey, which would have lowered his resistance ...'

And that somehow brought Alexander Yaroslavich five hundred years closer.

And that same scholar demolished the remaining interval completely when he—or was it another—tried to describe my future hero in more detail and said he had a beard 'a bit like Nekrasov's'.[11]

Work on Pushkin began after I had suspended my experiments on chromophonic counterpoint in the *Die Walküre*—experiments that I was bang in the middle of.

But, before going into that, I should say a few words about my work on Wagner.

In my production at the Bolshoi, which again was more a sketchy idea than a complete picture, Wotan's appearance was preceded by toppling pine trees.

Then, near the curtain, they rose up from the ground once more, joining the Valkyries' final upward flight and their divine father's furious departure.

I had identified the Valkyries with pine trees.

Probably because I first heard their frenzied flight on someone's piano among the giant pines in the forests of Finland.

The chords carried the warrior maidens off up to the crowns of the trees at Raivola station.

And I came to know the structure of leitmotif and counterpoint among the bases of even greater trees—the famous redwoods around San Francisco.

TOP. Eisenstein, Williams and Shpiller during the production of *Die Walküre* in the Bolshoi Theatre.

BOTTOM. Rehersal for *Die Walküre*.

I rested for a week in their cool shade, far from the heat and commotion of Hollywood; I gnawed the sweet fruits of knowledge and drank the subtle poison of Joyce's *Ulysses* and the commentary by Stuart Gilbert.

Autumn 1930.

It was from ... literature that I mastered the obvious tangibility of the technique of musical counterpoint.

This was probably not only correct, but natural too. Because I came to it after mastering visual counterpoint.[12] I needed the bare bones of counterpoint, separated from what was customary and usual—the world of sounds.

In a form in which they could become the backbone of what was new, unprecedented.

And it was very appropriate that they were encased in a literary form.

The more so as I was holding a quite remarkable piece of literature.

Which was devised not simply as 'music', but in strict accordance with musical canon: exactly on the principle of *fuga per canonem*.

The Sirens' episode from *Ulysses*.

Tiny squirrels hopped about gnawing nuts at the feet of these gigantic trees.

The crowns of the giant redwoods vanished in the blue sky.

And the multiple passages of regular, intricate constructions from the chapters of this novel's exceptionally musical prose whispered the secrets of these melodic structures in my ear one by one.

The chapter begins with bronze by gold: two heads of hair, Miss Lydia Douce's and Miss Minna Kennedy's.

It takes place in the Ormond Bar.

The girls are working in the bar.

But our interest in what happens here goes beyond the girls, the visitors and potential drama of premonitions.

It lies in the way this complex network of different personal experiences and personalities dissolves in a strict pattern of musical writing.

Stuart Gilbert, one of the most reliable commentators on Joyce, said:

> The episode of the Sirens opens with two pages of brief extracts from the narrative which follows. These fragmentary phrases appear almost meaningless to the reader till he has perused the chapter to its end; nevertheless they should not be 'skipped'.

In a footnote, Gilbert wrote:

> So curious is the language of this episode that, when it was sent by the author from Switzerland to England during the Great War, the Censor held it up, suspecting that it was written in some secret code. Two English writers (it is said) examined the work, and came to the conclusion that it was not 'code' but literature of some unknown kind.

What are these two pages?

> ... They are like the overtures of some operas and operettas, in which fragments of the leading themes and refrains are introduced to prepare the hearer's mood and also to give him, when these abridged themes are completed and developed in their proper place, that sense of familiarity which, strangely enough, enhances for many hearers their enjoyment of a new tune ...

Another expert and devoted follower of Joyce, Professor Curtius, reacted with critical disapproval to these attempts by Joyce, when he underscored the link between the structure of this chapter, and Wagner's way of working:

> ... These two pages of seemingly meaningless text form in reality an extremely carefully calculated composition, which can only be understood when the reader has perused the whole chapter and perused it with the greatest attention. The literary technique employed is an exact transposition of the musical technique. To be more precise, the technique of Wagner's leitmotif. But there is this difference, that the musical motif is complete in itself and more satisfying; I can listen with delight to a Wagnerian leitmotif, even if I cannot place the allusion (Valhalla theme? Walsungen theme?). But the word motif, unintelligible in itself, acquires meaning only when I relate it to its context... Joyce has deliberately ignored the essential difference between sounds and words, and for this reason his experiment is of questionable value ...*

Stuart Gilbert met this objection by suggesting that in music too the first notes of a theme are equally fragmentary and supply no more than do the initial, 'truncated' phrases of Joyce's text.

More important of course is the fact that this section too, like all the other chapters of Joyce's *Ulysses*, is immensely exaggerated.

Everything that subtly informs (to a lesser or greater degree) the style of this or that variety of literary writing, is here a *ne plus ultra*, the peak of material tangibility and clarity.

That same hyperbole that led to 735 pages of narrative being devoted to the events of one day in the life of an exceptionally modest, insignificant Dubliner—the advertisement canvasser, Leopold Bloom—is also manifest in the technical devices and the method of writing.

* Ernst Robert Curtis, *James Joyce und sein Ulysses* (Zurich: Verlag der Neuen Scweizer Rundschau, 1929), pp. 54–5. [E's reference]

Stuart's research into the nature of music and the observance of the laws of music in the writing of this chapter is compelling and scrupulous.

It probes every essential element of 'strict writing'. And it takes delight in each essential encounter with the most unlikely features and canonical figures.

It traces the path of music, from the structure of the chapter as a whole, to its influence on all the particularities within the writing; and it discovers verbal correspondences to *fermata* in music and explains how, by using abridged names, he achieves the effect of simultaneity, which corresponds to what is called *stretto* in a fugue. Etc., etc.

There would of course be no point in enumerating all these now.

I will confine myself to purely general notions.

...The language and content of this episode (its technique is the *fuga per canonem*) are throughout handled in a characteristically musical manner. The theme is rarely simple; there are generally two, three or four overlapping parts, which, synchronized by intertwinement in the same sentence, or closely juxtaposed, produce the effect of a chord of music. He who reads such passages as certain cultured concert—goers prefer to hear a fugue-with the parts kept mentally distinct in four, or fewer, independent horizontal lines of melody-will miss much of the curious emotive quality of Mr Joyce's prose in this episode. For most of the sensuous value of music, the enthralment of the Sirens' song, is missed by the musical 'high-brow' who forces himself to analyse the sounds he hears and separate the music into independent lines of horizontal parts. To enjoy to the full the emotion of symphonic music, the hearer should be aware of it as a sequence of chords, listen vertically as well as horizontally. And this holds good not only for the romantics such as Beethoven and Wagner, who (especially the latter) 'think in chords', but also, though in a somewhat less degree, for counterpoint fuguists like Bach . . .

This is all elementary stuff for musicians, of course.

For people who study literature, it is the very limit of compound structural writing.

But I am writing a traveller's notebook, not a textbook; it is my aim to map the crossroads, the highways and byways I travelled on as I sought to master the different means of influence outside my amazing art.

And at these crossroads I thought that the bases of musical rhythm could be applied to architecture; the shifts in tonality taking the place of the Gothic arches of Chartres Cathedral, the *pleinchant** perceived through moonlight shining through the thirteenth-century stained glass, counterpoint which I adored in the work on the pontoon bridge and the harmony of movements in space and in time, and the fugue, shown in the paradoxes of Joyce's prose. All these enriched and expanded my films, giving them a breadth of expression that they would never have acquired from a familiarity with the classicism of Bach or Taneyev alone.[13]

The last notion to enter my memory positively as I sat with the squirrels busy cracking nuts while the trees rustled high above my head, was the concluding paragraph of Stuart's chapter:

> . . . In no other episode, perhaps, of *Ulysses* has Mr Joyce attained such a complete 'atonement' between subject-matter and form. To Professor Curtius the experiment appeared 'of questionable value', and if it were a mere *tour-de-force*, an artificial grafting of musical on verbal idiom, musicoliteral virtuosity, his doubt would be well founded. But here

* In French in the original.

the musical rhythm, the sonority and counterpoint of the prose are evocative of the theme itself, the Sirens' 'song of enthralment'. This episode differs from most examples of 'musical prose' in that the meaning does not lose but is, rather, intensified by the combination of the two arts; sense is not sacrificed to sound but the two are so harmonized that, unless his ears, like the Achaeans', are sealed with wax against the spell, the reader, hearkening to 'the voice sweet as the honeycomb and having joy thereof, will go on his way the wiser'. (*Odyssey*, XII, 186–8)

The great Bach understood the interplay of separate passages within the seemingly highly abstract composition of a fugue in a way that was profoundly humanistic.

He heard the 'voices' of living people.

Together, these voices sounded like an excited confabulation on a matter of great mutual interest.

When someone had nothing to contribute, he remained silent.[14]

'Uncle Vanya'—Ivan Lebedev[15] is the legendary wrestling referee, and hero of my (and many others') childhood—would 'line up' all his 'alumni'.

Murzuk and Lurikh.

Zbyszko-Cyganewicz and Cyclops. Aberg and 'Black Mask'.[16]

They all passed before the cheering crowd, before grappling with each other in bridges and double-nelsons and turning into an indissoluble counterpoint of overstrained muscles, arched spines and bloody necks with the dull thud of skulls thrown back against the matting.

Some Japanese came.[17]

They were led by Sadanji, the 'Stanislavsky of Tokyo'.

The classical canon of his acting gradually became disturbingly innovative.

The concentrated beam which transmitted the plot according to the canon was sometimes diffused by an unexpected, unforeseeable and inappropriate psychologism.

In plays which were written in a more orthodox way, however, he was more strict.

Such as the performance of *Narukami*.

But, taken as a whole, the plays preserved the sheen of classical perfection.

They were also preceded by a line-up.

Here it was called *kumadori*.

To do it, the audience had to be introduced to a number of essential ideas about the play which would later develop into satin raiments embroidered with silk, knots of tightly coiled black wigs which spilt out of their bronze bases, which lay on the actor's shaven head (turquoise enamel was a fair representation of the bluish stubble; it filled the area between the white painted face and the silhouetted horse's mane, bound in a headband).

This was similar to the way the cast of characters in Elizabethan theatre disported themselves before the tragedy began, supplying the audience with details about themselves.

'King Maximilian' and his rebellious son 'Adolf' were presented to the audience.[18]

And the individual cogs of their complicated manoeuvres, Scribe and Labiche, Dumas *fils* or Sardou, were introduced by the leader of the chorus.

This is just the same as Joyce's juggling with truncated phrases to introduce the tonic characters of the Sirens' episode into the emotional fabric of verbal counterpoint.

And I, the youngest offspring of these glorious old lines, threw spots of colour, the first dancing colour frames of a dance in the Alexandrov sloboda—abstractly, like a dance of colours—into the beginning of the episode so that the golden horde of *oprichniki* could later arise from the gold and change into the theme of golden majesty and the wisdom of heavenly azure; shirts would develop out of the red and blood, in the candle-light; the spots of black would quench, like ash, the light of progress, reinstating the darkness once more.

And this was much later.

But then my telephone rang.

And I consented over the phone to a production of *Die Walküre* in the Bolshoi . . .

Children sometimes ask: 'Why is there a light?'

Equally valid would be the question: 'Why *Die Walküre*?'

'Because.' It is hard to think of a more logical answer.

I think it must have been the most unprepared, on-the-spot response I have ever professionally given.

Made while Williams and Samosud,[19] who had decided to butter me up for some reason with this production, were speaking on the phone.

Their flattery paid off.

I could not of course stand in the way of 'The Ride of the Valkyries'.

But this apparently chance, subsidiary exercise then became, of sheer necessity, a part of a solution to audiovisual matters which I had been obsessed by since my experience with audiovisual work on *Alexander Nevsky*, which concluded what Meisel and I had been working on in the score for *Potemkin* all those years ago.

(Not to mention even earlier quests on the same lines in the Proletkult theatre.)

In any event, at almost the same time as the work on Wagner, I was offered the chance of working seriously in colour, for colour cinema.

As was only to be expected of course, the proposal stipulated a natural 'wide spectrum of colours'.

The best subject, in that it had the widest range of colours, and was, at the same time, interesting and acceptable ideologically for the leadership, was the highly colourful Giordano Bruno.[20]

Italy, of course . . .

Renaissance dress . . .

A fire . . .

Two other themes were taken on board at the same time. One presented itself.

Colonel Lawrence and the Arab revolt in the Middle East.

The psychological aspect of Lawrence is bound to interest the reader familiar not only with *Revolt in the Desert*, but also the terrible inner confession of nihilism, moral bankruptcy and the Dostoyevskian character of the *Seven Pillars of Wisdom*—his record of his wartime exploits.[21]

True, the only colour here is in the green of the Prophet's flag and the green turbans of the generals.

And also the remarkable description of the old Arab woman, who had never seen blue eyes before and asked the intelligence officer whether his eyes were blue because the sky shone through them.

In fact, the green turban comes not from the Colonel's writings but from an English novel with a similar theme.

And in order to treat the material more freely, the film was not to be too factually biographical; the setting had to be a different, but no less popular, base for the mysterious colonel's activities—Iran.

Again history was a different theme.

Invariably, the colourful past would be looked for on the cusp between the Middle Ages and the Renaissance.

One of the reviewers for the Committee on Cinema Affairs came to me with this theme like a fox terrier carrying a slipper, all because of the bright colours of the costumes.

The theme was . . . the plague.

Why the plague?

Why the plague, rather than cholera, smallpox or typhoid?

In fact, it was not the colourfulness of this theme that appealed, but something quite different, although the appeal lasted only for a short period, until I had finished the graphic sketch.

It was the possibility of devising a film showing how the 'variety of colour', so dear to the leadership's heart, could be consumed by blackness as the plague spread.

Using different material, another aspect of this theme of the sensual (and colourful) wealth of life being consumed, turning into stone, excited me for quite different reasons. That was how I solved the knotty problem of gold in my planned film (and completed screenplay) of Blaise Cendrars' novel *Sutter's Gold*.

I had wanted to produce a romanticized version of Captain Sutter's life for Paramount while I was in America.

And also the destruction, caused by the discovery of gold on his Californian estates: it led to his prosperous farms being ravaged and to his own death. I wanted to express this with the vivid impression which the drags of the Californian gold prospectors have left on me to this day.

Mountains of spoil still stand where they were flung up from the half-excavated mines; as in Sutter's time, they bury the lush greenery of the fields around the mines.

Beneath the soulless layer of stones lay once-verdant orchards, fields, pastures and meadows.

Implacably, constantly and inexorably the wall of stone advanced, encroaching on the green and ruthlessly crushing living, vital shoots for the sake of gold.

The 1848 Gold Rush sent hundreds of thousands of prospectors to California in search of the valuable metal which so amply rewarded the effort of extracting it.

It is difficult to imagine how it was; to picture oneself in the throes of this maddening fever.

But a modicum of personal experience makes it easy to see how this elemental pursuit of gold must have raged like a typhoon, a hurricane, a welter of passions.

Considerably later, I happened to wind up in the mountains in the Kabardino-Balkarian Republic, at places which had only just been discovered by the prospectors.

A narrow gorge.

A rivulet.

A few home-made, rickety, shallow vats.

My travelling companion and guard (no doubt on the pay roll of the Republic's NKVD)[22] stooped to gather a handful of muddy earth.

The clods were put in a tin, bowl-like vessel.

The earth was carefully washed by rocking the vessel.

And suddenly some small specks appeared at the bottom. Gold!

The ground seemed to shake underfoot, opening up to its depths; and through the surface of dark mud, overgrown with turf, I could see millions of barely detectable grains of gold-dust!

You can easily imagine how people might fling themselves to the ground with arms outstretched, trying to amass it in their hands; people, made drunk by their contact with this wealth lying scattered under the soles of their boots; people ready to kill anyone who dared to walk on this sea of gold lying beneath the topsoil; people quite prepared to pan this amoral and lecherous rich earth in the warm blood of any rival trespassing on excavated grains of gold which were invisible to the naked eye . . .

The feet of thousands of such madmen trampled over Sutter's land; thousands of hands ran through it and turned it over; thousands of people raced towards this spot, coming from all corners of the globe and ready to tear each others' throats out for the sake of a tiny clod of this earth which bears so strange a crop in its core . . .

The flourishing paradise of Captain Sutter's Californian groves and pastures was trampled underfoot and crushed by filthy crowds lusting for gold.

Sutter was ruined . . .

But then, with fresh determination, the proud old man threw thousands of writs at these dirty invaders who had appropriated and occupied his land.

Sutter's estates at that time were extensive and prosperous.

Over the course of a few years, San Francisco grew up on those estates, expanding from a small mission into a large and bustling city.

The town grew in an unexpected and strange way.

You can see how it happened from old engravings. Flotillas of barges and boats blocked up all the available moorings and clogged the bays.

The boats dropped anchor and remained in the bays there after.

The gaps between the boats were bridged with gangways and ultimately silted up.

Shacks were built on the decks.

Bungalows at first; then two- and three-storeyed dwellings. The holds became cellars.

The decks dovetailed together, forming streets and alleyways.

The intruding holds and decks absorbed the surface of the bays as the slagheaps had done; the greenery of the gulf was buried by the secretly whispering sand which turned the once lush paradise into a saltmarsh hinterland, such as you might find in Central Asia.

When suddenly, one man, old and decisive, threw down the gauntlet before this town of boats and barges, which had worked its tentacles deep into the fissures of the coastline like an octopus and frantically dug into the shore and surrounding hills.

And another swarm gathered over California.

This time, a black one.

The attorneys' dress was a long jacket and tall, long-fibred topper—as we know from photographs of Lincoln and his colleagues in the legal profession.

Thousands of black jackets and toppers swooped down on San Francisco, like a flock of ragged crows.

An unprecedented battle was imminent: one man against an entire city.

And a third flock, black and ghastly, silhouetted between the yard-arms and lanterns in the coastal fog and blackness of the Californian night, spread itself over the once fertile, flourishing soil of Captain Sutter.

The image of a black flock is a vivid one which continues to attract me.

Perhaps because it is essentially a living impression.

Where would you have to go now (or even before the war) to see scores, if not hundreds of black toppers, wandering among the old low houses, vanishing into the twilight and then suddenly reappearing, lit by pinpricks of yellow light from small barred windows?

Does such a place exist outside Daumier's engravings—in real life, can you see such a fantastic sight?

Oddly enough, yes.

True, you won't see any beards or moustaches beneath the hats.

There is little more than down on upper lips, in fact. True, the people who wear them are unlikely to be of mature years.

I shouldn't think the oldest is as much as twenty.

But the mysterious twilight hides their age: only the general out-line is visible and the figures of the younger, juvenile, top-hat wearers in these alleys and mysterious pools of light only serve to intensify the fantastical element. They might be gnomes spirited from a Hoffmann story, or strange inhabitants of Poe's terrible stories.

But they are just whippersnappers.

Or more accurately, young gentlemen, scions of privileged families with the means to send them to Eton.

I did not mention Windsor Castle, nearby; or the white, round turned-down collars and morning trousers: that would have given the game away too soon.

After our tour of Windsor Castle, where Da Vinci's notebooks and Holbein's paintings are kept, my friend Professor Isaacs—with the bowler, red sidewhiskers and inevitable brolly—and I visited neighbouring Eton. This is the first link in the chain of English education; its discipline and atmosphere knocking the fragile, degenerate or excessively plump and indulged boys into stern and implacable, soulless and callous gentlemen, who do not go about bragging that they rule the world as the less prudent Germans do, but firmly believe that they do nevertheless and act with unwavering wholeheartedness for the glory of Britannia, Ruler of the Waves.

This type of gentleman, first sketched in the paradoxical silhou-ette of a young Etonian in his top hat, is refined still further in the chilly rooms of Cambridge and Oxford which are clad in the masonry of Tudor (and earlier) times, in refectories, where the ceilings vanish in the darkness, in the towering naves of the chapels, but also in the best-equipped physics, chemistry and electromag-netics laboratories.

And in the third link of a career which almost always stretches from Eton to Parliament via Oxford or Cambridge, this fully fledged gentleman displays to the world the strange spectacle of the perma-nency of Cadogan's policies, irrespective of whether the springs of happiness have revealed a Tory or a Labour government in the ballot boxes . . .

The avalanche of blackness consuming colour remains an enduring image of mine, one of my favourite ideas.

It is fed, from time to time, by new, associative impressions such as the trip to Windsor, a page from Cendrars' novel, a slagheap near Sacramento, or even a flock of black eagles—*zapilotes*—circling above the carcasses of horses in Mexico who died in bullfights and were dragged out into the yard at the back.

The eagles perched decorously on the fence around the yard to the rear of the arena in Merida, capital of Yucatán.

They were waiting . . .

However, Giordano Bruno, Lawrence and the plague promptly made way for another candidate on the list of projects I was to undertake.

The hero was virtually calculated mathematically.

In the same way, I think, that a displacement in the orbits of other luminaries postulated *a priori* the presence of another planet—Uranus[23]—long before ultra-powerful telescopes enabled man to see it.

What was the order of the day when sound came to cinema? The lives of musicians.

And when colour arrived, what then?

The lives of . . . painters.

What should one not attempt with both colour and sound?

Neither of these!

So what should one do?

Neither.

There is a third.

Not the life of a painter,

nor the life of a musician,

but the life of a . . . poet!

Which was how I hit upon the idea of making a film about Pushkin.

I intend to devote this third letter about colour to other and of course basic and crucial motives that led to this idea.

'The Letter That Was Not Sent' will use concrete examples to show how I envisaged the composition of the whole, according to the idea of a film entirely shot in colour.

Here, I shall just say that *Pushkin* shared the fate of the *Plague*, *Bruno* and *Lawrence*.

He remained in the 'ideas' section of my archives.

Front-line intelligence revealed that colour film was not yet ready.

There were problems that were insurmountable for the time being.

Colour was not an obedient servant, running to do the bidding of the questing craftsman: it was a terrible and savage tyrant who demanded so much light that it damaged the actors' costumes and melted their make-up; it was a scoundrel who wrung the heart of the colour idea dry; a vulgarian who rode roughshod over perceptions of colour; an idler who was unable to achieve even one per cent of the idea, the fantasy, the flight of what had been imagined in colour.

Then *Ivan* appeared.

Then war came.

Then victory.

And out of conquered Germany came an avalanche of the colour abominations of German cinema.

Then came three-layered colour film.

And this marked the beginning of a new chain of chance happenings which, after the war, took up a series of plans for colour which had been compiled before the war.

Of course, the yearning for colour arose spontaneously from my work on audiovisual counterpoint.

And of course only colour, colour and again colour is really capable of solving the problem of commensurability, of finding a common denominator for sound and vision.

Enthusiastically greeting the arrival of sound (Pudovkin and Alexandrov signed the article 'Statement On Sound' with me),[24] I once wrote very condescendingly about colour and three dimensionality in cinema, believing they could contribute nothing new in principle to the mastery of cinematic form.

People could then only guess at the possibilities of audiovisual counterpoint in cinema.

What was then being portrayed on the screen had only be gun to be mirrored by the sound.

Now, the practice of audiovisual cinema has made a real contribution to the development of cinema.

And sound, striving to find a visual image, beats powerfully in the confines of black-and-white, where it is forced to blend entirely with what is bdng portrayed.

The highest forms of organic kinship between the melodic pattern of the music and the tonal structure of a system of successive colour frames are only possible with the advent of colour.

But it is time to move from general phrases to the matter in hand, from the manifesto, to a plan of action, from loud declamations, to the practicalities.

From a tirade, to a history of those ups and downs, which were comic and sad, enjoyable and maddening, exciting and joyous (but more frequently infuriating) which we experienced during our actual work with colour on the two scenes in Part Two of *Ivan the Terrible*!

Was anything here not left to chance?

The fact that Prokofiev left Alma-Ata before me.

But *Ivan the Terrible*'s feast and the dancing could not be filmed without the music, composed and taped.

Which meant that we had to film the feast and the dancing in Moscow.

But Prokofiev fell ill and he was unable, working as he was to meet deadlines for *War and Peace* and *Cinderella*, to give me the score I needed that summer.

Autumn came, winter was not far off.

The set had been ready since the summer.

The score was further delayed.

Meanwhile, Dom Kino held a conference on colour.

No spectacle is less enjoyable than arguments and debates about things which no one has actually experienced first-hand.

It is futile, irksome.

But what irritated even more was the free supplement:

watching specimens of colour work by Americans, Germans and the few other courageous types who pushed the pre-war two- and three-film system beyond its limits and then had the gall to strut before us, amazed that we could show on our screens 'that wretched colouring of costume' and 'those fake complexions'.

Anger is a very good creative stimulus.

Unexpectedly among all this shoddy tat from abroad, we saw a documentary.

Filmed in colour.

The Potsdam Conference.[25]

The colour in this film was terrible and inconsistent.

Faces changed from brick-red,

to violet.

Green fluctuated from spring onions, to the oxide on old bronze coins.

Two-thirds of the spectrum were impossible.

No—Perhaps half.

But next came a series of interiors at Cecilienhof.

And some rooms.

A vivid red carpet filled the whole screen.

A row of white easy chairs picked out in red formed a diagonal.

So, red could be done!

More than that—we saw a few shots of the Chinese pavilion at Sanssouci.

When I was looking over it once, I saw Potsdam and some other relics of Frederick the Great's reign in real life.

The Chinese gilt figures also came out well.

More than that, there were also a green cast and reflections from the white marble steps.

Red was possible. Gold worked.

If I could assume that blue would work . . .

I could always risk it . . .

The set for Ivan's feast had been up since the summer. The feast had to be an explosion, between the dark scene of the plot against the Tsar and the murky scene of his attempted murder.

Why not resolve this explosion in colour?

The colours would burst into dance.

And fade at the end of the feast, imperceptibly resolving into black-and-white photography . . . the tone of the tragic and chance death of Prince Vladimir Andreyevich at the hands of the murderer sent by his mother to kill the tsar.

This was perfectly in keeping with my style and mood! In the preceding episode, in colour, the black of the cassocks first engulfed the gold of the robes of the *oprichniki*; then *oprichniki* in their black robes covered the gold of Vladimir's mantle; and finally the whole mass of black *oprichniki* swamped the inside of the cathedral. In its dark belly, they—and their even darker shadows—were swallowed up in the night; among them, was Vladimir, pitiable and helpless, his groan barely audible.

THE PRIZE FOR *IVAN*[1]

Khmelyov's coffin stood on stage.

He was once in one of my films—*Bezhin Meadow*.[2]

And later, in 1942, he burst into my hotel room hurling drunken accusations at me for not casting him as Ivan in my picture.

Now he was in a coffin.

The corpse had already been cleaned of make-up; the beard had been peeled off, the costume of Ivan the Terrible—robes, ring, wig and crown—had been taken away.

He had died during a rehearsal.

In the midst of the vicissitudes of Ivan's fate, Alexei Tolstoi died on the stage.

Yuzovsky recently came to visit me in the Kremlin hospital.[3] He recalled with horror a telephone conversation we had had, on 1 February.

We had laughed as we talked of the fateful danger facing people working on *Ivan*.

Tolstoi was dead. Khmelyov was dead.

'"But I'm still alive!" You laughed into the receiver,' Yuzovsky told me the next evening . . .

At the height of the banquet in Dom Kino, these vehicles had come for me, from the hospital.

My arms and legs had gone.

I remembered Arliss' *Old English*, except my arms had gone limp, instead of stiff.[4]

I did not go in an ambulance.

I walked to my car.

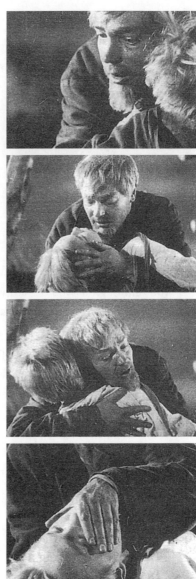

Nikolai Khmelyov playing the
father in *Behzin Meadow*
(second version, 1936–37).

Perhaps it was subconscious? Perhaps, for reasons I could not understand, I remembered another evening. Also in winter. The year before.

In Barvikha.

When another of Ivan's victims was being borne out of a neighbouring building.

I had never liked the Count.[5]

Neither as writer,

nor as a person.

It is hard to say why.

Perhaps, for the same reason that Quakers and Sybarites instinctively avoid each other, or Colas Breugnon and the ascetics?[6]

And, although I would hardly lay claim to the title of St Anthony, I felt something of an old maid when I was in the company of the Count . . .

The vast, white, dusty and completely flat, salt surface of land, somewhere near the aerodrome near Kazalinsk, or Aktyubinsk.

I flew back to Alma-Ata in 1942 and the Count accompanied me as far as Tashkent.

There were no bushes. Not even a blade of grass. Not a fence. Not so much as a stump.

We managed without a stump, then, a short distance from the plane.

We returned.

'Eisenstein, you are a pessimist,' the Count told me.

'In what way?'

'There is something in your face . . .'

We were somehow, tacitly, alien, even antagonistic to each other.

So it was with complete indifference that I looked at his body, lying in the small bedroom off his hospital room.

His jaw was bound up in bandages.

His arms were folded across his chest.

The white of cartilage in his pinched, bruised nose.

His wife and sister were crying.

Also present was a general with two ladies.

More interesting than the dead Count were the details. Such as the coffee.

His sick-nurse continually poured coffee out for all who wanted it, and all who did not as well.

They were about to take the body out.

Clear the ward.

And that night the body was flown to Moscow.

The next morning, the room would have a new occupant.

There was no need to worry about the tablecloth.

The coffee was poured out quite carelessly.

As if to splash the cloth deliberately, so liberally was it be spattered with pools of the dark liquid.

A smashed jug of cream lay under the table: a jarring note. But the nurses had arrived.

They covered the body with a grey army blanket.

With half his head sticking out from beneath it; deep-sunk eyes.

They got it wrong, of course.

They tried to carry him out head first, of course.

The legs stuck up, comically, until one of the elderly nurses intervened.

They turned the trolley so that his feet faced the exit. They were still on the first flight of stairs when someone turned on a tap in the bathroom, breaking the silence.

And a cleaner, with bucket and mop, almost bumped into the trolley as she squelched about in her bare feet . . .

Day and night, mattocks and spades scraped away in the belly of Moscow.

They were building the metro.

Girls dressed as miners walked evocatively across Theatre Square.

Underground Moscow had its own life.

It was at this period that I met Pasternak.[7]

He lived on the Arbat.

He lived above the tunnelling.

He wrote by night.

And the subterranean scrapes, cracks, clanks and squeals distracted him.

Urbanism was burrowing its way beneath the poet.

One morning he could not leave his flat.

The building had subsided.

It had started to bow.

And this prevented the door from opening.

Pasternak leant out with his elbows on the broad windowsill.

It was evening.

And we were somewhere high above Moscow, visiting someone.

In the night air you could hear the piercing and plaintive whistling of the trains.

'Trains,' Pasternak remarked, 'are the only honest people around. They're having a hard time, but they don't try to conceal it.'

He looked at me with his wide brown eyes above his negroid lips.

'Eisenstein, you are like an undecorated church . . .'

In those years, the years of *Counterplan* [*Vstrechnyi*, 1932] and *The Happy Guys* [*Veselye rebyata*, 1934], *Petersburg Night*

[*Peterburgskaya noch'*, 1934] and *The Storm* [*Groza*, 1934], my position in cinema was just that.

But now what?

Churches have been resurrected and the domes of the Kremlin cathedrals have been gilded.

Chiaureli,[8] with *The Vow* [*Klyatva*, 1946] took his place among the patriarchs of cinema.

I am last, apart from Simeon the Stylite![9]

We all, in some way at some time, play at being great historical figures.

I have described somewhere my and Pudovkin's first meeting with Dovzhenko, whose career was just beginning.

And I related how we assigned to ourselves the roles of various titans of the Renaissance. Pudovkin got his teeth into Raphael. Dovzhenko was allotted Michelangelo. And I was Leonardo . . .

In her relations with me in the 1920s, Esfir Ilyinichna Shub[10] probably saw herself as some kind of enigmatic George Sand.

Although it would be difficult to find anyone bearing a fainter resemblance to Chopin or de Musset than me, short-legged and corpulent as I am. But why else would she have advised me to read Tynyanov's *A Nameless Love*, when I was struggling to find the dramatic kernel of the plot for my already prepared general, lyrical conception for my film biography of Pushkin? Did she really, in the spring of 1940, see herself playing Karamzina to my . . . Pushkin?

But why did I instantly, with burning, unreserved resolve, latch on to that very notion? It was as though I had just seen that very drama being screened before my eyes.

A picture of such a love.

A love hidden and illicit. But illicit rather than hidden.

But of such strength.

And inspired.

Esfir Shub.

A love which strove to immerse its unattainability in the flour-ishes of the endless Don Juan catalogue, which could catch up with Pushkin's, and even outstrip it.[11]

Charlie Chaplin!

'In the purple rays of sunset.'

Hollywood ...

Candles burning down after dinner.

1930.

However ...

I have not yet explained how the conception of making a film about Pushkin came about.

How I wrote a screenplay on just one theme without even having the time to find a subject. How Tynyanov suggested a plot for the screenplay.

I have already written of my great capacity for envy. Further, this envy takes the strangest forms.

For example, I was terribly envious of a famous joke about Deburau.

A tall, thin, pale person, seized by a terrible melancholia, went to the doctor.

The doctor advised him to go out and have a good time. Have some laughs.

'Go and see Deburau.'

'I am Deburau . . .'

Yesterday, a very similar thing happened to me.

My heart is very weak.

The doctor advised me to take a break from my usual activities and mental pursuits.

'Take up photography!'

Ha, ha, ha!

Some diversion: at the very roughest guess, I must, during my lifetime, have taken some 15,000 photographs, counting each sequence—never mind the ones between them—as a separate photograph.

Apropos the melancholy of jokers.

I know one pretty closely.

The very greatest of his time.

Charlie Chaplin.

It is now hackneyed to say that his films are a mixture of smiles and tears.

As he is in life.

I remember a terrible evening in Beverly Hills.

As ever, we were playing tennis.

Apart from us, the three Russians, on that occasion there were also three Spaniards.

And Ivor Montagu.[2]

The Spaniards were somehow importunate and suspicious.

The Russians were boring.

Ivor was a particularly outspoken Englishman from Cambridge. Chaplin was doing his best to keep his end up in a 'highbrow English conversation'.* Then he started clowning around.

That day he was especially animated and mischievous. Especially playful, especially entertaining.

When you are with him, he is not still for one moment.

He has a medieval *horror vacui*: he is scared of the empty moment, a second of unoccupied time, intervals in the endless succession of *lazzi*, 'practical jokes'* or puns.

One moment he dances to the radio, parodying oriental dances.

And the next he impersonates the King of Siam, whose nose would barely reach the table top.

When they came to administer extreme unction to Rabelais, he tossed the blanket back and lay there dressed as Harlequin.

Of course Chaplin's Harlequin does not conceal a dying body.

But a spirit deeply affected by the long, cold fingers of the winged angel of melancholy, as depicted sitting sorrowfully, cheek on hand, in Durer's woodcut.

This angel is Marion Davies.[3]

Marion Davies is Charlie's one and only real, long-lasting love.

But Marion belongs, to Hearst. And, once Hearst has his hands on something, he will not let anyone else have it . . .

* In English in the original.

This evening Chaplin's playfulness is especially highly wrought: the Harlequin costume has been pulled on with even more nervousness than usual, to hide as much as possible of the sad little figure who has borne such unconsolable sadness since his Whitechapel childhood.

When he was at the Nezhin secondary school, Gogol began writing humorous stories to dispel the melancholia that afflicted his brother and himself.

Chaplin is afraid of solitude. He grabbed his guests.

He was like a child scared of being alone in the dark.

He asked us to stay for dinner.

His man Kono[4] and the other Japanese glided through the dining room.

Superficially, it looked like an improvised feast.

'The purple light of sunset' played on the silverware.

Then the sun set and candles were brought.

And a strip of purple sky led Chaplin to reminisce.

Three Russians and three Japanese sat facing each other like wooden figures on the right and left.

The Englishman from Cambridge sat opposite the host. The laughter died away.

The sunset and the motionless figures reminded Charlie of something.

The same sunset.

The same still figures.

Except wrapped up in red blankets, coats, sarapes.

The small church in a rocky hinterland near the small desert station in Mexico.

The still figures were there as witnesses.

Before the altar stood the priest, impatient.

Chaplin stood in one corner of the church.

A photo presented to Eisenstein by Chaplin.

A photograph sent to Pera Atasheva with the inscription 'To my best friend
in the USSR together with my best friend in the USA'.
Hollywood, September 1930.

And in the other was a young maiden with her mother. The priest held a bible.

The dying rays of the blood-red sunset shone through the roundel above.

Inside the church was the deep blue of twilight.

The groom was Charlie.

And the bride was Miss Grey.[5]

The priest impatiently Shifted his weight from one foot to the other like a horse trampling the ground.

The bible banged against the worn red velvet screen. At home, a rich red-pepper soup was awaiting him. The witnesses wore red sarapes.

The last rays of the blood-red sunset in the round window above.

A Study in Scarlet?

Why not?

That was the first detective story by Conan Doyle that I read. It was my first encounter with Sherlock Holmes.

But you do not have to be Sherlock Holmes to deduce that a marriage is about to take place.

Everyone was at their place.

The priest.

The groom.

The bride.

The two rings.

The Bible.

The two Mexicans, silent witnesses.

Why did the ceremony not begin?

From deep within the church came the harsh, persistent sound of an argument.

Everyone listened attentively.

With the possible exception of the Madonna and the two Mexicans who were supremely indifferent to it.

All they cared about was the handful of pesos they would take home for their wasted time.

The voices belonged to two attorneys.

They were very angry, forgetting where they were.

They waved their arms about as if they were in their own offices.

In the twilight, the two pairs of pince-nez glinted aggressively as they jumped up and down.

The rays of light intersected as the two pince-nez wearers pounced on each other.

And it seemed sometimes that it was not rays of light, but the sparks that fly when blades are crossed.

At night, the shadows were like crêpe. In English, shooting crap means playing with marked cards.

In this game, the two attorneys tried to beat each other: faithful guard dogs defending the interests of their respective clients.

Charlie sighed.

Charlie the narrator.

Probably, Charlie uttered sighs like that when he was taking part in that ridiculous ceremony.

Chaplin looked at a crucifix and probably found much in common between the life of the protagonist in the Bible and his own.

He almost met his Calvary, on any number of occasions . . . The Madonna sank into the darkness.

There was just enough light to make out the face on the crucifix above.

The man on the cross looked reproachfully at the money changers in the temple.

His hands were nailed to the wood.

He could not take a knotted cord and drive both attorneys out on to the street as they blasphemously raised their voices in the temple.

Two documents lay beneath the prominent noses of the perspiring attorneys:

A marriage document.

And a divorce document.

Both were drawn up for the same people.

For Charles Spencer Chaplin and Miss Lita Grey.

Then the priest pronounced a short prayer and bound the couple, who at that moment were exchanging rings before him, together for all time, for this world and the next.

They signed the first document.

And a moment later, the second.

Joined by God for all time, they would now be torn asunder by the hands of these two lawyers.

Prince Louis Bonaparte, after his first unsuccessful coup, was sentenced to life imprisonment in a fortress—for ever.

'How long does eternity last for, in France?' The prince asked and escaped from the fortress to pull off a successful coup.

Eternity is even shorter here.

And it would have been shorter still but for some clause in the document regarding money which obliged those zealous attorneys to lock antlers once more.

But this too was settled.

They all bowed their heads.

Hastily the priest said all that he had to.

Two signatures on one document.

The marks of witnesses in confirmation.

The ink was barely dry on the first document when the signatures were put to the second.

Which annulled it.

Nevertheless St Peter has been given the prerogative to tie and untie.

'And what is tied on earth shall be tied in Heaven.

'And what is untied . . .'

Nobody has ever said anything about the interval between these two procedures.

I forgot to clarify just one detail: whether the same witnesses put their marks to both documents, or whether there were two pairs of witnesses.

And when they said their congratulations.

In the middle of the ceremony.

Or at the end.

Or twice.

The scene before the altar is always the traditional 'happy end'.*

So it is now.

This is the happy end of a long and cunning intrigue.

The ending cost Universal's best comic roughly a million dollars.

Chaplin may have regretted this million as he told us all about it in the dining-room, with the candles, many years later in Beverly Hills.

This drama extends further back.

There was a similar reverse narrative in a novella by Flammarion, I seem to remember: *Lux*.[6]

The premise is that the speed at which particles of light from Earth travel to a planet increases at a constant rate.

So that what happens on Earth appears, to the observer on another planet, to happen in reverse.

---

* In English in the original: the form *kheppi-end* is used in Russian for 'happy ending'.

With delightful Gallic brilliance, Flammarion introduced all manner of bizarre happenings which might result from this.

He made human life flow backwards before the eyes of the observer.

Events acquired a new, engaging logic.

People, attired in mourning black, sob at the graveside, which torchbearers of gloomy aspect dig up in order to condemn someone to life in this Vale of Tears.

Husbands and wives, having annoyed each other for a great many years, embrace fondly and with a tender 'first kiss', thank each other for their newly restored freedom. After a phase of friendship and a first meeting, they part joyfully.

And on reaching his life's end, man vanishes in a strange way, with the help of a . . . midwife.

Ves' klass
prosit vas
v poslednii raz
*prochest' rasskaz.**

These immortal lines are chalked on the blackboard, twice a year without fail.

Before the end of the second and fourth quarters of the school year—the end of the first and second terms.

A school tradition allows—nay, insists—that the last lesson of each term be devoted to a story read by the teacher.

I remember the reverse action of Flammarion's novella having heard it just once, in one of the junior years at the Institute in Riga, where I first tasted the fruits of knowledge.

It made a strong, indelible impression, despite the fact that all the others were completely forgotten about—no amount of cudgelling my mind can recall them.

* Russian: 'The whole class / Says you must / Read your story / For the last time . . .'

Why?

I think because Flammarion's plot is not the only one of its kind.

The device of reverse action is a very popular one in a certain new art form, whose first impressions only take the form of running pictures (and I do mean running and bobbing up and down) jumping on a white canvas hung in flats with knocked-through walls—the first 'bioscopes'.[7]

Apart from Méliès, whose work I saw in Paris when I was eight, my first impressions of cinema came from short films in 'The Royal Bio' in Riga.

The first, which was memorable for its repulsiveness, was of Mounet-Sully's acting; he was filmed as Oedipus reciting a monologue and jam flowed thickly from his eyes.[8]

The second, which came before Max Linder, Pockson and Prince, was of races and it looked as though the projectionist was drunk.[9]

The horses took the fences.

Then they came to an abrupt halt in mid-air (the projectionist was staring at a girl).

Then the horses were madly transported in the opposite direction—backwards.

(While staring at the girl, the projectionist had absentmindedly begun cranking the apparatus in the other direction.)

He saw everything back to front.

In a restaurant, the patrons carefully removed sausage sandwich after sausage sandwich from their mouths and also carefully replaced a succession of leaves back on the branches as the leaves flew obligingly up from the gravel path and into their hands.

And then suddenly a grand vista of crazy 'traffic'* on a city street, all hurtling backwards.

* In English in the original.

I was for a time denied admission to the bioscope then.

Die Damen werden aus dem Café gehoben.*

I remember this last subtitle as if it were yesterday; it was not on the screen, but read out by a special announcer attired as a circus ringleader, standing to one side and explaining the action as it unfolded.

I was hurriedly taken by the arm and led out—the subject matter was not for one of my years.

The women rebelled and did what the men had done.

They began to frequent cafés.

Talk politics.

Smoke cigars.

While their husbands sat at home doing the washing.

And went for walks in an endless chain of prams.

Then the men rebelled.

They burst into the cafes.

They grabbed the ladies and triumphantly bore them out on to the street.

Die Damen werden aus dem Café gehoben.

'They are carrying the ladies out of the cafe,' announced the man in the uniform.

I was (all but) carried out of the cinema.

I held on to a chair. I did not want to leave. My eyes were glued to the screen.

To no avail.

I shall never know what finally happened to the poor women.

A Man's Fate in Yevreinov's Distorting Mirror Theatre, the ancient Greek buffonade by John Erskine and finally [. . .], the

---

* German: 'They are carrying the ladies out of the cafe.'

author of *Tonner*, later put the finishing touches to the fantastical situation of lords changing places with their ladies, although it becomes difficult henceforward to trace the line of my interest in the question of bisexuality, when it enters clearly the area of ecstasy.[10] Huysmans wrote of Sainte François and Saint Thérèse, thinking that this designation was more appropriate to the psychological cast of mind of a saint, who acts more like someone of the opposite sex.

Some of St Theresa's admonitory letters to nuns make amusing reading: domestic and administrative instructions are interspersed with frequent ripostes and earthy, Rabelaisian, redblooded humour!

The film about the liberated women's ill-fated escapade (it took place at the same time as the suffragettes' public displays and only just anticipated the fashion for ladies' *jupes-culottes*)* is in one respect immediately linked to films where sequences run in reverse order.

There is the same inversion of opposites.

The women take the place of their partners, just as here forward motion became backward motion.

Both films prepared the ground for Flammarion's story. Sterne's novel (*Tristram Shandy*) is written from start to finish.[11] Alice's adventures through the looking-glass.

Poe's doctrine that novellas, if they do not actually start at the end and work backwards, are nevertheless written that way and ought to be written that way.[12] It is all so much flowers and ribbons, interwoven into a wreath of first impressions, which end up with the actual principle of the comic structure being that same 'reverse', the simplest comic effect, broadened, heightened and then applied to any philosophical concept that is dominant at a particular historical period.

A hotel is burgled.

* In French in the original.

The police cordon the building off. The commissioner has all the exits covered.

The criminal has vanished.

'Might he have left by one of the . . . entrances?'

A policeman hazards.

Surely this 'unexpectedness' negates the unassailable status quo, the fixed predictability of Kant's metaphysical universe, which made him find funny even the premise that there could be something funny?

Surely the illogical negates logic (the dominant principle of one epoch) and is considered the basis of comedy, in exactly the same way that the period of *élan vital* supposed mechanicism to be the basis of what is funny (because it negated the basic doctrine)?[13]

Are they not simultaneously equal and inverse; as a door is both an entrance and an exit, representing two different approaches from two different directions, to the same phenomenon—even the yawning gape of an aperture in the flat surface of a wall?

And is it not just the same in the simplest comic trick of reversing the motor in cinematography, consolidating a favourite psychological 'game' from one's childhood into a technical device?

A rider galloping under his horse.

An axe using the carpenter to chop.

Fish pulling anglers out of the river.

And other such delights from the embellishments and folklore of childhood, collected in Grandville's *un autre monde* in order to spill out in a cascade of unexpected results from between the covers of that mad book.

However, the principles of comedy have their own place in their own book.

And I only mention them here, *en passant*, because it is precisely here and now that the two elements—reverse filming and the nature of the actual principle—have joined together to make one whole inversion.

The unity of the nature of tickling, the physiological mechanism of laughter, the structure of wit, the principle of humour, were all felt much earlier.

However . . .

In the best traditions of primitive comic film, like the race horse frozen in flight above a fence, we have left Chaplin and his young bride—bride and divorcee—hanging in mid-air, beneath the vaults of the little church in Mexico.

We set the wheels in motion. In reverse, as we said.

And now there is no longer a church before us, but a small railway halt.

A long passenger train at the platform.

The staid Kono strolled officiously along the platform.

He had evidently got off the train to have a breath of fresh air.

Such was the general verdict of the hundred-odd reporter who did not let him out of their sight as they stayed on board.

A whistle.

He climbed back on board.

And the train pulled out.

Further into the heart of Mexico.

Away from Los Angeles.

The reporters sank back into their seats and made them selves comfortable once more.

Not here, then . . .

Busy watching Kono as he got off the train, they did not notice what was happening under the carriages.

The endless corridor between the wheels of the train.

Stretching in both directions.

A lady with her daughter ran in one direction, bent double. And, pressed to the ground on all fours, a great comic actor made his way in the other direction in a degrading farce, this time not on the screen but for real.

Traditionally the groom and bride arrive at the church from different directions.

Here, both had to run away in different directions before meeting at the altar, which in this case involved a hasty separation of the newly-weds, forever, as in Flammarion's novella!

They had to avoid meeting reporters and journalists before the affair could be made lawful; before the affair could be recognized by a *de jure* marriage; before the divorce could be processed.

No one should know when the second followed the first and that 'both the two' after the marriage are *de facto*.

This *de facto* could cost Chaplin not only a paltry million.

But . . . a lifetime of hard labour.

The girl, the 'victim', was only sixteen.

And the rape case could also be treated as the seduction of a minor.

'You must understand me!' Chaplin said, anguished by the mere memory of it. 'Imagine, a blossoming young girl, as tall as a grenadier.

'And me, next to her . . .'

We vividly pictured this puny little manikin next to a larger than-lifesize Venus de Milo.

'Can you see me as a rapist?

'Can you imagine me with her in my arms?'

We agreed it was not easy.

And the mystery of Venus's missing arms, this time at least, seems a perfectly apt image for the embraces which so easily swept the little man up in the air as he stood enraptured in the web of his own sensuality.

But this case involved not only the two deft arms of the young Venus herself.

There is a third arm too and it played a key part: it was the protagonist.

Charlie sighed.

'Her documents said she really was sixteen . . .'

The hand of Moscow!

To this day, Anglo-Saxons, on either shore of the ocean which lends its name to a certain treaty, look for the 'hand of Moscow' everywhere.

As happened earlier too.

Moscow, involved in this?

Yes—the hand of Moscow.

But a friendly hand, which Anatoli Vasilevich Lunacharsky[14] extended across the seas and oceans.

The invitation to drop everything and come to the Soviet Union.

Here, as always, the hand of Moscow opposed the Hearsts, giving them a rap across the knuckles.

It was Hearst who obligingly set the sixteen-year-old adventuress Lita Grey on a collision course with Chaplin.

It was they who helped ensnare Chaplin in the web of intrigue.

The boycott of his films had just begun.

'The Daughters of the American Revolution', a term that is for women what 'sons of bitches' is for men, were already blowing their trumpets of jericho, which resounded across all America, carrying the message that the little man with the bowler and the moustache was breaching the citadel of American morality.

He could see even at this early stage the rippling mirage of scandal: a court-case and penal servitude.

The sluice gates of filth were opened, ready to ruin and drown this diminutive character who made the whole world laugh, feel happy and cry.

At the last minute, Hearst himself threw the lever of his all destroying machinery and called off his pack of newspapers and newshounds.

Chaplin slid out from under the looming court case which would have spelt ruination and ignominy.

Money and the press are omnipotent in America.

Hearst runs the press.

Chaplin holds the money.

A million or so.

Nothing!

'This will teach the boy to forget about Marion Davies . . .'

Hearst thought.

Chaplin slid off his chair.

Ran upstairs.

We waited a little while.

Then we left.

We didn't see Chaplin again that evening.

We saw him then as few people see him.

Pale, suffering, his face crumpled.

He remembered a lot that was difficult and painful.

But it takes even more pain and hardship to forget about something . . .

I cannot undertake to confirm all the above details on oath. Whether both the attorneys wore pince-nez.

Whether there was a velvet screen before the altar.

Or if there was, if it was worn.

Whether the priest was in a hurry to get back to his red pepper soup.

And exactly how Randolph Hearst expressed his thoughts about Chaplin and Marion Davies.

And I am quite sure that Charles Chaplin did not look at the crucifix.

I am just retelling a story.

And an impression received from a story, at that. Furthermore, a story I heard all of sixteen years ago.

But one thing I can guarantee:

The atmosphere of the story.

And the atmosphere of the setting where it was told. Chaplin's heart-rending melancholy, which took the upper hand in the farcical situations between Charlie and the 'grenadier', the two haggling lawyers or Kono's air of concentration which distracted the reporters.

And the purple rays of sunset which played on the silverware and triggered Charlie's reminiscences of this whole epic.

[Now around me is the dazzling gold of the midday sun. Yet I am burdened by melancholy.

We all have our Marion Davieses . . .]

I have never had a good ear. I have always found it difficult to remember a tune so that I could recognize it again.

And as for remembering it well enough to be able to sing it myself that was out of the question.

But there have been exceptions.

I remember rocking on my bed all night after *The Tales of Hoffmann*—which I had seen and heard for the first time in Rigaand singing the 'Barcarolle' over and over again.[2]

And even now of course I can sing the waltz from *The Dollar Princess*, if not aloud, then to myself; it amazed me when I heard it for the first time, also in Riga, probably aged about twelve.

I remember the words:

Das sind die Dollarprinzessen,
Die Miidchen von vie-ie-lem Gold
Mit Schätzen u-u-unermessen . . .*

But these pages will not deal with my first impressions of operas or operettas.

I shall set out elsewhere the details of my first encounter with *Eugene Onegin* at the amateur dramatic society in Riga, where all the usual 'romance' of the sets in Act One looking now through the colonnades on to the endless fields (Rabinovich at the Bolshoi)[3] were summarily replaced with a green garden seat pushed against the back of the stage.

Similarly, I shall talk of the first theatre comics to fascinate me—Fender, Kurt Busch and Sachsl[4]—in the German Theatre and

---

* German: 'These are dollar princesses, / The girls with lots of gold / And treasures beyong measure . . .'

Opera House in Riga, the scene of my introduction (at a tender age) to the repertoire from *Hansel and Gretel*, to *Götz von Berlichingen* and from *Wallenstein's Death* to *Der Freischütz* and *Madame sans gêne* (the unforgettable Fender played the cobbler and had three words to say; and to this day, I can still recall the floating arabesque as he uttered the phrase '*Wie eine Fee*',* referring to the imminent entrance of the Marshal's wife!), *Around the World in Eighty Days*, and the operetta *Feuerzauberei*.

I also saw the latter before the war (I mean the war of 1914!). But I cannot be more precise than that, since, as I recall, after 1914 another of my favourites, Sachsl, who played Bonaparte himself in *Madame sans gene* and here the part of an actor playing Bonaparte in a film who rode a white horse on to the stage towards a model film camera (this was the first film sequence that I saw) was suspected of spying and interned!

Before that scene, Fender sang

Und die Mühle
Und sie dreht sich . . .†

against a backdrop of a landscape, with a model windmill. The vanes of the windmill began turning in the background, in time to the music . . .

The *Schlager*‡ dominated the whole scene:

In der Nacht, in der Nacht
*Wenn die Liebe erwacht . . .***

and

* German: 'Like a fairy'.
† German: 'And the windmill / How it turns . . .'
‡ German; 'Hits'.
** German: 'At night, at night, / When love burns bright . . .'

Kind ich schlaf' doch so schlecht
Und ich träum' doch so schwer . . .

I repeat:

I remember *The Dollar Princess* from a quite different occasion.

When I met a real dollar princess very many years later. Principally because this meeting quite unexpectedly opened my eyes to the cause of the age-long trauma of the ugly duckling, which I mentioned earlier.[5]

And it certainly went a little way towards overcoming this trauma.

When I realized what it was, it was already late: But in the final analysis, an abstract structural schema frequently held as much pleasure for me as did an actual fact.

German: 'Child, I sleep so badly, / Tormented by terrible dreams . . .'

KATERINKI[1]

We will try to fictionalize one's tragic romantic experience.

Let's see how the symbolizing machinery works. Millionaire's daughter made ... princess (*notez*: *Die Dollarprinzessin*).

The movie director builder of 'Canvases' made—Cathedral Builder.

His inability to talk and to make conversation we transform into a literally swallowed tongue.

He swallowed his tongue and talked through his cathedrals.

Now elaborating this image we set:*

Les piliers de ses cathédrales fûrent ses consomnés.
Les rosaces—ses voyelles.
Les battements de son coeur—les roulements de l'orgue.
L'étendue de sa pensée—le dome recouvrant sa nef.
Les sons des cloches—la voix de son message.†

And, hiding somewhere in the foundations of the crypts of cathedrals he had made, he sent into the world an ever-increasing number of arches, gallery after gallery; enfilade after enfilade of vaults; and he spoke through the coloured patterns of the glass.

Through the spires of his belfries he summoned people to elevated thought.

His organ music drew people to feel the majesty of emotions.

He himself was mute and without a tongue.

And so he became the guardian of his own works which spoke on his behalf.

---

* The basic language of the text so far has been English.

† French: 'The pillars of his cathedrals were his consonants. / The stained glass windows were his vowels. / The beating of his heart was the peals of organ music. / The breadth of his thoughts was the dome above his nave. / The ringing from the belfry was the voice of his message.'

As dancers are the slaves of their own feet, girls slaves of their own voices accompanied by the lute and, as those whose expertise lies in plucking the strings of a harp become slaves to their hands, he himself spent some time in the darkness, whispering to himself or writing in the dust with an unsteady finger:

'Who am I? No more than the steward of my thoughts, the resigned servant of my works ... A bell-shaped vessel through which the people—my brothers—speak. I myself am nothing.'

And once a Little Princess came to the last cathedral that he had built.

She walked along the vaulted galleries.

And through the rays shining through the stained glass. And she glanced into the crypt.

She took him by the hand and led him to a great feast.*

The Little Princess and the Great Cathedral Builder Who Swallowed His Tongue

Once upon a time there lived the richest little princess in the world.

Never married,

afraid,

and so she whored around and especially with a red-headed lad of the lowest grade, famous for his voice that carried over the oceans, and by his force that could overturn anything in the world.

On the other end of the great big world there lived the famous Cathedral Builder who had swallowed his tongue and talked through the edifices he built.

At high table were the greatest Grands of the world at that time.

The Chinese prince besides her father,

Earl Venceslas with his fair-haired spouse—Pearl of the East.

---

* The basic language of this section was Russian but the rest is in English.

Sir Archibald native of Schottland.

They drank the health of the Builder, but he couldn't say a word since ['and' in Russian] he had no Arches, Pillars and Counterforts.

So he was mute.

Then the Princess asked him to deliver her of a drunken beastly baron trying to seduce her by his love proposals.

Asking her to dance with him.

So he delivered her and explained that there remained no need for dancing.

'Let us drink to springtime in the Great Builder's heart,' said her Father the King, but being a Magician and not being it enough he couldn't break at once the spell resting on the poor little Great Builder.

But time went on, and the Magician's words like seeds began to flourish.

And the poor little Builder saw that his spell and the spell on the little princess were nearly the same.

When somebody looked at him, he thought they looked at his Cathedrals.

When somebody looked at her, she thought they were hunting for her millions.

So he ran to her and wanted to tell her—sister, don't we suffer of the same?

And shouldn't we go together?

Aren't we really worth nothing at all, you for yourself, and me for mine?

But never, never could he get in touch with her. Fate was against them. And so she went away with her Fatum. And he remained muter than ever.*

* This section in English.

A POET'S LOVE (PUSHKIN)[1]

... I was looking for material for a colour film.

For a film with music, one would 'naturally' pick a biography of a composer.

And for a film in colour, doubtless the story of a painter.

Which is why, for a film uniting colour and music, I chose neither one nor the other.

I chose the life of a man of letters. Pushkin.

But of course, there were other reasons.

Because it was precisely a colour film of Pushkin that could impart the same moving drama of colour, the same movement of the chromatic spectrum, to the tone of the poet's fate as it unfolded; just as Gogol's creativity may be discerned not through his life, but in the succession of his works.

A curious colour shift occurs throughout the entire corpus, which includes the entire range of tones at the start with *Evenings on a Farm Near Dikanka* and ends with the second part of *Dead Souls*.

If the author's tragic history emerges through the fabric of his works, his youthful wholehearted dedication to a full life, shifting towards an ascetic darkening, represented by a shift away from the rich fullness of colours towards a severe monochrome, such as we see on a screen, then the same dramatized shift in colour could reflect the environment in which the poet's fate so tragically unfolded; from the carefree, wide-open spaces of Odessa, to the cold shroud of snow by the Black Brook.[2]

Images from his life intermingled with ideas represented in colour.

Here is the rich palette of oils, at the most auspicious of beginnings.

Tsar Boris, clad in thick gold, with flecks of silver in his black beard.

Here is Tsar Boris' monologue, which could be portrayed cinematically as a nightmare ('beholding the blood-soaked infants')! The red carpets of the cathedral. The red candlelight. And, illuminated by it, seemingly splashed with blood, the icon frames.

The Tsar rushes about his aparunents.

Dark blue. Cherry red. Orange. Green.

They rush to meet him.

The multicoloured brightness of the aparunents and towers of the Kremlin palace burst upon the tsar, a nightmare of colour, as the camera lunges this way and that.

The poet saw the character of the tsar-cum-regicide, Alexander, in Boris.[4]

In the fireplace at Mikhailovskoye, smouldering embers flare up.

Nicholas seems to be looking out at the poet from the fire (superimposition, quite permissible in film).

The poet's hand doodles on a sheet of paper.

A gallows.

Gallows, gallows, gallows.

'And perhaps, I ... me also ...'—nervouslywritten between these recollections of the Decembrists.

Staring into the fireplace.

The vision of Nicholas, returning his gaze from the flickering embers.

The paper is crumpled in his fist.

Like Luther's inkwell hurled at the devil, the ball of paper flies at the ominous vision.

The vision fades.

The paper, with the ominous gallows, flares up, devoured by the last tongues of flame in the dying hearth.

In a burst of light, there comes the startling knock of a policeman's sword.

The first bloody highlight—the newly—kindled flame gleams on the policeman's helmet . . .

Summoned by Nicholas, Pushkin gallops to Moscow.

The theme of blood is identified with the colour red. In the 'Requiem', it is Danzas' red cap-band.[5]

The animated flow of skaters moving towards the islands.

Although 'flow' is a bad metaphor, as this is in winter, on snow and in sleighs.

No one pities him.

Nor, of those who were to see him a few hours later when his blood formed a red wreath on the snow, would there be many to mourn.

No one feels any sorrow for him.

And he is satisfied.

He politely exchanges bows with those he passes in his sleigh; he caustically tells his companion [. . .].[6]

His companion can hardly hear him.

He fidgets on the seat of the sleigh.

He is preoccupied by a strange, thankless task.

He is trying to attract the attention of those he passes to what he is holding in his hands.

But in such a way that his companion does not notice.

The object is a flat case, for carrying pistols.

But the people he meets, though unfriendly, are invariably attracted to his companion's curls which flow from beneath his top hat.

One more unsuccessful attempt to attract attention to the case in the officer's hands.

And yet one more caustic comment from his curly-haired companion.

No one pities him.

And he is satisfied.

He is going to a duel.

And he is delighted that no one stands in his way.

A very smart sleigh passes by.

Inside, a well-dressed lady.

But she is shortsighted and does not recognize the curly-haired gentleman.

Although the curly-haired poet is her husband.

But did I say that the gentleman going to a duel was a poet?

I have always pictured Pushkin's duel, like all duels, as taking place in the morning.

Like the duel between Onegin and Lensky, in the operaversion.

This duel though takes place in the afternoon; between four and five o'clock, to be more precise.

And Pushkin and Danzas (he is the nervous officer doing all he can to draw people into the affair, since he cannot openly tell them of the impending tragedy) are proceeding to their rendezvous through the glitter of elegant skaters, among the islands of St Petersburg.

Bah! All the faces are familiar.

There is not one person one could stop at.

Not one person one could stop . . .

Danzas testified that Natalya Nikolayevna was among those who met Pushkin.

Because of her poor sight, she did not see or recognize the poet.

The sounds of dancing, the cream of Petersburg society happily skating, ring out with greater urgency.

And the strains of Prokofiev's 'Requiem', as yet distant, will mingle with it, an increasingly ponderous and gloomy musical subtext.[7]

For Pushkin is travelling to his death, through the round dance of Petersburg's elite.

The 'Requiem' swells . . .

It is intensified by the dancing.

It diminishes, fades. The external motif is the pale blue chill in the air, which dulls all colour; hoarfrost, which tones down the ruddy glow of moustaches and sideburns, the snow falling from the branches, and hangs like a new kind of lace before the fireworks, deadening their colours.

The flickering light of the cherry satin, Natalya Nikolayevna's muffler—she is 'the madonna with a squint'.[8]

The final range of colours is misty grey.

And harsh black and white.

Snow.

The duellers in silhouette.

One spot of colour.

Bloody.

Red.

Not on his chest.

Not on his shirt.

Not on the poet's waistcoat.

In the sky!

The blood-red disc of the sun.

Not radiant.

But that same dark red colour as it shines low above the horizon, visible on frosty days among the black silhouettes of trees, the

LEFT. Natalya Pushkina-Goncharova. (Watercolour by Karl Bryullov)
RIGHT. Baron George d'Anthès-Heeckeren, who killed Pushkin in a duel.

Empire-style palings of Petersburg, the outline of lamp-posts behind
the spire of the St Peter and St Paul Fortress . . .

A red diamond of light shines through the particoloured pane
of the door in the mezzanine and falls on Natalya Nikolayevna's
fingers, which are white with dread.

The poet has been brought home.

And the first woman he wanted to see was not her, his wife. The
first woman he called for was . . . Karamzina, the historian's wife.[9]

The red diamond could be blood.

Natalya Nikolayevna hides her hands.

But now her magnificent white dress is covered in a cascade of
diamonds—now of all the colours of the rainbow.

And Natalya Nikolayevna's pure white dress (which she wears in all the pale violet scenes of her love affair, courtship and marriage, including the inauspicious omen of the dropped ring) suddenly becomes the motley costume of Harlequin.

As she jumps up from her seat to admit Karamzina, dressed entirely in severe black, Natalya Nikolayevna is lit up by all the colours of the glass panes as the light filters through them.

And her white dress suddenly becomes something resembling that masquerade costume of a lady Harlequin, which she wore when Pushkin was experiencing pangs of particularly acute jealousy at the masked ball, when he and d'Anthès were consumed by jealousy of a third man.

But the blood-red velvet of the royal box and the black, still guardian angel, Benckendorff's spy, maintain an enigmatic silence above the stage, which has been arranged according to Lev Tolstoy's observations on Nicholas I's amorous encounters ...[10]

Thus, the colour leitmqtifs of the themes were woven into the subtleties of the action.

And also scenes began to wind themselves around a certain central core.

This core for me had to be the most beautiful, strict and magnificent, of all possible themes using the material of the poet's life—Yuri Tynyanov's theory about the 'nameless love' Pushkin had for Karamzin's wife.

I do not know how much of this is fact and how much fiction.

But I know that this theory holds great possibilities for the plot.

And I think the theory holds the key (Tynyanov does not write about this) to understanding that thoroughly incomprehensible, inexplicable and blind love Pushkin felt for Natalya Niko layevna.

The key to the bewildering number of Pushkin's escapades. Donjuanism (after all, did not Pushkin write *Don Juan*?) is often interpreted as unsuccessful attempts to find the one woman who is inaccessible.[11]

The line of women is varied.

Laura, with the flaming hair.

Donna Anna, beneath her severe veil.

But not even the thousand and three (*mille e tre* on Don Juan's list) can provide an exhaustive variety of shades of hair, timbres of voice, waistlines, or angles of the arms.

And one woman is sought for among all these.

Is this one like her?

But they are all different.

Yet nevertheless.

This one's hair. That one's walk. A third has dimples. A fourth, full lips. A fifth, wide-set eyes, at a slight angle. There, well-rounded legs. Here a curious waist. Voice. Way of holding a handkerchief. Favourite colours. Laughs easily. Or eyes which always fill with tears at the same harpsichord music. The same cascading ringlets. Or a similar flash of earrings, reflecting crystal chandeliers.

The chains of associations which enable one suddenly to sub-stitute one being for another, purely on the strength of the similarity of a microscopic feature, or on the basis of a fleeting community to replace someone with somebody else—even sometimes to change two people around because of a barely noticeable trait—are complete mysteries.

And probably only this can explain his blind, incomprehensible and monstrously misplaced attraction to Natalya Nikolayevna.

It is doubtless true that Natalya Nikolayevna embodied to a very considerable degree those features of the older woman which had left an indelible impression on the unbridled, impassioned emotions of the lycéeist. He was in love with the wife of a much respected man, who read to him, in his wife's presence—and I think, even with

Emperor Nocholas I.

her participation—an ironic lecture on the inappropriateness and absurdity of his fascination.

And later, many many years later, in his apartment in Tsarskoye Selo, Karamzin showed Count Bludov the cushion on the divan where, as a a pupil at the lycée, the now universally famous writer and poet had sat sobbing . . .[12]

Key periods in the romantic peripeteias of Pushkin the man and Pushkin the writer are slotted into this central pivot of his secret, lyrical drama, which was to last all his life, but which had been hidden behind his debauchery and turbulent Donjuanism and the final tragic story of his marriage.

The periods indissolubly appeared not only in bright colours, according to a strict spectrum; they even seemed painterly in their execution.

After the brief prologue around the divan at Tsarskoye Selo, which assembled around a bouquet the passionate young lycéeist, the cold, ironic man who was to be the official historian of the Russian state and Yekaterina Andreyevna Karamzina. with her unexpected and unfinished outburst of regret ... (this lady apparently lived by the motto 'but I belong to another and will always be true to him').[13]

Alexander Sergeyevich reappeared in the south. Among the tents of 'The Gypsies'.[14]

It was he who left their intimate canopy when Aleko returned unexpectedly with the bear in the pale dusty watercolour softness of the terrain of the southern steppes and plunged into the gaudy, Bryulovian brightness of oriental .watercolours at the start of the nineteenth century, in teeming, polyglot Odessa ('a sandpit in summer and an inkwell in winter').[15]

The spurs of Tatyana's husband from the forthcoming *Onegin* were on Vorontsov's boots.

'The locusts flew, flew ...'[16]

Pushkin was 'an Arab devil'.[17]

A murkiness spread over the potentially colourful water colours of the south ... The golden grape, the robes, striped turbans and yellow silks ...

The grey and milky blue motif of the blizzard and the devils, which musically and visually anticipated the future blanket of snow of the duel and the pandemonium of high-society loathing, harmonized with the bells on the carriage which brought Pushkin at full tilt to his incarceration at Mikhailovskoye.

As the bright flame in the grate follows the darkness of a blizzard, so the period of artistic maturity was painted with thick strokes of rich colour: Boris succeeded Ruslan.

The spectrum is full, saturated with colour. The texture of the oily sheen.

The southern haze has lifted.

Maturity.

There is a similar richness in the people around.

The senior priest of the Svyatogorsk monastery—the future Varlaam.

Arina Rodyonovna.

His affecting, rustic love for her niece.[18]

Kern.

(I am not setting down the plot. This is not how the biography would develop. It is not rigidly consistent. It is just certain areas, how I would resolve them.)

A summons to Moscow.

Istomina from *Eugene Onegin*.

A fateful meeting with Natalya Nikolayevna. Entrancement, leading to the poet's ensuing pale violet courtship.

A discordant note is struck (beyond the shot) by the click of the abacus in the Linen Factory[19] which was expecting to be able to balance its books, at the expense of the poet's inspiration if need be.

The discord peaks, drawing the violet and white into the silvery top of an iconostasis, orange-blossom, wedding veil and the ominous dropping of the ring . . . and the line leading from the Linen Factory, to the hasty note (the day before the marriage) requesting money (nothing to pay for the carriage to ride to church in).

St Petersburg.

The deep blue and indigo which consumes the colourful sportiveness of the full range of colours.

By degrees.

With jealousy mounting with each turn of the plot and inseparable from the scorn of society and his worries about money.

As once-in my earliest sketches for colour projects—I had an idea for a film about the plague in which gradually the blackness spread and overran the joyfully coloured landscapes, the costumes of those dining, the luxuriance of the gardens and the radiant sky itself.

Jealousy is the plague, in this case.

And the frames are dark rectangles with one or two spots of colour torn from the darkness. The green baize and the yellow candles in the casino where, in the mirror, fingers held up behind the poet's head look like horns.

The blackness of the night surrounding Golytsina's orange apartment—she had turned night into day after being told that she would die in the middle of the night. Meeting his rival.

The line—Pushkin—d' Anthès—Nicholas.

The bronze horseman.

The circle of the moon in the raven-black night. Nicholas's bronze face.

'You just wait!'[20]

The theme of Othello.

More gypsies. Not in the unconstrained south, but in a poor gypsy apartment by the Black Brook.

Pancakes in the morning.

The gypsies sing Pushkin his song from 'The Gypsies'. 'Old husband, grim husband . . .'[21]

As they sang songs to Ivan in his old age; epic tales and stories about him and Kazan which he captured.

Now he himself is the 'old husband' (despite being only thirty-seven), the 'grim husband'.

The Order of the Cuckolds.[22]

The duel theme develops, gathering momentum.

The sleigh ride, as narrated.

The colours fade.

The blanket of snow.

Silhouettes of trees standing like symbols of death.

Like a spot of blood on the blanket is the dead, crimsondisc of the sun, against a dull winter sky above the rimed tree tops.

The flat blackness of the coffin, stolen from the burial service and driven off into the night.[23]

Watercolour has a soft register. Oil has a rich one. Again the soft, pale and lyrical register. Then high-society dazzle. The black-and-white woodcut with its spot of colour. A reprise of the high-society dazzle. A sharp black line against the whiteness of the background. Strips of light against the blackness at the ending . . .

A haywire, unsystematic retelling of a screenplay and the ideas a director had about colour, for a theme that was never to be realized.

We are said to be still technically incapable of making colour films.

My next film was also made in colour and in black and white—*Ivan the Terrible*.

AFTER THURSDAY'S SHOWER[1]

This small, ridiculous woman died today, Thursday evening.

She was seventy-two.

And for forty-eight of those seventy-two years she was my mother.

She lay in a room downstairs.

I was upstairs.

And it would have been hard to say which of us was the more dead.

She and I were never close.

Our family broke up when I was very young.

It was one of those breaks that take years to heal.

The sort of break that destroys natural bonds, natural instincts the feeling of family closeness.

When we were alive, we got on badly.

I hardly ever went to see her.

Now that she was dead, I was drawn towards her room. And in death we were both at peace and close to one other. The barrier, which when we were alive kept our too similar natures apart, no longer stood between us.

She was eccentric.

I was eccentric.

She was ridiculous.

I was ridiculous.

Now we were both silent.

And we understood each other as if for the first time.

And nothing held us apart: we were as we had been once; before she was a mother, before I was a child.

TOP. Little Sergei with his mother in Riga.
BOTTOM. With his mother, 9 May 1932, the day of his return to the USSR after working abroad.

LEFT. Yulia Ivanovna as a young lady.

RIGHT. Photo presented to her son after the premiere of *The Battleship Potemkin*, inscribed: 'My pride. Mama. 1926'.

I read somewhere that the gulf between mankind and the higher primates is narrower than the gulf separating the primates from common monkeys.

I was somehow remote from the living: that distance was greater than the one separating the living from the dead.

Hence, both were equally close . . . or distant from me.

And perhaps the dead were even closer than the living.

But there was no difference between them.

The living seemed ghostly.

Ghosts seemed to be alive.

And in life—three days earlier—Yulia Ivanovna had perhaps been less real than she was now in imagination and memory.

The late Khmelyov was somewhere with me, although when he was alive we barely acknowledged each other.

Vsevolod Emilevich, Nemirovich, Khazby or Kadochnikov, Stanislavsky and Yelizaveta Sergeyevna . . .[2]

The remoter, the less real, the less tangible they were, the nearer they seemed; and those whom I did see, appeared unreal.

I remember travelling in a narrow berth, from Moscow to Vladikavkaz.

I had just been separated from a little child, a Mexican.[3]

And the sobbing in my chest: schizophrenia, most likely.

For my heart cannot distinguish between an objective image and an image in my imagination.

So they revolve around me, the shades of the living and the dead, intermingling, possessing equal weight, all seemingly just as alive (or just as dead).

Yulia Ivanovna groaned continually.

Her pulse beat more slowly, then stopped.

The groans came mumed through the floor of my room on the first floor.

Our dog howled in the distance.

Zholtik.

He had bitten someone.

So in those days he was on a leash.

I went out into the garden.

Yulia Ivanovna was a great believer in planting bushes and trees, but she had no overall plan.

We argued a lot.

In her siting of shrubs, there was no consideration of how they would look together. We agreed on one thing.

We both liked bushes in thick clumps.

Especially at the back, near the fence.

Yulia Ivanovna planted this area with clumps of rudbeckias.

These have yellow spherical flowers in autumn, at the end of a very tall stem.

Why did my hand want to reach out and snap them off? . . .

I returned.

The porch was rotten and sagged.

Yulia Ivanovna dreamed of converting it into a verandah. There was not enough money that year.

I sat down heavily on a straw-filled chair on the porch. The chair had lost its sheen. It was discoloured.

It had always been left out in the rain.

I looked at the flowers in my hand.

There were seven, as it turned out.

Seven fatal yellow globes.

Seven.

Yulia Ivanovna Eisenstein in old age.

I listened hard.

And there . . .

Quietly, quietly—almost silently, the door slowly opened. That had never happened before.

The door slowly opened—unusual for a door opening of its own accord, more usual if someone is pushing it.

Behind it was the plain white surface of the second door. Who came through that area of white and opened the outer door?

An aspen stood near the rotten porch.

It was once an unprepossessing bush; but it had grown into nothing short of a tree during the war.

Yulia Ivanovna had wanted it felled.

I had wanted it left.

Then, just as mysteriously as the door opening and taking just the length of time needed to go those three steps, between her and the aspen, a branch began to rustle, long and eloquently.

The branch was saying something—a rushed farewell, then silence.

Where did that breath of wind come from, on that still day?

Wotan spoke through such a rustle, in the branches of the ancient ash: words of approval and farewell to Sigmund, his son.

And so Yulia Ivanovna took her leave of me, walking unseen through the doorway and rustling something distinctly and hurriedly, as if someone was already waiting for her at the gate, through which a small bird flew a minute or so later.

Was it really over?

I went through the doorway.

In the distance, indistinct moans.

I held the yellow flowers.

And in front of me were feathers, feathers, feathers.

Black ones.

Ostrich.

They lay everywhere.

On armchairs. On the divan. On the beds.

Little Sergei, playing, had scattered a collection of black ostrich feathers, torn out of a hat and boa from the 1890s . . .

I went into Yulia Ivanovna's room.

She was holding out a hand towards me.

Her speech was rapid, but it was already incoherent, without words.

All in the same rhythm, forced out in starts where once there might have been an intonation.

For her distinct words had already flown, rustling the branch above the porch.

Her eyes were probably sightless.

Although only half covered by her eyelids.

She could not see, but she sensed my immediate presence. And her muttering was just her worrying about me.

I put her hand on her cold forehead.

She grew quiet . . .

I took it away.

And suddenly, then, for the first time, I felt something in my heart, my throat . . .

I went down to Yulia Ivanovna's room a second time . . .

I looked round to see that the room was not entirely empty. The first time it looked as if everything had been taken out. But now I could only see the couch; it took up the middle of the room.

She slept on this couch once, when I had measles.

I pulled back the blanket.

The tip of her nose was slightly darker.

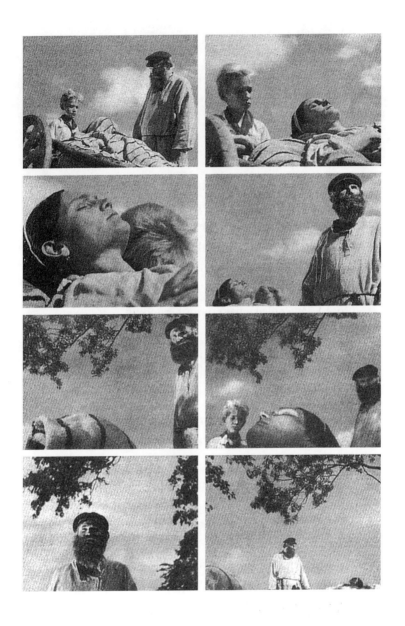

Stills of the episode 'The Mother's Death' from *Bezhin Meadow* (first version).

I looked at the coins on her eyes.

For some reason, I thought they were British pennies, with Britannia on one side and the characteristic profile of the young Queen Victoria on the other.

I used to play with old coins like that once.

But these were not pennies.

But five-kopek pieces.

On the right eye—darkened by oxidation—was the number five, a sickle and the year 1940 underneath.

I pulled the blanket down further.

She was cold, even through the dress.

A cushion had been placed between her chin and her chest.

It was embroidered.

Once I had copied a pattern for her to sew.

Richelieu stitching.

Now the cushion was to stop her jaw hanging open.

Below were her hands.

Yulia Ivanovna's hands.

I never saw them stop moving, all month.

Carrying a tray, at morning, afternoon and night.

Or darning.

Or moving deftly between the raspberry canes as she picked the fruit.

Or getting her accounts book muddled—Yulia Ivanovna got hopelessly lost with that.

Or measuring out my medicine drops.

They were once the hands of a lady.

With manicured nails.

Pale.

That month I saw them sunburnt, but strangely soft, not coarsened as they moved before me.

Only their outline had been broken.

There was some disfigurement (from gout?).

Going down to see her the first time, I kissed her forehead. Now I kissed her hand . . .

A small, white, old lady lay before me.

In some ways very distantly reminiscent of Grandmother, as I remember her.

Yulia Ivanovna always dreamed about Grandmother, when ever some disaster or unpleasantness was in the offing.

Now Yulia Ivanovna was quiet, severe, still.

Eternally serious, with the dark spots of coins on her eyes. The coins blurred and looked like the dark shadows eye sockets above white lips clamped severely shut.

I had, to my horror, known all month that Yulia Ivanov was dying . . .

Doing exercises in style for my forthcoming memoirs, I jotted down a page.

There it is, later on.

It contains a fateful slip of the pen.

'Of how to say simple things in a complicated manner.'* Leonardo da Vinci would have put it thus:

People throw off the pelts which they put on, and bury them in the ground.

But the pelts become animals once more, and hide from people, when those people (after some years have elapsed) dig the ground up again.

* In English in the original.

Before the evacuation, Yelizaveta Sergeyevna had buried her new sealskin coat somewhere near the veranda of Olga Ivanovna Preobrazhenskaya's dacha.[4]

When Ye. S. died, Yulia Ivanovna wanted to dig it up again but it was not to be found.

Olga Ivanovna Preobrazhenskaya's caretaker knew about this sealskin coat, buried near the veranda . . .

'The gentle art of saying simple things in complicated ways.'*

I suddenly came to, crossed the name out and inserted the right one.[5]

The late Yelizaveta Sergeyevna.

But I felt that I could not erase what had come out on to the paper of its own accord. Death was waiting for Yulia Ivanovna.

And when, exactly three days later, completely out of the blue, she told me that she had had a small fit, I knew deep down that it was only the first.

And there would be a fatal one. . .

* In English in the original.

Among the stories, myths and plays which I not only loved when young, but which went on to form a set of ideas, aspirations and 'ideals', I remember very distinctly three that undoubtedly had a profound effect on me.

The first was not so much a story or a legend, but a line of thought perhaps from Marie Corelli's. *Grief of Satan*, or one of Victoria Cross' novels (she wrote *Six Chapters of a Man's Life*).[2]

A notion about philosophy: philosophy is like cocaine—it can deaden your joy but at least it stops you feeling pain.

For me, this had fateful repercussions. The feeling of joy was rigorously killed off, but philosophy proved inadequate defence against the feeling of pain.

And heavens! Only I know the full depth of the feeling of pain, and the bitterness of suffering, through which, as through the rings of hell, my personal, all too personal inner world moves from year to year.

The second impression which struck me very early on (and very deeply, at that) was some legend or other, I think from a national Persian epic.

It concerned a certain strong man who would become a hero and who had felt, since childhood, a calling to accomplish some very great task.

Preparation for this future accomplishment meant conserving his strength until he had attained his full might.

He went to a bazaar, where some tanners, as I recall, pressed around him. 'Get down on your knees before us and lie in the filth of this bazaar, so that we can walk over you,' they jeered.

The last photo of Eisenstein.

And the hero-to-be, saving his strength for the future, humbly lay at their feet in the filth.

This is said to have happened as many as three times.

Later, the hero reached manhood, attained the full mastery of his unprecedented strength and performed all the feats of unheard of difficulty that lay before him.

I found this episode with the tanners utterly captivating: his unheard of self-control and sacrifice of everything, including his self-esteem, as he readied himself for the achievements to come, where he would accomplish what had already been primordially ordained and decreed.

This motif emerges clearly on two occasions in my work. In the unrealized part of my screenplay for *Alexander Nevsky*, where, after the Germans had been routed on Lake Peipus, the Tatar horde advanced on Russia once more, to exact vengeance.

The victor, Nevsky, hastened to meet them.

He walked submissively between the purifying fires in front of the Khan's pavilion and humbled himself on one knee before. the Khan. His meekness gained the time needed to build up strength so that later this enslaver of our land could be overthrown too, although not by Nevsky's hand this time, but by the sword of his descendant, Dmitri Donskoy.

The prince died on his way back from the hordes, poisoned, looking at the field—Kulikovo Field—lying before him. Pavlenko[3] and I had our holy warrior make a detour for this purpose, leaving the historic route which Alexander Nevsky actually took on his way back and so he did not reach his own home.

It was not my hand that drew the red pencil across the page after the scene where the German masses were put to flight.

'The screenplay ends here', I was told. 'A prince as good as that cannot die!'

But, if my hand humbled a prince and a saint in the name of a higher purpose, Tsar Ivan the Terrible did not escape the same fate either.

Immediately after reaching the height of his glory in the thundering of kettle drums, against a background of racing clouds and the roar of cannon over the victors' heads, the victor of Kazan attained an even greater degree of glory in the next scene. Grief-stricken, he abased himself, falling down before the gold brocade hems of the boyars' furs, tearfully beseeching the stony cohort not to hack Rus up after his, the first god-crowned autocrat of the Russian state's, imminent, feverish death . . .

In my personal, too personal history I have had on several occasions to stoop to these levels of self-abasement.

And in my personal, most personal, hidden personal life, this was perhaps rather too frequently, too hastily, and almost too willingly done—and also to no avail.

But then, 'in the course of time', I too was able to chop heads off as they stuck out of their fur coats; Ivan and I rolled in the dust before the gold-stitched hems but accepted this humiliation only in the cause of our most passionate longings . . .

For my part, of course, this chopping was metaphorical. And more frequently, as I witdded the sword above some one's head, I would bring it crashing down on my own instead.

The third impression was Bernard Shaw's *The Chocolate Soldier*. This was in my very tender, romantic, heroically inclined years: by a merciless twist of irony, it would seem, I had cooled my youthful bent for pathos permanently.

And then I spent my whole life in heroic-pathetic drudgery, with screen 'canvases' in the heroic style!

Let a description of my visit to Bernard Shaw in London, 1929, follow here. This happened after he had sent me a cablegram which overtook me exactly halfway across the Atlantic Ocean when I was sailing to America. He proposed that I film *The Chocolate Soldier*, 'on the condition that the entire text be altered not one jot'.[4]

Hence, retrospective interpretation of that tireless atmosphere of persuasive charm, which he showed me throughout my stay. The great honour of this proposal, coming as it did point blank, and from someone who had never, for any sum, sold anyone the right to film one of his works.

On a par with Maxim Gorky, another major writer whose proposal to film one of his works I 'turned down'.*

And here naturally I must describe my trip to Gorky to see Gorky, to hear the screenplay he wanted filmed by my own hands.

And even before his death the old man could not forgive or forget this 'outrage'*—and I saw him several times in the interval.

* In English in the original.

THE TRUE PATHS OF DISCOVERY[1]

Torito

It is seldom an easy matter to untangle the knot of secondary associations, early impressions and the facts of a previous experience which are found in the plot that inspired me and which assist in the realization of the composition.

To give an example: take one of the shots in our Mexican film. It is recognized, by people who have a thorough knowledge of Mexico, to be one of the more successful photographic recreations; to have captured the physiognomy of the country particularly profoundly. Probably because of the impression these compliments have had on me, I immediately attempted to analyse it, to see what made the substance of this photograph so typically Mexican—how it captured the country's style, spirit and physiognomy so well.

I still have a diary entry for 16 August 1931, With my notes on that theme which I had made almost on the day of filming.

(I must note in passing that the style of shot composition was one of the basic problems of form in our Mexican film. For despite the piquancy and typicality of things Mexican, it was extremely difficult to find ways of showing them so that they would convey the style and spirit of Mexico. But this comes elsewhere. The point has been made that we worked long and hard over problems of style).

And so, Martin Fernandez, playing Sebastian, stood before us in the straw hat and white sarape of the peons. *Torito* is the traditional firework on Mexican national holidays. It is worn on the head, parodying the bullfight. It shoots rockets (the really powerful ones are fired from horns). In the background was the portico of the same hacienda where pulque—Mexican vodka—was distilled in huge bullhide vats. Everything was purely Mexican. But what was it that led, to all the elements being together, in that combination, within the frame of a single photo? (It should further be noted that. the scene itself is intermediary. The chief subject—with the *torito*, which the rebellious peons used to burn the hacienda down—went further. This was simply the first encounter with it).

The key compositional combination for *torito* and the hacienda block at Tetlapayac turned out to be a reconstruction of a very old, plastic memory from childhood.

I remember when I was a young child that my room was hung with tinted photographs. Father brought them back from his travels abroad: Venice with the Doge's Palace and the Lion of St Mark.* Somehow, when I was young, they formed a familiar pattern. So much so that even twenty-five years later I had only to see a lancet window, a portico and a cardboard bull, with a vague semblance of wings on his back, to feel an insuperable longing to combine them all into a single composition. Characteristically, there was even a stone barrier in the foreground, reminiscent of an embankment. This is a clearly 'Venetian' motif: the buildings rising up sheer on the edge of the embankment. This inevitably made me want to place the *torito* at the top—it had to break the skyline. This new exigency was dictated by the Lion of St Mark, silhouetted against the sky.

The plastic positioning of the portico itself in precisely that compositional arrangement was based on another 'irritant'. More precisely, it was based on that same childhood memory which had been taken up by a new visual impression.

Indeed, why had those landscapes, typical of de Chirico,[2] affected me so strongly, when I saw them in Paris in the previous year?

* Sadly, I no longer possess these photographs; they were destroyed in Riga during the occupation. But the attached photos of the same subjects give a very good impression of them. [E's note]

The still of the *torito* from the film *Que Viva México!*

St Mark's Square, Venice.

I saw them as some sort of link between the real and the Venice I remembered from childhood. They (or landscapes like them) proved so memorable because of the Venetian motifs which I remembered because of the specifically Italian shade, which so closely resembled the spots of colour and the outlines of shadows on sunny days in Mexico. (Some frames in the film were based on this too.)

One more plastic notion from that series was woven into the complex. I can remember seeing most clearly on Boulevard Montparnasse, in a bookshop window, a recently published album of Max Ernst's surrealist montages (*La Femme aux 100 têtes par* Max Ernst). It was open at a page showing a portico with skeletons, which was the backdrop to a tall lamp with butterflies. Again that compositional pattern: a portico and something with wings! (Incidentally, the composition of this illustration coincided almost completely with qline). But here a new motif also had been included: death and skeletons. (And this gallery of skeletons is very similar to a gallery on the cover of one of the earlier Pinkertons which also made a powerful impression on me in my delicate childhood). And this motif of doom and death links this montage directly with my theme. The sensation recurred a year and a half later in the composition of a particular frame, for the fate of the peons who had revolted and their deaths were essential to the plot of the film.

According to the screenplay, the peon Sebastian took Maria, his bride (seen at the back of our screen) to the *hacendado* for his permission to marry her. A disagreement flared up over the ancient *ius primae noctis* which still obtained in Mexico before the 1910 revolution and this led to the peons' revolt and their flight. Ambushed in a field of agave, they were caught and suffered a bloody retribution. A sense of doom hung over Sebastian and a group of his friends. And under the influence of this motif, from the entire rich variety of colours and styles of Mexican dress, I chose white: the white sarape. This theme—the link between white and death and also mourning—dates from my earliest sensitivities and memories. I was once astonished to learn that the Chinese wear white, not black, for mourning. More significantly, I recalled that in the last act of the opera *Khovanshchina*, all the Old Believers who had been condemned to death and who burnt down their hut while still inside, wore white shirts.[3] And from somewhere came a fragment of religious verse (possibly from the same opera, or a romance): 'Clothe yourself in white raiment.' At least this fragment was never far off, during all of my immersion in things Hispano-Aztec-Toltec, when we were deciding which costumes the doomed peons should wear.

I distinctly remember also another 'key' moment, which seemed to influence the return to the white shirts of *Khovanshchina*, redesigned into long sarapes. I saw in Mexico a flier advertising subscription to Webster's *Encyclopedia Americana*. Every means of attracting subscribers was resorted to: from the astronomical number of words and illustrations contained within, to the etymological derivations of words. And there it turned out that the well-known word 'candidate' comes from Roman times and is closely connected with the concept of purity and innocence (what irony!). In the pre-election practice of those days, that quality was represented by the candidates' wearing togas of dazzling white. It symbolized their probity, honesty and purity. The white of Chinese mourning. The white shirts of the doomed Old Believers. The white togas showing the purity and honesty of the Roman candidates. Each idiosyncratic quality merged with the others, into the white sarape of the Mexican peon-far from 'formalistically', as we can see, but in a way that was connected with sense and subject to a profound degree.

(Incidentally, white sarapes in Mexico, although not unheard of, are nevertheless few and far between, chiefly because of their impracticality and tendency to stain. And the light grey sarape, as seen in the frame, was far from being my first 'impressionistic' adaptation, but it was something that was fundamentally 'emotionally charged', demanded by circumstances, but as I remember, hard to find and not a simple solution).

There was another moment in the peons' tragic fate that was linked to Paris and my childhood. The rebellious peons fled from their pursuers into the agave fields that stretched far to the horizon; they were caught and taken to be executed. How to show the exchange of fire? Should they be filmed among the bushes of agave, defending themselves? A proper siege?

I see on the pages of my director's notes the terse note: 'Sebastian and his comrades are in a giant maguey plant . . . Fort Chabrol.'

That's a great help!

Not many people have seen maguey. And by now, probably, no one can remember what Fort Chabrol was. One thing I can say in advance, and that is that it has nothing to do with Mexico, maguey, peons or agave. Strictly speaking, I did not know Fort Chabrol proper; I only found it in phrases like 'the Fort Chabrol of such-and-such a street' (like the Lady Macbeth of such-and-such a district).[4] The matter led to a small page of a pre-Revolutionary edition of *Ogonyok* [The Torch], or *Sinii zhurnal* [The Blue Paper], with touching descriptions of a besieged house on a 'certain' street which bandits had occupied. For three whole days, armed with guns, they fought off all attempts the police made to seize them. 'Fort Chabrol' became firmly welded, in my imagination, with the val our (naturally valour) of the three men surrounded by *force majeure* and heroically returning fire. My notions about Fort Chabrol were tinted with heroism . . .

At the right moment, a pencil mark introduced the complex of these touching sentiments into the screenplay, linked as they were to a heroic spirit I had long held in awe. It was not the 'Fort' that was of importance, but the fact that the entire complex of emotions associated with this exotic name should emerge here, in the scene which really proved to be one of the most powerful and heartrending.*

As regards the heroism of Fort Chabrol—the grandfather of that scene which I filmed under that name in the heroic episode of Mexico, an 'irony of fate' decreed that it should be absolutely, utterly and completely . . . the reverse.

I learnt the details of the history of Fort Chabrol much later. It turned out that the real Fort Chabrol was one of the last rumblings of the storm precipitated by the . . . Dreyfus affair. It was a challenge by a clique of antisemites and monarchists, who were quartered in a villa on the Rue Chabrol and who were resolved to defend the president of the . . . Anti-Semitic League, a Jules Guérin. Guérin was meant to testify before the Supreme Court, as was Déroulède,[5] who appeared in court before Guerin, on 12 August 1899, charged with treason. The militant antisemites and monarchists withstood a drawn-out siege, and caused Paris much mirth at the expense of the police, who seemed unable to sort them out. More accurately, the police would have treated this affair much more seriously had it been a group of revolutionary workers. The entire history of this scandal

* In this respect, it is characteritic that the associations followed in this line rather than superficial, situational and perhaps more spontaneous and immediate lines—Bancroft, who shot at the police (a film I saw much later) or the ruined fort of Vaux near Verdun. [E's note]

The rebellious peons in the maguey undergrowth. Still from
Que Viva México!

and its dramatic conclusion have been dramatically described in Paul
Morand's book, *1900*.[6]

In any event, these compositional associations, diametrically
opposed though they were in form and content, merged quite
seamlessly with the Mexican models. I ask you to bear in mind that
the hacienda building, Sebastian, the *torito*, the stone barrier and the
time of day for filming all had to be assembled and composed. They
were composed directly, according to some vague, unwritten code.
One integral picture was arranged with an utterly brutal regularity,
with all the details pinned on to it until the hoped-for effect was
achieved; and only in that form could it liberate all those impressions
which, as can be seen, had been shelved for years, their energy
accumulating in my consciousness and creative stock.

The success of this episode, which despite all the antisemites,
Old Believers, Surrealists and skeletons was purely Mexican in its

resolution, can of course be explained by the fact that the associations were not deployed mechanically but as the principal point, the chief, fundamental idea—in Goethe's words, 'opportunely'.[7]

Of course, one cannot always have those essential supporting elements at one's fingertips: the essential 'scaffolding', made up of a stock of resonances, compositional schemes, or templates for working from. Sometimes there is nothing for it but to cast about, searching hurriedly for such elements which have the right resonances, or templates. This happens in those cases where there is an agonizingly acute desire and a thematic need to express an idea plastically with precision; that idea which at a given moment possesses you, but which is absent from the stock of essential material. Off you go to find it. Not in search of the 'unknown', but of that which definitely and concretely accords with the vague image which hovers before your consciousness and emotions.

The Tale of the Vixen and the Hare

An example.

In *Alexander Nevsky* there is the charming figure of Ignat, the linkmail maker.

It would have seemed natural for this representative of the artisan class to have been present right at the start of a depiction of 13th-century Rus in its most diverse aspects.

Perhaps, according to an *a priori* sociological scheme, Pavlenko and I had such a representative. I do not remember! But, if that was the case, then it was so abstracted that I do not even remember it and that would have been impossible if this had been a living image.

So he can be taken as someone who never existed: either factually, or 'in essence'—if he existed in rough drafts as 'a space allocated to the artisan class'.

In either case, how he came into being was exactly as follows.

Athena was supposed to have been born from the skull of Zeus. Ignat, the armourer, had a similar fate.

With just this difference: that here it was Alexander's skull.[8]

And not so much the skull as Nevsky's thoughts of a strategy.

I had an insuperable desire to make Alexander a genius.

In everyday thought, genius is always (and wrongly) linked to something like Newton's apple, or Faraday's mother's jumping teapot lid.[9]

Wrongly, because the ability to extrapolate a universal law from an individual case and subsequently to find a useful application for it, in derivative spheres of every kind of activity, is really connected to one of the features which comprise the complex psychological apparatus of a genius.

In an everyday context—in its obvious aspect—it is believed to be simpler: the ability to apply conclusions about something chance and insignificant to something unexpectedly different and weighty.

Something concerning a falling apple, to something concerning the globe and the law of universal gravity.

If the hero does something like that in the film, then the viewer will very rapidly 'reflexively' come to find the associations which usually surround the question of genius.

And the stamp of genius is as clearly marked on this prince as a halo.

We had only one opportunity in the film for his genius to dazzle —that was in the strategy of the Battle on the Ice, the famous pincer movement in which he crushed the 'iron swine'*—the Teutonic Knights—the pincers entirely surrounding the enemy.

---

* This is a manoeuvre known as a cavalry wedge, which aims to force its way through the enemy lines and make the breach increasingly wide. The Russian word *svin'ya* also means 'pig' or 'swine'. [Trans.]

Ignat tells 'The Tale of the Vixen and the Hare'. Scene from *Alexander Nevky*.

This is a manoeuvre all generals throughout history have dreamed of; it brought unfading glory to the first person to employ it (apart from Alexander): Hannibal, at the battle of Cannae.[10] It brought hundred-fold more glory to the generals of the Red Army, who employed it even more brilliantly in the battle of Stalingrad.

Hence the film's business is clear: a 'Newton's apple' had to be found which would reveal to Alexander, as he deliberated on the imminent battle, a picture of the strategy for the Battle on the Ice.

Situations like this for showing inventive cunning are extraordinarily difficult. It is harder than anything to 'invent' an image, when the spontaneous need for it has been strictly formulated. Here is the formula for what we need: now go and find an image for it.

The procedure advances organically and especially conveniently: a figurative sense of the theme and the gradual crystallization of the formula of an idea (thesis) move, as though merging together and being wrought into one, at the same time.

But when such a formula is already complete and articulated, it can be very difficult to steep it in a soup thick with images of spontaneous, primary, 'inspired' emotional feeling.

This is what causes many dramatists and writers, past and present, great misery. Having made problematic plays, plays *à thèse*, their speciality; or plays designed to demonstrate, through the fate of the characters and performance of the actors, a ready-coined thesis, or 'clause', the natural life of the play itself is suffocated; the thesis is not polished smooth to come across as a particularly acute coining of the theme's overall sense, nor the ideas which gave rise' to the thing. Moreover, sometimes posing the question in this way can lead to clearly preconceived 'discoveries' which in essence are purely mechanical.

There was nothing to be done: that was how it happened. The formulation of the copy-book 'order' preceded the natural evolution of the scene itself, owing to the spontaneity of the internal need; it bypassed the formula and immediately demanded that a figurative form be found for it.

There was nothing for it!

I had to 'seek solutions', 'try them on', and conductconsciously the play of 'proposals and selection' that happens almost uncontrollably, when you take both horses of a pair of bays—conscious and figurative thought—in one, levelly tightened bridle and make them gallop abreast towards the one common goal—the wise imagery of the whole.

You begin with trial and error, measuring for size.

What did Alexander have to see on the eve of battle that could enable him to conceive a plan of action for the easiest destruction of the Germans?

Furthermore, the plan was well known, *a priori*.

Not to allow a wedge to break through the army.

To make the wedge stick fast.

Dmitri Orlov as Ignat.
Scenes from *Alexander Nevsky*.

Then to fall upon it from all sides and the rear.

And strike, strike, strike.

A wedge. A wedge, sticking . . .

Pavlenko thought of an 'image' instantaneously: the night before the battle. There would be campfires, of course. Logs, of course. Chopped, of course.

An axe strikes a knot. It is wedged . . . and sticks fast.

The lively beginning grew cooler and cooler. It was so dull, so lacking in visual appeal. So wrong, too. You can imagine Russian camp fires in a forest, piled up with well chopped logs, like the ones we placed on the tiled stove in Pavlenko's flat, which was in an out-building of the house which, according to tradition, belonged to the Rostov family. It now houses the Writers' Union. In the very same wing where, according to tradition, Andrei Bolkonsky lay severely wounded . . .[11]

We were embarrassed; we immediately made our excuses. One of us had quite forgotten that he was expected somewhere else and the other really had to be going.

The next day, no one mentioned firewood.

Perhaps Alexander's thoughts should not turn to a wedge stuck fast? Perhaps, he should think about ice being too thin to bear the weight of the knights? (Alexander's plan took account of this circumstance also. And the ice did indeed crack when the knights retreated, panic-stricken, sealed inside their heavy armour, just when they were piled up against the high bank of Lake Peipus.)

Well now, let's see.

An 'image' is instantly ready: at the edge of the ice walks a cat.

Ice is thinnest at its edge.

The ice . . . shatters . . . beneath . . . a cat . . .

This proposal was so cretinous we almost choked.

Again, we had both completely forgotten. Pavlenko was already very late . . . I had to be making my way . . .

A few more days.

And more of the same. I do not know about Pavlenko, but I could not sleep at night.

Everywhere axes were sticking in logs, cats slipped on ice; then axes shattered the ice and cats were wedged into logs.

To hell with it!

All sorts of mad ideas come to mind when you cannot sleep and lie tossing from side to side.

I reached out for the bookcase.

I needed something to take my mind off things.

I picked a collection of 'cherished', 'adult' Russian folk tales.[12]

Almost the very first was 'The Vixen and the Hare'.

Well now!

However did I come to forget my favourite story?

One jump took me to the telephone.

I roared triumphantly down the receiver:

'Got it!

'Someone begins telling the story of "The Vixen and the Hare" by the camp fire.'

How the Hare jumped between two birches.

And the Vixen chased after him and got stuck, wedged between those two birches . . .

After half an hour or so of great exertion, the fable took on the form that it has in the film.

['So the Hare jumped into a gully and the Vixen, she came after him. Then the Hare jumped between two birches. And the Vixen, she came after him—and stuck fast! Try as she might, she was wedged between the birches and could not move an inch. It was all up for her. Then the Hare, who was' standing close by, he looked at her seriously and said, "Perhaps I'll bust your maidenhead, now . . ."

'The soldiers around the camp fire laugh. Then Ignat-continues: '"Oh, don't do that, I could never bear the shame. Have pity!"'"You had no pity for me," said the Hare, and he bust it.']

Alexander hears the story being told at the campfire. (The Prince's mingling with his troops will look good. The proximity between the general and his soldiers).

He interrupts to ask:

'Stuck between two birches?'

'And he bust it!' answered the storyteller, jubilantly, to much laughter.

Of course, Alexander had long borne in mind the image of an encirclement.

Of course, he did not learn this wise strategy from a fable.

But the distinct dynamic of the situation in the story provided Alexander with the trigger necessary for him to deploy his actual fighting force.

Buslai lets the swine's snout snuffie around.

The snout sinks in . . .

Gavril Olexich's troops secure the flanks . . .

And the irregulars strike at the rear!

Inspired now, quickly, precisely and covering every contingency, Alexander sketches in the outline for the next day's battle.

Alexander says to Gavril and Buslai:

[Drawing himself up, Alexander turns to the soldiers and says: 'We will fight them on the ice . . .

Eisenstein enacting the moment of Ignat's death (Mosfilm, 1938).

'There, by Raven Rock, will be the vanguard ... You, Gavril, take the regiments on the left. I'll take my men on the right, and the Prince's Regiment. And you, Mikula, take the peasants and the ambush force. We know the Germans will strike in a wedge, there, by Raven Rock, and the vanguard will bear the brunt of that.'

Buslai asks:

'Who will take the van?'

Alexander answers:

'You will. You have run all night, now you can rest for a day. And bear the full brunt, giving no quarter, until Gavril and I press them in on the sides, from left and right. Got it? Let's go.'

Alexander leaves.]

In the satisfaction with what has just been achieved there is a passing recognition that a general rule might be deduced from what has just occurred.

All our attempts were unsuccessful so long as we tried to find a similar plastic prototype for a plastic image of the battle: logs, a cat.

The key material was supplied by another dimension: narrative, storytelling.

I suspect a certain natural truth underlies all this. It is the dynamic outline which fits the fact or subject, rather than the details themselves, that should lead to the conception.

And, if the fact or subject is of a different, order—for example, not plastic but auditory—then the sensation of this dynamic schema is more acute as the brain can transpose it into another area—more acute, and much more efficacious.

Perhaps we are dealing here with a law characteristic of inventiveness as a whole?

And my own 'representative' case, showing how Alexander 'invented', sheds light on the mechanism of inventiveness in general?

Surely everyone knows that, according to Gutenberg's testimony, the complex invention of book-printing by means of setting each letter separately, came about as a result of three completely and absolutely indirect impressions; the dynamic essence of each of these was abstracted and then 'mixed' with another area and another set of actions.

How was this remarkable art invented?

We know about this from the letters Gutenberg wrote from the banks of the Rhine, in the middle of the fifteenth century, to monks of the Cordelliers' Brotherhood[13] (*Histoire de l'invention de l'imprimerie par les monuments*, Paris, 1840).*

* E's reference.

I shall quote extracts from them, pedantically preserving their idiosyncratic form, their repetitiveness and tone, at once artless and passionate. The anomalies in the way he set down his thoughts convey beautifully the inventor's inner turmoil; at every step, he is tortured by an impatient longing to succeed.

We can follow these stages in his quest and the gradual development of his discovery.

a) First—the burning desire, 'the *idée fixe*': to shorten the copyists' lengthy labours.

Gutenberg was burning with longing to achieve this.

For a month, my head has been hard at work; thought must emerge from my skull fully-armed like Athena . . .

I want to inscribe with one action of my hand, one movement of my fingers, in one go, with one expulsion of my thought everything a large sheet of paper can take in terms of lines, words and letters, that the most industrious of clerks could accomplish in one day (or in many).

(From the first letter)

But what method should be used? Playing cards and small pictures of saints suggest the method to be tried first:

b) The first thing that led me to the method was playing cards and small pictures.

You have seen, as I have, playing cards and pictures of saints . . . These cards and pictures have been engraved on small wooden blocks and below are words, whole lines, which are also engraved. A layer of viscous ink is put on top of this engraving; a sheet of slightly dampened paper is put on this layer of ink, and that paper is rubbed and rubbed until it begins to shine. Then the sheet is lifted clear and you will see on the other side a picture which looks as if it has been drawn on, with words which look written on. The ink was transferred to the paper, leaving the engraved block, drawn by the paper's elasticity and held by its dampness . . .

Renewing the ink on the block and repeating the process, you can make hundreds and thousands of identical prints.

So. What you have done for a few words, a few lines, you must learn how to reproduce on to whole, large sheets printed sheets; large sheets, covered with letters on both sides, making whole books and the first book of all: the Bible.

How? There is no point in thinking about how to engrave 1,300 pages on these boards; no point in attempting to obtain these prints by rubbing the reverse side of the paper, since the second side can only be covered with words at the expense of the first side, which will have to be rubbed . . .

How to proceed? I do not know, but I know what I want to do: I want to copy the Bible; I want the impressions ready for the pilgrimage to Aix-La-Chapelle . . .

(From the first letter)

And so, the urgent desire usefully to serve religion is also expressed in his letter. But there now emerges a second phenomenon which led him to the means of realizing his wish: minting.

c) Minting is the second key phenomenon.

Each coin starts off as a stamp (die). The stamp is a small steel rod with one engraved end which takes the form of a letter, a few letters, all the symbols that are to appear in relief on the coin.

It is dampened and driven into another piece of steel, giving it depth (*un coin*). Small gold discs (blanks) are set into these, also wetted, and when they are hit hard they become coins.

(From the second letter)

d) The third key phenomenon: a press and printing.

But the idea of minting gave rise to the idea of pressure, as the die is pressed into the steel. Two memories—of a wine-press and printing—complete the picture, combining an additional principle of repetition. Gutenberg wrote:

I attended a wine-making, and I saw how the grape juice runs. Working backwards from effect to cause, I was preoccupied with the press's strength, which nothing could resist.

One could create such pressure using tin. A simple substitution, and light dawned. The pressure which the tin exerted would have to leave a mark behind on the paper. The inventor exclaims triumphantly:

'So that's it! God has revealed a secret to me, as I had besought him . . . I ordered a great quantity of tin be brought to my room: that was the pen I was going to write with.

'But the handwriting, engraving and pattern: how would they look?'

Then he had the idea of the possibility of repeated use.

The big monastery seal which the monks affix for signature was what prompted him.

'Does your seal not enable you to produce these signs and letters as often as you require?'

They had to produce similar ones for this new technique:*

---

* At that time, seals were engraved, to give a raised image on wax, like those that we use for sealing wax. They were like negatives of what is today a simple resin stamp, where letters stand out in relief, on the actual stamp. [E's note]

We must melt, forge, make a countersunk die, like your brotherhood has on its seal. A mould, such as that used for the casting of your chalices . . .

First, a relief made of steel; a *poinçon*—a rod with the letter proud on one end, then an incision made by a blow of the rod into brass. This is the mother's breast of the letter—the matrix . . .

Finally the letters themselves:

A sharp tap sends the molten metal into the very bottom of the matrix . . . you open the mould, take out the image of the steel rod realized in tin—a small tin rod with a delicate relief on one end, and the residue on the other, which you will need to file away. They are as alike as sisters, these letters: they all bear the likeness of the *poinçon*, their father.

(Fifth letter)

Hence: independent letters, all alike:

. . . Movable letters. That they can be moved is of course the real treasure I have discovered while seeking the unknown via the unknown. From these letters and blanks between to establish the spacing, I can make words, etc.

(Letters eight and nine)

The full picture of the invention is just the same as the one we traced just before as I went through all the phases of our search for a composition.

First, the most acute desire to realize a definite idea, which has possessed the inventor. The needs of his like-minded associates—making the Bible more widely accessible—were concentrated in this idea. (There was also a more circumscribed and precise task: to contribute, morally and economically, to the success of the pilgrimage to Aix-La-Chapelle.)

The seeker's personal inspiration turned out to be the expressed command of a social group whose interests he shared.

The elements that could enable the invention to be realized practically, but represented only in vague outline, were sought feverishly.

When possessed by a theme, consciousness only registers those features of a chance phenomenon that can, one way or another, lead to the realization.

To sum up, we have found three basic characteristics of this invention: the results of the future apparatus will resemble the reproduction of engravings. The future apparatus will print, by applying pressure to paper (the technique of printing for preparing a pictorial engraving was then unknown—see above); the apparatus will be able to reproduce the image of the actual letters by a method completely new to woodcut printing at that time (it will not be necessary to engrave each letter afresh, as is the case with engraving blocks: using a mould, each letter can be reproduced as often as needed).

These three crucial moments arose from his own experience and the principles of three analogous technical situations: playing cards and images of saints gave him the idea of the woodcut printing technique for drawing the letters; the winepress and the monastery seal gave him the idea of the using tin as the material for the letters; finally, money and minting inspired a similar apparatus for forming letters. And the principal features of these three partially analogous phenomena merged into a new, independent invention.

Then there is the famous case of Otto von Guericke, who made the Magdeburg hemispheres.[14] It was a rose, whose scent he drew in through his nostrils (that is, he created an artificial vacuum which nature rushed in to fill—bringing the scent with it!), which led him to the idea of a pump that could extract air.

Surely the same thing happens in art?

The painter, Repin, heard Rimsky—Korsakov's *Vengeance*[15] and his response was not an imitative piece of music, but a painting: Ivan the Terrible standing over his murdered son: the colour and actions of the characters embodied the same dynamic of emotions that he felt in the music.

And the encounter with the squadron in *The Battleship Potemkin*, is *sui generis* a new version of the traditional 'chase' sequence, taken from a quite different point of view, and interpreted according to the subject of the material, observing precisely the rules which generally govern the traditional build-up of suspense and dynamic!

… But there is no time for meditating here. We have more work to do on the screenplay.

The first thing that emerged from the above-mentioned resolution was an order to the wardrobe department.

In order to 'drive' the link between the plan of battle and the story into the consciousness, the peasant irregulars would wear giant hare-fur ear muffs as they drove a wedge into the Germans' rear.

But a 'chain' reaction of inventiveness is hurtling off with particular impetuosity in another direction.

How the image of the storyteller was formed.

The fable had to be told well, dramatically.

Who was our best actor for narrative and storytelling? Who?

Dmitri Nikolayevich Orlov, of course.[16]

No one who has listened to his inimitable rendering of Dogada can be in any doubt about that.

Orlov had all the wisdom, archness, seeming naivety and calculating cunning that you would expect to find in a Russian peasant of the middle orders; an artisan, or craftsman.

Stop!

We had in our list of *desiderata* for the film a vacancy for just such a person.

By that point he was faceless.

That is, not counting the face of one of the figures with a funny basin-crop on the Korsun Doors of St Sophia in Novgorod.

The style of the story and Orlov's particular arch innuendo with his eyes screwed slyly up, breathed life into the outline of this representative of Novgorod craftsmen, a social category indicated in the cast list by the general heading *desiderata*.

Orlov was to be a linkmail maker.

More shrewd than the simple young soldiers.

No wonder he teaches them, albeit with crude fables.

And so that the fable should not stand out from the general flow of his talk, the style of his talk should be in character: from embellishment to his patois; from folk sayings to proverbs.

And so that the story would not sound simply crude, but crude only in the way it was told, it was important that Ignat (his name had already been found, but goodness knows where it came from!) should be a truly Russian man and patriot.

And so when arguments broke out on the town square about 'whether it was worth fighting for some kind of unified Rus'—which is how the conservative propertied classes of Novgorod viewed the national business, it fell to none other than Ignat to summon the people of Novgorod to fight the Germans.

And now Ignat comes forward with a call to arms.

But so that it should not sound mere rhetoric, he must be a patriot in deed as well as word.

And he leads the town's metal-beaters day and night, forging swords, lances and mail. But his 'activism' must not be confined to his professional work.

It must fill the breadth of his soul.

He makes presents ('take them all') of everything that has been made, forged and wrought.

And so this does not leave the aftertaste of a banal, theatrical gesture, we will earth him with a gentle irony, which begins to make its presence felt in his sayings. Let his tongue run away with itself in his generosity; let him be too extravagant.

Let the metal-worker end up without any mail, because, he has given it all away.

Let him be left with nothing.

(The defenceless armourer' is such an innovation that it would not be proper for the traditional 'barefoot cobbler' to pose too.

We will not leave Ignat without boots, therefore; we have already learnt something about the methods of 'transplanting' situations—not for nothing did that cat of ours dive under the ice!).

But perhaps that would be overstated.

We shall not leave him without mail. Better, more amusing, to give him a coat the wrong size.

'It is too short!' He will say, slightly perplexed, rather distressed and confused; he will be left with a short coat after giving all the others out.

But then, looking at the dramatic necessities from another angle, the viewer's hostility towards the Germans must be assured.

A positive hero had to die.

When Pskov was sacked, the only people who died were those who had done nothing to win the viewer's sympathy: they were merely his compatriots—Russians—people from Pskov.

The sack of Pskov did not strike the viewer with sufficient emphasis—there was no element of personal fate to involve the audience closely.

'The coat is too short! The coat is too short!' It has a good ring to it, it stands repetition.

A refrain.

All the rules governing refrains dictate that there must be a new light cast on the subsequent repetition-it must be interpreted differently.

On one hand, 'the coat is too short!'; on the other, one of the film's heroes must die.

Not Alexander.

Nor Buslai.

Gavril Olexich almost dies, as it is.

But both must be alive at the end.

'The coat is too short!'

But the coat could offer insufficient protection in other places than at the bottom.

It might not cover the throat properly . . .

Comedy can turn into tragedy.

And if what is tragic echoes what was comic, the grief is deepened, and anger mounts at the cause of that grief . . .

And the funny 'the coat is too short!' is said first self-consciously and then with dramatic urgency as he pulls the collar up higher than the murderer's knife . . . whose knife?

Of course, the most treacherous of the enemy host: Tverdilo, the turncoat governor of Novgorod.

'The coat is too short!'

Repeated as a refrain, the second time as the last breath of this likeable character—this witty, sly, selfless servant of Russia; this ardent patriot and martyr of the common cause.

So, out of the needs of the whole, the live features and necessary qualities of a new character develop organically within the work; just as the situation and unique conditions of an historical event stir up the people's hearts, calling them to action, throwing up unexpected heroes and revealing those traits of character and deeds which bathe the people in the rays of undying glory . . .

And the actor Orlov walked around the huge Mosfilm hangar on Potylikha, from episode to episode, following the dramatic fate of his chainmail maker, continually bending over to the tip of Ignat's boot.

There was a crumpled and greasy bundle at the end of the boot: this was the verbal tissue that fleshed out his role.

Orlov would stoop down to add a new saying to the list:

'Birds of a feather . . .'

One more for his stock.

He had read it somewhere.

And something had reminded him of it.

He had learnt it from someone.

Or he would stoop down to pull out an apposite saying—he had found the part in his role where he could slip it in.

One would be most appropriate before his death: overconfident talk. His guard was down. He missed the ominous glint of a knife.

Orlov walked around Mosfilm, croaking and bending over, arguing with himself as Ignat about which lines fitted best where.

Constantly and conscientiously.

What a shame I did not find this one saying earlier:

The mushrooms have eyes:
They put them in pies
And eat them alive
In Rya-a-zan . . .

I can almost hear you saying that.

But it is too late.

Hard to believe though it is, we made that picture eight years ago . . .

Layout

In real creative work, of course, this progress is far from gradual and intelligible.

The plastic perception of the parts, the calculation of the correlations, the possibilities for the spatial coordinates, the points where the juxtapositions of *mise-en-scène* are particularly expressive: all these hit you from all sides, in a highly dramatic manner.

It is like lava which hurls itself at you, surging up from all sides-part of the calculation for the finale, a convenient aspect of the climax, the dynamic flourish of a chance sequence, the angle of a certain grouping.*

What comes first, what follows, what comes earlier, what later, it is impossible to establish any of this as the first, general, chaotic sketch of the whole spills out on to the page.

When it settles on the paper with its platforms, bridges and staircases, the environment of the conceived scene is like an 'impress' formed by the whirlwind of activity which fashions for itself a pedestal and supporting sides; crossbeams holding the action together; surfaces, for the broad scope of the action; or slopes, along which it might develop upwards, or which it can gradually descend.

Sometimes even in this mad gallop, a cavalcade of the future 'acting workshop' as it is formed in your senses, its separate elements which have just settled can anticipate you and introduce changes to situations, calling for new, unexpected episodes: inset platforms

---

* Many of the scenes in *Ivan the Terrible* were drawn up before being written. If it is done normally,
1 theme
2 content
3 subject
4 layout
then the commonest procedures are: 1-4-3-2-; 3-2-4-1; and even 4-3-2-1. [E's note]

intensify the drama of conflicts. Bare surfaces, created for the essential parts of a certain scene, beg to be used differently elsewhere. A detail that seems to have arisen quite by chance becomes the place for applying successive, unforeseen changes of direction in developing scenes, as they come together in counterpoint.

It is more or less impossible to establish such a 'flight' in one's notes.

And the cascade of notes on the following pages is an attempt to record (if not completely) a wholly improvised initial outline in the form in which I tried demonstrating it at one of my lectures.

I had tried to switch on the 'whirlwind' at once, 'at all points'; that is, to give free rein to the new 'urges' that each new element of the scene, the *mise-en-scène* and the situation includes and provokes: these influenced each other in turn; so the dynamic of the situation grew, illuminated at the same time by the growth of the static component of *mise-en-scène*—the picture of the scene in relief, as if it had taken its shape from the forms underpinning the whirlwind dashes of *mise-en-scène* as they race after each other sequentially.

First of all.

The chaotic dynamic formula of the key whirlwind. The invariable 'primordial element'.

Someone speaks to his followers.

The opposition bursts in.

The speaker is quietened.

No more for the time being.

So:

A high point.

Its base.

Something for them to rush out from.

Towards the speaker. His audience. The supporters. The opposition.

The Plan of the Battle on the Ice on Lake Peipus, sketched by Eisenstein

So, A.

And its base, B.

How best to burst in?

'Bursting in' means through an opening.

A round opening is an extreme case.

Round gates of Chinese palaces?

No! They would not be of use to the running crowd, because of the lower section.

Retain the idea of a round opening, but adjust the lower part to make it easy for the people to run through.

An arch!

A—He is talking.

B—They are listening.

C—They burst in.

Next—The overthrow.

DIAGRAM 3:

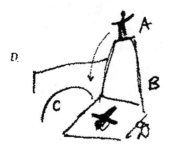

So. He is lying down.

Lying is materially important.

He must be seen.

D—The platform at the base needs to be raised.

DIAGRAM 4:

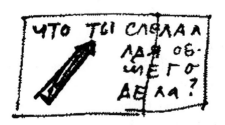

In order for it to be seen distinctly, an arrow will have to be affixed.

As on posters:

What have you done for the common cause?

DIAGRAM 5:

Fix it scenically, with a 'look'.

She (who?) should come out after his fall.

Obtain the maximum effect from this by having the sightlines on a diagonal.

DIAGRAM 6:

She has to come out.

She needs her own small arch. (If the first, gently sloping, then large; or if vertical, small.)

Arch C is narrower than the bridge.

More precisely, she enters—that's the first thing. Then she sees him.

There are two points on the bridge, a and c.

The tug towards him grows stronger.

They draw near.

A look.

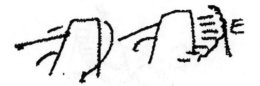

It only remains for her to descend.

Their look is direct.

The descent towards him must be circuitous.

The line in the air needs to be underpinned.

So, a staircase down comes into being.

DIAGRAM 8:

She has made the descent.

She lies over him.

They form a cross.

The platform, D, is inclined.

The outward appearance is beautiful. They need to be in differently coloured clothing, to emphasize that they are lying across each other.

Take an extreme case: *blanc et noir.*

He is in black.

She is in white.

Is he a monk? Savonarola. Campanella. Bruno.

Is she a convert? St Genevieve? Beatrice?

The platform is clearly ideal for an audience.

They listen, en masse.

Not chance bystanders, but adherents.

One mass, forged from many people.

The outward appearance is good: those nearer the back (from the viewer's position) are higher.

Those who are to overthrow him race up staircase E.

This is preceded by a brief struggle.

His adherents are scattered.

The *mise-en-scène* is destroyed.

The opponents burst in, forming a ring around the followers.

The opponents press in, taking over the platform.

The followers turned round on the spot. Their attention was focused on the speaker, at the back—high up. Now it is on the 'footlights'— on the opponents.

DIAGRAM 12:

The opponents break in from the right, throwing the followers down off the platform.

DIAGRAM 13:

The followers are scattered.

Necessity demands some details of construction in the foreground, on the left and right. Steps down into the pit, or a barrier running the length of the footlights.

DIAGRAM 14:

The left flank of those bursting in rushes towards the speaker (the left route is greater—more clearly distinguished). Those on the right may be occupied with ending the fight.

DIAGRAM 15:

The end of the tail—those on the right cross over to the left—catches the defeated man. This is how the overthrow happens:

1. The platform is surrounded.

2. They climb on to the platform and surround him.

3. They lift him up.

4. They throw him down.

5. Raised arms emphasize the fall.

The Speaker vanishes in the pile of captured people.

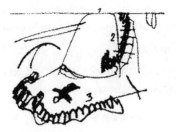

He is thrown up out of the crowd.

They run this way and that as he falls.

Some have remained at the top and on the staircase.

Those at the base throng around the platform, a ring of black.

DIAGRAM 17:

She appeared in the archway. She is seen in sequence by (1) those at the top; (2) those on the staircase; (3) those at the bottom.

Those in black—who burst in—apprehensively back away from her.

DIAGRAM 18:

Perhaps she is . . . blind?

Her unseeing eyes are even more terrible when she 'feels', up above, that he is somewhere down below in the deathly silence?

Perhaps it is his mother?

She appears at point b the moment after everyone gathered in a crowd in the right (struck by a superstitious horror).

DIAGRAMS 19 AND 7:

When she stops at point b—the wild rushing back of those in black, under the arch (19).

After their escape, her descent towards him (19 and 7).

DIAGRAM 20:

Two possible ways for her to approach him: A and B.

B of course is better. Falling on her knees, and then falling across him—in front of the audience. This is visible. This bypasses the 'exchange of looks' (or, if she is blind, the sensation of his presence. Perhaps, she bent over at an angle, perhaps she is on her knees, feeling, probing . . .).

Here she has fallen on to her knees.

Stretching out.

And the black ring of the enemy looks like a funeral ring (wreath) around her.

DIAGRAM 22:

Obviously, the black figures on the right will need to be surrounded by details of a city: porticoes, loggias, flat roofs, windows and so on.

DIAGRAM 23:

But now she rises up.

And her mute call is answered: from every corner, her followers begin to return, gathering in strength.

DIAGRAM 24:

And now their arms are raised in anger.

And the black ring of their enemy hides, cowardly.

And the funeral procession bears off the body of the dead man. The Speaker.

DIAGRAM 25:

And only she, she alone is left, sobbing at the base.

Deep in shadow . . .

Or she stands at the top end of the platform of the tower, her arms raised in anger; the scarlet rays of sunset bloody her white clothing.

Cast dark silhouettes of sails against the backdrop, or the funeral crosses of mournful pennants, and you will be ready to write a play around the central scene we have just prepared . . .

THE AUTHOR AND HIS THEME[1]

Twenty Years Later
(1925–45: from *Potemkin* to *Ivan*)

Twenty years have passed . . .

Two decades.

That is twice the time allowed for by the law of prescription: after that period, a guilty man is freed from any obligations before the law and anyone seeking justice no longer has a valid claim.

I think this entitles me to talk about *Potemkin* and the author in the third person, as I would of any extraneous object, of an object and person with an objective existence outsicle myself. It is only thanks to happy (?) chance that I know of them, more or less and in greater detail, than do many other researchers.

I will therefore speak of the author and film impartially, not fighting shy of the affection I feel for them both. And I shall take advantage of my access to a significant amount of material unknown to anyone else—after all, no one else had any access to it.

And as I have already resolved to write of the author of *The Battleship Potemkin* as I would of someone I did not know, I will try to do so according to the criterion which none other than Belinsky insisted upon:

> Contemporary criticism should reveal and lay bare the poet's soul in his works. It should follow his dominant theme, the thought governing his whole life, his whole existence. It should observe and elucidate his inner contemplation and his spirit . . .
>
> (*The Poetry of Baratynsky*, 1842)*

* E's reference.

Of all the questions which lend themselves too readily to disorganized screeds of writing, a very popular one is:

the author and his theme.

Whether authors have such a theme running 'through' all their works, or not; whether it always exists; what relationship does an evolving series of works bear towards it; etc., etc. All of this is certainly not very well known, and so it is an unbelievably rich vein for endless inferences and guesses.

But there is one thin element of truth, however.

Some researchers find this confirmed even in the simple comparison of titles.

Thus for example Krzhizhanovsky, author of *The Poetics of Titles* (now long out of print), adduced a list of examples of this from Russian and foreign literature.[2]

Jack London's basic theme is family and stock; the overwhelming majority of his titles are precisely to do with this.

With regard to Goncharov, the author goes even further, holding that Goncharov's theme is even linked to a particular auditory symbol—'Ob'.[3]

This sound symbol recurs in a series of the author's key works (*Ob-ryv* [The Precipice]; *Ob-lomov*; *Ob-yknovennaya istoriya* [A Common Story], and one work which should, in its inner workings, have broken the run of this series (and which was not realized) would have had an exceptional title too: *Ne-ob-yknovennaya istoriya* [An Uncommon Story].

Similar examples are titles which adhere closely to a given formula. This is the case with one of the best and most prolific writers of detective fiction, from the golden age of the genre in America: S. S. Van Dine (in the 1930s).[4]

All the titles are variations on one theme: *The Canary Murder Case*, *The Dragon Murder Case*, *The Kennel Murder Case* and so on.

But there is more to it than that: in each title, the one word which defines the distinguishing incident has no more and no fewer than. . . six letters. Canary, dragon, kennel, garden, scarab, casino, Benson (a surname), Greene (ditto), Bishop (a complex pun which throws red herrings the detective's way, as it can be read as 'Primate', a surname and finally as the chess piece) and so on.

In one article, the author of these novels (a middling art critic and a failure at serious literature, but who went on to make a fortune from detective fiction) commented on this circumstance.

He explained it as superstition: the first such title brought him good luck and he clung fervently to the formula of his first literary success!

Of course, this discourse on titles only covers the superficial aspect of the question, the heart of which probably lies very deep.

I am not about to solve this question. And I want to limit myself to just one example of a theme running 'through' my work, as I am already beginning to find it fascinating and tempting to analyse the case of an author who was responsible for such works as *The Battleship Potemkin* and *Ivan the Terrible*, whose themes are seemingly incompatible.

What could be more startlingly different than the themes and treatment of those two works, separated by an interval of twenty years?

The first had a collective and a mass of people.

The second, an autocratic individual.

In the first, there was something resembling a chorus, a monolithic and united collective.

The second was about a sharply defined character.

The first showed a desperate struggle with tsarism.

The second showed tsarist rule being established for the first time.

Eisenstein editing *October*, 1928.

If here, at these extremes, the themes appear divergent, polarized, then what lies between seems, at first glance, unimaginably chaotic: themes thrown together haphazardly.

It would seem funny to think that this author could have a unified theme, one that ran 'through' his works; it would be naive to talk of it in that way.

Indeed!

If we consider my planned work as well as the work I achieved, there are: a short story about one, unique strike (*The Strike*); a wreath of exotic novellas situated in a Mexican landscape (*Que Viva México!*); there is the epic exposition of the October Revolution, 1917 (*October*) and—an odd juxtaposition—An *American Tragedy* (based on Theodore Dreiser's novel); the history of a black ruler of Haiti—Henri Christophe, the liberator-turned-despot of his island; Alexander Nevsky's heroic struggle against the Teutonic interventionists who invaded in the thirteenth century—'the German dogs'; the introduction of a collective economy into a backward rural setting (*The Old and the New*); the history of Captain Sutter, on whose Californian estates gold was first discovered in 1848; the history of a mutiny on a battleship; a screenplay about the building of the Fergana Canal (1939), an idiosyncratic historical triptych (Part One included episodes from Tamerlane's campaigns, printed in *Iskusstvo kino* [The Art of Cinema], in 1939); there is in my files a detailed treatment of a screenplay about Pushkin in colour, an intimately personal view of the poet's life. It took as its theme Tynyanov's brilliant article mentioned for the first time: *Bezymennaya lyubov* [A Nameless Love] (*Literaturnyi kritik* [The Literary Critic] no. 5, 1939) and then significantly less interestingly developed in the third part of *Pushkin* ... And finally a film about a historical colossus—Ivan the Terrible and the establishment of autocracy in sixteenth-century Muscovy!

The most casual observer could tell at a glance that this resultant mass is composed of irreconcilable and incompatible elements.

Only the most driving obsession could force you to look for a unity of theme in this particoloured mixture; to look for the one theme which informs this whole disparate variety.

To palpate the author's one pervasive thought which 'dominated his entire life' (well, perhaps not all, but a twenty-five-year-long section of it at any rate: 1920–45).

Let us remember for the time being this tendency—to look for that one thing in this many-coloured variety. We shall find those things that concern a driving obsessiveness repaid with interest later on.

We shall now avail ourselves of a little patience and look at what each of these works was examining, in greater detail.

As we do so, we shall distinctly remember that this has nothing to do with the different costumes and robes, historical situations or the stance of this or that film, nor with chance ethnographic variations. In each and every case, it has to do with those elements within the theme which emotionally drew the author to deal with this or that subject, the majority of which were his free choice. There was always a 'personal turn' within the theme anyway and, in every case, the actual material of the film was written independently.

This is irrespective even of whether the film was commissioned by the State—for in that case, the episode on the *Potemkin* is an episode from *1905*—or whether the film was an adaptation from a book, in which case the author would have to have been very keen on it, either for the way the events unfolded (Blaise Cendrars' *Sutter's Gold*), or for the psychological actuality of a thing (indicated by Tynyanov in *Pushkin*); or whether the choice of theme was entirely free (*Que Viva México!*).

Unity

If I were an impartial researcher, I would say of myself: this author appears to be constantly fixated with one idea, one theme, one subject.

Everything he has thought up and done, not only within the different films but through all his plans and films, is in each and every case one and the same thing.

Almost invariably, the author uses different periods (thirteenth, sixteenth or twentieth centuries), different countries and peoples (Russia, Mexico, Uzbekistan, America), different social movements and processes within the shift towards different social forms, as different masks covering one and the same face.

This face is the realization of the ultimate goal—the attainment of unity.

With Russian revolutionary and socialist material, this is the problem of national and patriotic unity (*Alexander Nevsky*) or state unity (*Ivan the Terrible*), or collective or mass unity (*The Battleship Potemkin*) or socioeconomic unity (*The Old and The New*), or Communist unity (*Fergana Canal*).

Abroad, this is either the same theme, in a different guise suiting the national aspects, or the seamy side (which is always tragically coloured) of the same theme, which sets off the positive side of the whole opus. This happened in *Nevsky* too: the bright theme of patriotism is underscored by the darker episodes of the Germans' reprisals at Pskov, which represented Russian unity.

The tragedies of individualism, planned during our tour of the West, were: *An American Tragedy*, *Sutter's Gold* (the paradise of primitive patriarchal California being destroyed by the curse of gold which had completely corrupted the moral and ethical system of Captain Sutter, who opposed the gold), *Black Majesty* (hero of the Haitian revolutionary wars of independence, fought by the Haitian slaves of French colonists, and who was a comrade-in-arms of Toussaint L'Ouverture and who became the emperor of the island: Henri Christophe, who perished after an individualistic split from his own people), *Fergana Canal* (another 'hymn' to collectivist unification through socialist labour) the only means of bridling the forces of nature—water and sand—which were unloosed by the human discord of Tamerlane's wars in Central Asia. When his state collapsed, the desert came into its own. The peoples of Asia languished under the tyranny of nature as well as under the tyranny of tsarist Russia, and this first tyranny was overthrown too.

Finally, *Que Viva México!* This was the history of cultural changes, but not presented vertically—in years and centuries—but horizontally: as utterly diverse stages of culture, coexisting in the same geographical area, next to each other. This is what makes Mexico such an amazing place. Some provinces (Tehuantepec), built on a matriarchal system, lie next to provinces which virtually achieved Communism by revolution in the second decade of this century (Yucatán, Zapata's programme, etc). The central episode of Mexico concerned the idea of national unity—historically, the 'United Entry' into the capital—Mexico. This was the combined forces of Villa, who came from the north, and Emiliano Zapata, who was from the south. The central figure in the plot was a Mexican woman—a *soldadera*—who moved, with the same concern for her man, from faction to faction of the Mexican soldiery that were fighting each other and riven with the contradictions of civil war. It was as if she physically embodied the image of the one; nationally united, Mexico, working against the international intrigues which were attempting to carve the nation up and to play the different sections off against each other.

At this point, you will retort all the more fiercely that this only goes to show that all the observations made relate only to me, the author, who is now absolutely *toqué*,* fixated on a single, albeit respectable, idea—and that one only.

And I must answer all the more truculently that this is not at all the case; and again, 'in the case we have examined', we have only an example of a particularly, perhaps, emphasized feature, which is absolutely general.

And again, perhaps, only more glaringly obvious . . .

The process of assimilating material, i.e. making it 'one's own', happens at the moment when, coming into contact with reality, it begins to set itself out according to a grid of outlines and sketches of the same special structure as that in which one's consciousness was formed.

It makes no difference whether this encounter is with a new land and milieu; with a picture of a bygone age; or happens face to face with one's own epoch, the present.

I became acquainted with all the aspects of such encounters: with an unknown land which suddenly appeared before me; with a past age which suddenly unfolded before me; or face to face with my own times.

I also encountered different possibilities within these encounters. With imaginary coincidences of my matrix with the outline

* French: 'touched'.

of the phenomenon I met, and with the morbid streak in my works; with still unresolved meetings and the great feeling which accompanies an absolute coincidence. I speak of this from personal experience.

There is in each of us something like those complex knots that Leonardo designed for the Milan Academy and that he drew on the ceilings.

We encounter a phenomenon.

And the plan of this knot seems to be laid over this phenomenon.

The features of one coincide, or otherwise.

They coincide partially.

Here and there.

They do not coincide.

They clash with one another, striving for coincidence.

Sometimes breaking the structure and the outlines of reality, in order to satisfy the contour of individual desire.

Sometimes violating individualities in order to 'synchronize' with the demands of what they have clashed with.

I cannot actually remember any examples of the latter from my own personal practice; but then I could give plenty of examples illustrating the former . . .

P.S. [1]

P.S. P.S. P.S.

Of course—P.S.!

On 2 February this year, a heart muscle ruptured. There was a haemorrhage. (An infarction). By some incomprehensible, absurd and pointless miracle, I survived.

All the facts of science dictated that I should die.

For some reason, I survived.

I, therefore, consider that everything which happens from now on is a postscript to my own life . . .

P.S . . .

And indeed, who, at the age of forty-eight, has read this about himself:

'Un des plus fameux metteurs-en-scène de son temps . . .'* (The monthly magazine of the Institut des hautes études cinématographiques, Paris, 1946, in the section 'Critique des critiques', on *Ivan the Terrible*).

Or (from *La Revue du cinéma*, 1 October 1946):

. . . La présentation d'un nouveau film d'Eisenstein suscite le même étonnement que ferait naître la création d'une nouvelle pièce de Corneille. On s'est tant appliqué a donner au cinéma une histoire qu'a force de traiter les metteurs-en-scène de classiques qu'il semble qu'ils soient d'un autre age . . . on pardonnerait volontiers à Eisenstein d'être encore en vie, s'il était content de refaire Potemkine *ou* La Ligne générale. *Mais* Ivan

---

* French: 'One of the most famous directors of his time.'

le Terrible *vient de bouleuerser toutes les idées saines et simples que la critique avait facilement dégagées de l'etude des grands auteurs du müet.**

I never imagined that this sort of thing would be written about me—certainly not before I had reached my seventies—and I thought I simply would not live that long!

And here, at forty-eight—

P.S.

P.S.

P.S.

* French: 'The showing of a new film by Eisenstein provokes the same astonishment that would meet a new play by Corneille. So much effort was used to invest cinema with a history, that it seems as if directors, proclaimed as classics, come from a different age. . . . One could readily forgive Eisenstein for still being alive, if he were content with remaking *Potemkin* or *The General Line*. But *Ivan the Terrible* has just overturned all the healthy, simple truths that criticism had easily drawn from studying the experience of the great auteurs of silent film.'

Eisenstein, October 1930.

NOTES

Eisenstein's own notes, and indications of those passages where English is the language of the original, are placed at the end of the relevant page.

Throughout the notes, Eisenstein is referred to as E and frequently cited works are abbreviated as follows:

ESW1 Sergei Eisenstein, *Selected Works, Volume 1: Writings, 1922–34* (Richard Taylor ed. and trans.). London: BFI, 1988.

ESW2 Sergei Eisenstein, *Selected Works, Volume 2: Towards a Theory of Montage* (Michael Glenny ed.; Richard Taylor trans.). London: BFI, 1991.

MONKEY LOGIC

1 Written on 22 June 1946 in Barvikha.

2 Grigori M. Kozintsev (1905–73), Soviet theatre and film director. He was named People's Artist of the USSR in 1964.

3 Mikhail A. Kuznetsov (1918–86) played this part in *Ivan the Terrible*.

THE HISTORY OF THE CLOSE-UP

1 E began this on 26 June 1946 in Barvikha but never completed it. He left gaps for quotations from examples that he had used elsewhere. Some of these quotations have been included where they are essential for an understanding of the general sense of the text. The final part, beginning with 'This was on another occasion', is taken from the manuscript for *Method*.

2 Kazusika Hokusai (1760–1849), Japanese painter and engraver particularly noted for his views of Mount Fuji, a considerable influence on the French impressionists. See also *ESW1*, pp. 211–12; *ESW2*, pp. 120–1.

3 E is referring to his work on 'The History of the Close-Up in the History of Art', which was completed in draft form in 1943 but which he continued working on until October 1947. Part of it was published as 'Dikkens, Griffit i my' [Dickens, Griffith and Ourselves].

4   The insect in Poe's story is in fact a death's-head moth.

5   The 28 mm wide-angle lens was the widest available in E's time. It preserved considerable depth of focus and therefore made it possible to pass from medium close-ups to deep-focus *mise en scène* shots.

6   E used examples from Pushkin's 'Poltava' in 'Pushkin the Montageur' and 'Montage 1938', translated by Michael Glenny in *ESW2*; the extract following in the text is from p. 222. E also used examples from John Milton's *Paradise Lost* for the first English publication of 'Montage 1938' under the title 'Word and Image' in *The Film Sense* (Jay Layda ed. and trans.) (London: Harcourt, Brace, 1943), pp. 52–7.

7   The following extract contrasting a scene from Gogol's *Taras Bulba* (1839) with Kuleshov's treatment is taken from E's unfinished 'Montage in Literature' (1941).

8   Lev V. Kuleshov (1899–1970), Soviet film director and theorist who first developed the notion that montage was central to the specificity of cinema. This quotation is from his *Osnovy kinorezhissury* [The Foundations of Film Directing] (Moscow: n.p., 1941), pp. 66–7.

9   Nikolai V. Gogol, *Polnoe sobranie sochinenii* [Complete Collected Works], VOL. 2 (Moscow: Akademiia nauk SSSR, 1937), p. 142.

10 Pathfinder was the eponymous hero of stories by American writer James Fenimore Cooper (1789–1851).

THAT'S JUST IT

1   This chapter consists of three fragments, the first of which is dated 28 June 1946.

2   A Russian omen.

3   Otto Weininger (1880–1903), psychologist of sex and author of *Geschlecht und Charakter* (1903), translated as *Sex and Character* (1906).

4   The Siguranrça was the secret police in the Kingdom of Romania. Henri Barbusse (1873–1935), French novelist and a member of the French Communist Party.

5   Grigori S. Skovoroda (1722–97), Ukrainian philosopher, poet and scholar. The epigraph is taken from his 'Dialogue or Talk about the Ancient World' and misquoted by Leskov:

Stand, if you will, on level ground and have a hundred mirrors placed around you. Then you will see that your body mass has a hundred aspects but, when the mirrors are taken away, all the copies disappear. Our body mass is however just like a shadow of the real person. This creature represents, like an ape, the visible presence of the invisible and individual strength and divinity of the person, of whom all our body masses are but shadowy reflections.

MONSIEUR, MADAME ET BÉBÉ

1 This text was written in two or three drafts. The date on the first page—14 July 1946, Kratovo—probably relates to the date of editing.

2 A jocular reference to the 'blue' and 'pink' periods in the early work of Pablo Picasso.

3 *La Nietzschéenne* was a popular novel published in 1907 under the nom de plume of Daniel Lesueur, the pseudonym of Henry Lapauze (1865–1927), curator of the Petit Palais gallery in Paris, and his wife, Jeanne Loiseau.

4 Pierre Coulevain was the pseudonym of Augustine Favre de Coulevain (1888–1913). Her novel *Sur la branche* [On the Branch] was published in 1904.

5 E's mistake: *The Semi-Virgins* was written by Marcel Prévost.

6 *The Stages of Vice* [Les Etapes du vice] is incorrect. The proper title of this work by the Marquis de Sade is *Histoire de Juliette ou Les Prospértés du vice* [The Story of Juliet, or the Joys of Vice].

7 Gyp was the pseudonym of the French writer Sibylle-Gabrielle-Marie-Antoinette de Riquetti de Mirabeau, Comtesse de Martel et Janville (1849–1932), who wrote popular and somewhat salacious novels.

8 Jean Moreau (1741–1814), French painter, engraver and graphic artist who illustrated the works of Molière, Voltaire and Rousseau. Charles Eysen (1720–78), French graphic artist. Gravelot, pseudonym of Hubert François Bourguignon (1699–1773), French painter, graphic artist and engraver.

9 Octave Mirbeau (1850–1917), French writer of erotica. Leopold von Sacher-Masoch (1836–95), Austrain writer of erotic novels involving self-abuse, from whom the phenomenon 'masochism' derives its name.

10 Alexander Meller-Zakomelsky (1844–1928) was the Russian imperial governor general of the Baltic provinces; he brutally suppressed the revolutionary events of 1905.

11 The problem of 'pathetic construction' began to interest E particularly after the success of *Potemkin*. In *The General Line*, he set out to introduce pathos into 'inherently non-pathetic' (rural) material. His first attempt to generalize theoretically from this experience was his unfinished essay 'How Pathos Is Created' (1929), later reworked into 'Pathos' (1945–47), part of *Nonindifferent Nature: Film and the Structure of Things* (Herbert Marshall trans.) (Cambridge: Cambridge University Press, 1987), pp. 38–199.

12 E's ironic term for the analysis of the derivation of words in the history of art.

13 See 'The Montage of Film Attractions' (1924) in *ESW1*, pp. 39–58.

14 At its fullest in the first part of *Direction* in 'The Art of *Mise en scène*' (as yet unpublished).

15 See *Nonindifferent Nature*, p. 27. We have preferred our own translation.

16 The Khlysts were a mid-seventeenth-century Russian religious sect who believed that by ecstatic rituals, including 'zealous whipping' (with a whip known as a *khlyst*—hence the sect's name) and 'running around in circles', they could drive evil spirits from their bodies and effect the resurrection and reincarnation of Christ in Man.

17 Frank Alexander (1891–1964), American psychologist, head of the Chicago school of psychoanalysis. *Imago* was the journal founded by Freud in 1912.

18 Sandor Ferenczi (1873–1933), Hungarian neurologist and pupil of Alexander. His *Versuch einer Genitaltheorie* (1924) has been translated as *Thalassa: A Theory of Genitality* (1949).

19 From Chapter 80, 'The Nut'.

PRE-NATAL EXPERIENCE

1 Written on 5 July 1946 and probably intended as an introduction to part of *Method*.

TO THE ILLUSTRIOUS MEMORY OF THE MARQUIS

1 Almost certainly written on 15–16 July 1946 and probably initially intended as an insert into '*Monsieur, madame et bébé*' but later grew into a separate chapter.

2 Nikita V. Bogoslavsky (1913–2004), Soviet composer, author of more than 200 songs, 8 symphonies, 17 operettas and musical comedies, 58 soundtracks, and 52 scores for theater productions.

3 Leonid O. Utyosov (1895–1982), leading Soviet jazz musician.

4 There is an untranslatable pun in Russian which plays on the two meanings of *polovoi*—'sexual' and 'waiter'.

5 Simon Bolivar y Ponte (1783–1830) led the struggle for the independence of Latin America from Spain.

6 John Grierson (1898–1972), British documentary filmmaker, theorist and producer.

7 See Matthew 13:45-6: 'Again, the kingdom of heaven is like unto a merchant man, seeking goodly pearls: Who, when he had found one pearl of great price, went and sold all that he had, and bought it.'

8 The German film film *Don Quichotte* was made in 1933 by Georg W. Pabst (1885–1967).

9 Vicomte Mathieu de Noailles, husband of the poet Anna-Elisabeth de Noailles (1876–1933), whose salon was frequented by Cocteau and Colette.

10 A play on Nekrasov's poem 'The Pedlars' which became a popular Russian song: 'Oh, my basket is full, full of calico and brocade.'

11 Margarita I. Rtishcheva, Russian popular entertainer who specialized in imitating singers of different nationalities. The actual inscription read: 'Here's a little book for your journey! Perhaps you'll be bored enough to read it and smile. It's eighteenth century. Who knows? Perhaps Pushkin held it in his hands and leafed through these yellowing pages! 19.8.29.'

12 See *Beyond the Stars, Part I*, p. 227.

13 Jean-Jacques Brousson (1878–1958) was secretary to French poet, journalist and novelist Anatole France (1844–1924) from 1902 to 1909.

14 The German translation of E's autobiography attributes this work to Victor Mirabeau, but he was an eighteenth-century French economist. The reference is almost certainly to Sibylle-Gabrielle-Marie-Antoinette de Riqueti de Mirabeau: see '*Monsieur, madame et bébé*', n. 7. In 1905 she published *Journal d'un casserolé* [The Diary of a Man Betrayed]. She is not to be confused with Octave Mirbeau (see '*Monsieur, madame et bébé*', n. 9).

15 Herbert S. Gorman (1893–1954), American literary historian, author of *The Incredible Marquis* (1929).

16 Flexatone was a trademark.

17 Walter Hasenclever (1890–1940), German expressionist dramatist and poet.

18 Diabolo was an early-twentieth-century game in which a two-headed top was spun, tossed and caught on a string attached to two sticks held in each hand.

19 E often makes metaphorical use of the terms 'left'—to denote an earlier, more primitive stage—and 'right' to denote a later, more developed stage. These usages possibly derive from his interest in graphology.

20 Marshall, *Nonindifferent Nature*, pp. 3–37.

21 See Matthew 27:51: 'And, behold the veil of the temple was rent in twain from the top to the bottom; and the earth did quake and the rocks rent.'

22 The Iberian Gate contained a chapel where the tsar always worshipped when arriving from outside Moscow before entering the Kremlin. It was destroyed in the reconstruction leading to the building of the Hotel Moscow between Manège Square and Okhotny ryad in 1930.

23 The *veche* was the popular assembly through which Novgorod was governed in the thirteenth century.

24 Nikolai N. Breshko-Breshkovsky (1874–1943), Russian journalist.

25 Nat Pinkerton was the fictitious hero of serial detective stories by anonymous authors. The character's name was widely used by the Russian avant-garde in the 1920s, especially as a generic term. *The Caves of Leuchtweiss* was a historical novel which also appeared anonymously. Nick Carter and Ethel King were the main characters in popular adventure stories.

26 Joaquín Amaro Domínguez (1889–1952), Mexican revolutionary general and military reformer. He served as secretary of war in the 1920s.

27 Francisco Villa (1877–1923), nicknamed Pancho, was a leading figure in the Mexican Revolution of 1910–17.

28 Materials for *Que viva México!* were edited without E's consent into *Thunder over Mexico*, which was premièred in May 1933. *Viva Villa!*, directed by Jack Conway, was released in 1934.

29 The action of Béla Bartók's opera *Duke Bluebeard's Castle* (premiered 1918) revolves around the mysteries concealed behind seven doors.

30 Joseph Schildkraut (1895–1964), American stage and screen actor of Austrian descent.

31 Robert François Damiens (1715–57), a French domestic servant whose attempted assassination of King Louis XV of France culminated in his notorious public execution. He was the last person to be executed in France by drawing and quartering, the traditional and gruesome form of death penalty reserved for regicides.

32 Ivan F. Gorbunov (1831–95), Russian actor and writer. *Evenings on a Farm near Dikanka* was a series of stories by Nikolai Gogol which included 'Sorochintsy Fair', 'Christmas Eve' and 'A Terrible Revenge'.

33 Armand Dayot (1851–1934), French art critic, art historian and leftist politician whose works include *L'Invasion. Le Siècle 1870. La Commune 1871* [Invasion. The Century 1870. The Commune 1871].

34 By 'Nuremberg Maiden' [*Nürnberger Jungfrau*] E means the 'iron maiden', an instrument of torture used by the Inquisition. It consisted of a kind of iron cupboard in the shape of a townswoman of the sixteenth century, lined on the inside with long sharp nails which pierced the incarcerated victim when the door was closed. One of the most famous of these 'iron maidens' was kept in Nuremberg, hence the reference.

35 The monastery of the Trinity and St Sergius at Zagorsk (now Troitse-Sergiyev Posad) was a centre of toy-making in Russia. The Museum of Russian Toys is now open next to the monastery. The 'Hussar', the 'Lady', etc. were standard toy designs from this town.

36 In the early twentieth century, Riga was predominantly a German-speaking port with a Latvian-speaking native population in the agricultural hinterland and a governing class of Russian civil servants.

37 Reference to the battle scene in *Alexander Nevsky* and to the third part of *Ivan the Terrible*, a significant part of which was to deal with the war between Ivan and the Livonian Order (1558–83) to secure an outlet for Russia onto the Baltic Sea.

38 Edmund Meisel (1874–1930), Austrian-born musician and composer who wrote scores for the German performances of these films.

39 The headquarters of the state cinema organizations Goskino and Sovkino in the 1920s and, indeed, still the headquarters of the State Committee for Cinema (by then once more called Goskino) at the time of the dissolution of the USSR in 1991.

40 Now Mezaparks to the north-east of Riga.

41 Major Frank Pease (1879–1959), self-styled 'professional American patriot' and president of the Hollywood Technical Directors Institute, an anti-communist activist organization during the 1920s and 1930s, led the campaign against E's presence in the USA, denouncing him as part of a 'Jewish Bolshevik conspiracy' to 'turn the American cinema into a communist cesspool'. See Marie Seton, *Sergei M. Eisenstein: A Biography*, REVD EDN (London: Grove Press, 1978), especially pp. 167–8.

42 Now Bulduri, part of the town of Jurmala.

43 Especially in the articles 'Vertical Montage' (1939–40) in *ESW2*, pp. 327–99, and 'Nonindifferent Nature' (1945–7) in *Nonindifferent Nature*, pp. 216–396.

44 Edinburg is now Dzintari. Maxim M. Strauch [also Shtraukh] (1900–74), E's childhood friend, was a Soviet actor and director who also worked under E at the First Proletkult Workers' Theatre in Moscow and then as one of his 'iron five' associates in film in 1925–28.

45 Vera G. Muzykant was an actress who worked at the Proletkult First Workers' Theatre.

46 Ivan A. Pyriev (1901–68), Soviet film director who acted in the First Workers' Theatre and the Meyerhold Theatre. He acted in E's production of *Wise Man* and his first film *Glumov's Diary*.

47 *Chasing the Moonshine* [*Gonka za samogonkoi*, 1924] was a short film made by Abram M. Room (1894–1976).

48 'Our Gang' was the name of an American comedy group consisting of six children and a dog, the heroes of a very popular series of films produced by Hal Roach.

49 Refers to Pyotr L. Kapitsa (1894–1984), Soviet physicist who worked with Rutherford at Cambridge.

50 Alexander G. Rzheshevsky (1903–67), who wrote the screenplay for *Bezhin Meadow*, was a firm believer in the notion of the 'emotional scenario'. The plot was based upon a real event: the murder of a Young Pioneer, Pavlik Morozov, by his relatives in September 1932 in the northern Urals because he had denounced his father to the village soviet for speculating with false papers for kulaks who had fled. In Rzheshevsky's version, Stepok prevents the kulaks from setting alight the crop fields of

the collective farm and is murdered by his father. In his film, E elaborated on this basic theme with emotionally powerful metaphors, such as Abraham's sacrifice of Isaac in the Old Testament, the New Testament collision between God the Father and God the Son, and a number of examples from Greek mythology. Mythological figures were also deployed, somewhat paradoxically, in the scene in which the church is converted into a club.

51 Louise Michel (1830–1905) was an active participant in the Paris Commune and the *pétroleuses* were the women who, following her call, preferred to set Paris alight rather than surrender.

52 Sadayakko (1871–1946) was a Japanese geisha, actress and dancer.

53 E is mistaken: the reference is to the Arab Emir Abd el Kadir (1807–83), who led the Algerian resistance to the French between 1832 and 1847.

54 Joséphine Beauharnais (1763–1814), Napoleon's first wife. Roustum Raza (1783–1845) was Napoleon's mamluk bodyguard and secondary valet.

55 *Up Front* by William H. Mauldin (1921–2003) was published in Cleveland and New York in 1948.

56 The *tricoteuses* (literally, 'knitting women') were the women who knitted while watching the executions during the French revolutionary terror. Théroigne de Méricourt (1762–1817), actress and courtesan who sided with the Girondins during the French Revolution.

57 Francisco de Zurbaran (1598–1664), Spanish painter, known primarily for his religious paintings depicting monks, nuns, and martyrs, and for his still-lifes

58 The St Bartholomew's Day massacre in 1572 was a targeted group of assassinations and a wave of Catholic mob violence in Paris, directed against the Huguenots during the French Wars of Religion. Emperor Rudolf refers to Rudolf I (1552–1612), king of Hungary and Croatia (1572–1608), who ruled as Rudolf II, the Holy Roman Emperor from 1576 to 1612.

HOW I LEARNT TO DRAW
(A Chapter about My Dancing Lessons)

1 Dated 17 July 1946.

2 Engelbert Dollfuss (1892–1934), Austrian chancellor from 1932, was assassinated by the Nazis.

3   Dolores Ibarruri (1895–1987), known as 'La Pasionaria', was one of the Communist leaders in the Spanish Civil War. After Franco's victory in 1939, she emigrated to the USSR, where E met her.

4. Maria Verkhovskaya was a prominent social figure in pre-Revolutionary Riga. Her salon was frequented by leading musicians and theatre people and E visited the house during his youth.

5   Wang Pi (226–149 BCE), Chinese philosopher. The quotation is from his *Basic Principles of the Book of Transformations*.

6   Olaf Gulbransson (1873–1966), German caricaturist of Norwegian extraction who contributed to the satirical journal *Simplicissimus*.

7   The pen name of P. P. Matyunin, a Russian caricaturist. *Vechernyeye vremya* was a newspaper that supported the tsarist regime and later the Provisional Government.

8   Dmitri Moor, pseudonym of Dmitri S. Orlov (1883–1941), poster and graphic artist and painter. The lubok that inspired his work was a traditional Russian woodcut that told a story.

9. The Wanderers were a group of socially conscious artists in early-nineteenth-century Russia. There is a play on words here between *Peredvizhniki* [the Wanderers] and *podvizhniki* [ascetics].

10 E suffered his first heart attack on 2 February 1946 while attending the official celebrations at Dom kino [Cinema House] in Moscow for the award of the Stalin Prize to *Ivan the Terrible, Part One*.

11 The rough draft for this chapter contained a plan for an insert entitled 'On the Break in My Drawing': 'There was an interruption and quite rightly so—in 1916. Minna Ivanovna and the painter Tyrsa: giveaway price. I abandoned it.' But in 1917 he began drawing again: at first, political caricatures and sketches for costumes and stage sets, later still real set designs. The big break in his drawing began in 1924, when he started to make *The Strike*, and he only began again seven years later in Mexico.

12 Diego Rivera (1886–1957), Mexican painter and muralist much inspired by traditional folk motifs.

13 A paraphrase of part of the introduction to Friedrich Engels' *Anti-Dühring* (1877).

14 M. Bardèche and R. Brasillach, *Histoire du cinéma* (Paris: André Marterl, 1935), p. 285:

All this matters little: nobody has aimed a more accurate and self-willed camera at the world. No Romantic (and he is a Romantic) has been more severe with himself, no sensualist (and he is cinema's greatest sensualist) has been more profoundly intelligent. In him abstraction and sensuality merge as they do in the greatest creative artists.

15 José Guadalupe Posada (1852–1913), Mexican political printmaker and engraver whose work has influenced many Latin American artists and cartoonists because of its satirical acuteness and social engagement.

16 Edith Isaacs was the editor of *Theatre Arts Monthly*, as it was actually called. E met her in New York in April 1932 on his return from Mexico.

17 Maurice Dekobra, pseudonym of Maurice Tessier (1885–1973), French writer of detective stories, including *La Madonne des sleepings* [The Madonna of the Sleeping Cars, 1925].

18 Valentin Ya. Parnakh (1891–1951), Russian poet, translator and choreographer, published a collection entitled *Introduction to the Dance* in 1925.

19 Vladimir Ya. Khenkin (1883–1953), Russian actor.

20 Pyotr K. Rudenko, alias Georges, Russian circus artiste and acrobat.

21 Leonid L. Obolensky (1902–91), pupil of Lev Kuleshov, who later became E's assistant at VGIK. His film *Bricks* [*Kirpichiki*, 1925], a light comedy, was made for the commercially orientated Mezhrabpom studio. Anna P. Sten (1910–93) played the leading role in Boris Barnet's *The Girl with a Hatbox* [*Devushka s korobkoi*] in 1927. In 1930 she moved to Germany and starred in *Der Mürder Dimitri Karamasoff*, directed in 1931 by her husband Fyodor Otsep. From 1934, she worked first in Hollywood and then in Britain. The State Film School in Moscow was known as GTK from 1925 to 1930, then as GIK till 1934, and subsequently as VGIK.

22 The mimes of the Atellans were popular comedies in ancient Rome in the first century BCE.

23 The Morozov villa (coincidentally just across the street called Vozdvizhenka from the cinema where *Potemkin* had its first run) was used by Proletkult in the early 1920s and it was here that E staged his production of *Enough Simplicity for Every Wise Man*. It had belonged to Ivan Morozov, one of the leading art collectors in pre-Revolutionary Russia. His home was sequestrated after the Revolution and his collection transferred to state

galleries. The villa was later the headquarters of the Society for Cultural Relations with Foreign Countries. The reception E refers to took place in August 1945 when J. B. Priestley (1894–1984) was in Moscow for the world premiere of his play *An Inspector Calls* at the Kamerny Theatre. *The British Ally* was a Russian-language paper published by the British Embassy in Moscow during the Second World War.

24 Mikhail M. Eskin (1903–25) acted with Proletkult. The Blue Blouse was the name of a popular troupe of travelling actors who performed agitational plays on current political topics in the early 1920s.

25 Vera D. Yanukova (1895–1939) played the role of Mme Mamayeva in E's production of *Wise Man*. Alexander P. Antonov (1898–1962) was one of E's 'iron five' group of assistants and also acted in *Glumov's Diary*, *The Strike* and *Potemkin*.

26 Yudif S. Glizer (1904–68), wife of E's lifelong friend and collaborator Maxim Strauch, became a leading stage actress, notably at the Theatre of the Revolution. In E's production of *Wise Man* she rode a camel. Her memoir, *Eizenshtein i zhenshchiny* [Eisenstein and Women], was published in *Kinovedcheskie zapiski* [Cinematic Notes] 6 (1990): 120–30.

27 Emile-Jaques Dalcroze (1863–1950) was the Swiss musician who originated eurhythmics.

ON FOLKLORE

1 Dated 19 July 1946, Kratovo. In accordance with E's intentions, a shortened extract from *Method* has been inserted in the middle of this chapter.

2 Nicholas Brady, pseudonym of John Victor Turner (1900–45), American thriller writer.

3 The *Kalevala* is the Finnish national epic, gathered together in the mid nineteenth century from songs and folktales.

4 The 'Songs of the Western Slavs' are a cycle of sixteen poems written by Alexander Pushkin in 1833 and published in 1835. Most of them are free versions of texts in Prosper Mérimée's volume of poetry *La Guzla*, supposedly based on Serbian and Croatian folklore. In addition, Pushkin included a number of authentic songs and themes from Serbian, Croatian and Czech folklore and two poems of his own.

5 Epic battle poem and classic of medieval Russian verse. Academia was a Leningrad publishing house.

6 The German director Fritz Lang (1890–1976) made his film version of the Nibelungen saga in Germany in 1924 in two parts: *Siegfried's Death* and *Kriemhild's Revenge*.

7 The *Eddas* were Icelandic sagas; Yggdrasil is the cosmic ash of German mythology, the tree of knowledge in which Odin/Wotan sacrificed himself to himself.

8 *The Golden Bough* (1890) is a study of early magic and religion by the Scottish anthropologist James George Frazer (1854–1941). Alexander N. Veselovsky (1838–1906) was a Russian literary historian. The reference to 'Sir Joshua' is presumably either a misnomer for James Frazer or a reference to the English painter Joshua Reynolds (1723–92).

9 Characters from Russian epic songs dating back to the eleventh century.

10 Aristide Bruant (1851–1925), French poet and cabaret artiste who wrote numerous songs in Parisian *argot* which he performed in this bar. In 1901, he published a *Dictionnaire de l'argot au XXme siècle* [Dictionary of Twentieth-Century Slang].

11 The original title for the third part of the novel. In the first published edition in 1846, Balzac called this part *Where Bad Paths Lead*.

12 In Egyptian mythology, Osiris is killed by his brother Seth and dismembered, only to be re-assembled by his sister-wife Isis.

13 Isidor Sadger (1867–1942), Austrain forensic doctor and psychoanalyst.

14 E is here referring to the essay by Freud on Da Vinci's recollection of a childhood dream. The correct title is *Leonardo da Vinci: A Psychosexual Study of Infallible Reminiscence* (1916).

15. Hanns Sachs (1881–1947), one of the earliest psychoanalysts, and a close personal friend of Sigmund Freud. For Ferenczi, see '*Monsieur, madame et bébé*', n. 18.

16 See G. K. Chesterton, 'Defence of the Detective Story' in *The Defendant* (1901).

17 Reference to a book that E valued highly and often cited: C. F. E. Spurgeon, *Shakespeare's Imagery and What It Tells Us* (1935). See *ESW2*, pp. 187–91.

18 Jacques Deval, pseudonym of Jacques Boularon (1894–1972), French author of comedies in the style of Sacha Guitry.

19 Sergei T. Konenkov (1874–1971), Soviet sculptor whose figures were based on folklore, myth and fairy tale.

20 The proceedings of the January 1935 Conference of Soviet Film Workers, including E's contribution, were published under the title *Za bol'shoe kinoiskusstvo* [For a Great Cinema Art] (Moscow, 1935).

21 Alexander R. Luria (1902–77), Soviet psychologist and pioneer of neuropsychology. The actual title of Goldschmidt's book is: *Ascaris. Eine Einführung in die Wissenschaft vom Leben für jedermann* [Thread-Worm: An Introduction to the Science of Life for Everyman].

22 Mei Lan-Fan (1894–1961) was a Chinese classical actor with the Peking Opera whom E met in Moscow in 1935. In his 1935 article 'To the Magician of the Pear Orchard', E explained: ' "Pupils of the Pear Garden" is an ancient title given to Chinese actors who are trained in the appropriate part of the Imperial Palace. Mei Lan-Fan's official title—First in the Pear Orchard—means that he occupies first place among China's actors.'

23 The harlequin (actually *manteau d'Arlequin*) is a curtain attached to a fixed wing and soffit painted to look like an open curtain. It hangs directly behind the main curtain and serves to restrict the view from the auditorium into the stage works. Mirror is the name given to the vertical front surface of the stage between proscenium and apron.

24 Richard Teschner (1879–1948), Austrian painter, graphic artist, set designer and puppeteer.

25 E is referring to the first volume of his planned textbook on direction to be entitled *The Art of Mise-en-scène,* the bulk of which was devoted to a detailed treatment of the theme 'A soldier returns from the front and finds his wife with a babe-in-arms'. The situation was treated successively from the standpoint of melodrama, pathos and comedy, and the different versions were analysed for the concrete solutions they offered and the associations they employed.

INVERSIONS

1 This chapter was produced on 30 July 1946. There was a note attached to the manuscript with a list of the basic themes and two remarks 'for myself'. One of these concerns the place the chapter should occupy in the *Memoirs*:

'Probably to follow *Skeletons*' [in English in the original], i.e. after 'On Bones' (see *Beyond the Stars, Part I,* pp. 443–50). However, the text is closely linked to the *Grundproblematik* and, for this reason, the Russian editors have elected to include it in the cycle of chapters from July 1946. E's second remark reflects his dissatisfaction with the literary quality of the text: 'Run out of steam—pretty bad—a lot of stylistic corrections.' The manuscript has no title and the Russian editors have selected this one from a reference in one of the drafts.

2   Aristide Briand (1845–1932), French statesman, prime minister, foreign minister and advocate of a United States of Europe. For Bruant, see 'On Folklore', n. 10.

3   André Gill (1840–85), French caricaturist.

4   Emile Bayard, *Quartier latin, hier et aujourd'hui* [The Latin Quarter, Yesterday and Today, 1924]. Bayard also wrote *Montmartre, hieret aujourd'hui* [Montmarte, Yesterday and Today, 1925].

6   José Guadalupe Posada (1851–1913), Mexican political printmaker and engraver known for his satirical acuteness and social engagement. He used skulls, calaveras and bones to make political and cultural critiques.

COLOUR

1   This text was probably written in early August 1946. The final sentences were written on a separate sheet of paper under the heading 'First Encounter' and at a different time. They were possibly intended as a link between the text and the cycle of chapters on the 'mastery of colour'.

GOGOL'S MASTERY

1   Undated and untitled. Possibly written as early as 1940 for the unfinished article 'Montage 1940' but more probably written in early August 1946.

2   Andrei Bely, pseudonym of Boris N. Bugayev (1880–1934), Russian writer and, in the pre-Revolutionary period, one of the leading figures in Russian symbolism. His best known work is the novel *Petersburg* (1913).

3   Taras is the Cossack hero of the story *Taras Bulba* (1835) by Gogol. Dovgochkhun is Ivan Nikiforovich, one of the two principal characters in 'The Tale of How Ivan Ivanovich Quarrelled with Ivan Nikiforovich' (1835). Chichikov is the charlatan who is the central figure of the novel *Dead Souls* (1842). Selifan and Petrushka are his coachman and servant respectively.

4 Petukh (literally in Russian: 'cockerel') is a landowner in Part Two of *Dead Souls*.

5 Andrei Bely, *Masterstvo Gogolya* [Gogol's Mastery] (Moscow: OGIZ/ GIKhl, 1934), p. 159.

6 The novel was dramatized by Mikhail Bulgakov and directed by Stanislavsky; the production opened on 28 November 1932.

7 E chaired an evening in Bely's honour at the Polytechnic Museum in Moscow in 1933.

8 The State Publishing House for Literature.

THREE LETTERS ABOUT COLOUR

1 Written on 20 August 1946 in Kratovo after 'The Springs of Happiness'.

2 Yuri Tynyanov (1894–1943), Soviet writer, literary critic, translator, scholar and screenwriter, died of multiple sclerosis in Moscow. In 1941, already seriously ill, he had been evacuated from Leningrad to Perm, where he had continued to work on his biographical novel *Pushkin* despite intense pain.

3 Mikhail I. Kalinin (1875–1946), Soviet head of state from March 1919 until his death, which was six years later than suggested here by E.

4 The title of Tynyanov's study of Pushkin.

THE SPRINGS OF HAPPINESS

1 The first part of this chapter is dated 3 July 1946; the second, 3 August 1946; and the insert on E's work on *Die Walküre* was probably written even later.

2 These boulevard romances were all published at the beginning of the twentieth century. The authors are: Mikhail P. Artsybashev (1878–1927), Yevdokia A. Nagrodskaya (1866–1930), Nadezhda A. Lappo-Danilevskaya (1874–1951) and Anastasia A. Verbitskaya (1861–1928).

3 Vsevolod A. Verbitsky (1896–1951), son of Anastasia Verbitskaya, acted with the Moscow Art Theatre for many years.

4 Edvard Munch (1863–1944), Norwegian painter, one of the principal inspirations for German expressionism.

5 In his three-volume theoretical work *The Theatre for Oneself* (1915–17), director and dramatist Nikolai Yevreinov (1879–1953) argued that every

individual was capable of metamorphosis and role-playing; everyday life could therefore be metamorphosed in theatre so that every individual could simultaneously be actor and spectator.

6   There is an untranslatable pun here: the Russian word *klyuch* can mean both 'spring' and 'key'. Similarly, the Russian word *schast'e* can mean either 'happiness' or 'fortune', so that what is here translated as 'The Springs of Happiness' would have a variety of alternative meanings to a Russian.

7   E's unfinished project for *Fergana Canal* dates from May to October 1939. See Werner Sudendorf, *Sergej M. Eisenstein. Materialien zu Leben und Werk* [Sergei M. Eisenstein: Materials on Life and Work] (Munich: Hanser, 1975), p. 228.

8   The production opened on 21 November 1940.

9   On 2 April 1923 in the Bolshoi Theatre, an evening celebrating twenty-five years of Meyerhold's theatrical activity included an extract from E's production of *Wise, Man* entitled 'Joffre off to Campaign'.

10   See 'A Miracle in the Bolshoi Theatre' in *Beyond the Stars, Part I*, pp. 193–4.

11   Nikolai A. Nekrasov (1821–78), Russian poet, writer and dramatist.

12   See *ESW2*, passim.

13   Apart from Bach's 'The Art Of Fugue', E had in mind the theoretical work by the Russian composer and scholar Sergei I. Taneyev (1856–1915): *Podvizhnoi kontrapunkt strogogo pis'ma* [The Moveable Counterpoint of Strict Style].

14   In 'On the Structure of Things', E quotes from the book by E. K Rozenov, *I. S. Bakh i ego rod* [J. S. Bach and His Kind] (Moscow; n.p., 1911), p. 72:

> . . . According to testimony coming to us from Bach's pupils, he taught them to look at the instrumental voice as they would a personality, and at the polyphonic instrumental composition as a conversation between these personalities, while setting up a rule that each of them 'speak well and in time, and if they have nothing to say, it would be better to remain silent or wait their turn . . .'

Quoted from *Nonindifferent Nature*, p. 4.

15   Ivan V. Lebedev (1879–1950), Russian athlete, referee and circus artiste.

16   These were all wrestlers at the beginning of the twentieth century. Cyclops and Aberg also appeared in circus acts. 'Black Mask' was the popular name for a wrestler whose identity was not known.

17 Reference to the visit by the Kabuki theatre to the USSR in August 1928 with Itakawa Sadanji (1880–1940), director, actor and dramatist. See *ESW1*, especially pp. 115–22, 181–94.

18 Characters from the popular medieval Russian *Play of King Maximilian* which had its roots in Byzantine mystery plays.

19 Pyotr V. Williams [Vilyams] (1902–47), Russian painter and set designer, principal stage designer at the Bolshoi Theatre from 1941 until his death. Semyon A. Samosud (1884–1964), principal director at the Bolshoi from 1936 to 1943.

20 E proposed a film on the Italian painter Giordano Bruno (1548–1600) to the Committee on Cinema Affairs in 1940 but the idea was rejected.

21 The proposal for a film about Lawrence of Arabia envisaged a script written by Lev Sheinin (1906–67), who had written the play *The Prestige of the Empire* about the Beilis affair in 1913, which E submitted as another film project at roughly the same time. On Sheinin's connections with the secret police, see: Leonid Kozlov, 'The Artist and the Shadow of Ivan' in Ricanrd Taylor and Derek Spring (eds), *Stalinism and Soviet Cinema* (London: Routledge, 1993), p. 244n13.

22 The NKVD was the People's Commissariat for Internal Affairs, synonymous with the secret police, which formed one part of its organization.

23 E's mistake: Levernier's calculations predicted the existence of Neptune, not Uranus.

24 See *ESW1*, pp. 113–14.

25 The first Soviet colour documentary film, made with Soviet three-colour stock and directed by Sergei Gerasimov in 1945.

THE PRIZE FOR *IVAN*

1 This chapter consists of three fragments written at different times. The first section, dealing with the deaths of Khmelyov and Tolstoi, was written in mid-June 1946 as part of another chapter from which it was subsequently removed. The text presented here is preceded in the manuscript by a few words from that chapter. The second section, entitled 'The Prize for *Ivan*', is dated 28 June 1946. The third section, with neither date nor title, links the other two with the theme of the search for a colour concept for 'A Poet's Love'.

2   Nikolai P. Khmelyov (1902–45), Russian actor and director, part of the Moscow Art Theatre troupe from 1924 until his death. He played the role of the father in the second version of *Bezhin Meadow* (1936–37), replacing Boris Zakhava, who played the part in the first version (1935–36).

3   Khmelyov died on 1 November 1945, shortly before the premiere of *Difficult Years,* the second part of the two-part drama *Ivan the Terrible* (1941–43) by Alexei N. Tolstoi, who had died on 23 February 1945 during the rehearsals for the first part of the drama *Eagle and Eagle-Woman* on the stage of the Maly Theatre. Iosif Yuzovsky, pseudonym of Iosif Ilyich (1902–64), was a literary and theatre scholar and critic.

4   See 'Bookshops' in *Beyond the Stars, Part I,* pp. 398–408.

5   That is, Alexei Tolstoi

6   The eponymous hero of Romain Rolland's novel *Master Breugnon* [French title: *Colas Breugnon*].

7   Boris L. Pasternak (1890–1960), Nobel Prize–winning Russian poet, translator and writer, author of the novel *Dr Zhivago.*

8   Mikhail E. Chiaureli (1894–1974), Georgian film director responsible for such key films of the Stalin cult as *The Vow* and *The Fall of Berlin* [*Padenie Berlina,* 1949].

9   Simeon the Stylite (390–459 CE) was the first of the pillar ascetics, spending the last 36 years of his life at the top of a pillar in northern Syria, ostensibly to avoid contact with the mass of pilgrims who came to see him.

10 Esfir I. Shub (1894–1954), compilation documentary film-maker. E worked with Shub on the re-editing of Fritz Lang's *Dr Mabuse der Spieler* (1921–22) from two parts into one for Soviet distribution. It was on this film that E cut his cinematic teeth.

11 Late in 1829 Pushkin wrote in the poetry album of his lady friend in Moscow, Yelizaveta Ushakova, a list of names of the women who had been the 'objects' of his passions: this later became known as Pushkin's 'Don Juan list'.

MARION

1   Written on 28 June 1946 in Barvikha. The final sentences, deleted from the manuscript, have been reconstructed, as they provide a transition to the following chapter. The last sentence probably read: 'And at midday I (?) feel the sensation of a flaming (?) sunset.'

2   The Hon. Ivor Montagu (1904–84), third son of the second Baron Swaythling and leading light in British table-tennis between the wars, also a filmmaker and writer, accompanied E on his travels in the West in 1929–30, and was co-author with E of the script for *An American Tragedy*.

3   Marion Davies (1898–1961), American actress, protégée of the newspaper magnate William Randolph Hearst (1863–1951).

4   Toraichi Kono (1885–1971) was Chaplin's valet and general assistant from 1916 to 1934.

5   Lita Grey (1908–95), American child film extra who appeared in Chaplin's *The Kid*. From 1924 to 1927 she was Chaplin's second wife, the mother of his two eldest sons. E's account of the wedding in this chapter is therefore erroneous.

6   Camille Flammarion (1842–1925), French writer, publisher and astronomer.

7   One of the many early words for cinema theatres: see Yuri Tsivian, *Early Cinema in Russia and Its Cultural Reception* (Chicago: University of Chicago Press,1994).

8   Jean Mounet-Sully (1841–1916), French actor who worked from 1872 at the Comédie Française.

9   Max Linder (1883–1925), French comedian, one of the leading comic actors of silent cinema. Pockson, pseudonym of John Banny (1863–1915), American film comedian. Prince, pseudonym of Charles Prince Rigadon (1872–1933), French film actor.

10 Nikolai N. Yevreinov (1879–1951), theatre director, dramatist, scholar, founded the Starinny Theatre in St Petersburg and from 1910 to 1917 was chief director of the Distorting Mirror Theatre, a theatre of miniatures in the same city. John Erskine (1879–1951), American novelist and scholar who wrote *The Private Life of Helen of Troy* in 1925. The title *Tonner* has not been traced and E has left the author's name blank, but the reference may be to Louis Delluc's French film *Le tonnerre* [Thunder, 1921].

11 What E meant to indicate here was that in Laurence Sterne's *Tristram Shandy* (1759), the hero/narrator is carried away by so many digressions that the novel ends with his birth.

12 Edgar Allan Poe, *Marginalia*: 'I cannot help thinking that romance writers in general might now and then find their account in taking a hint

from the Chinese, who, in spite of building their houses downwards, have still sense enough to *begin their books at the end.*'

13 Reference to the ideas expressed in *Le Rire. Essai sur La signification du comique* [Laughter: An Essay on the Signification of the Comic] by Henri Bergson (1859–1941).

14 Anatoli V. Lunacharsky (1875–1933), Soviet People's Commissar for Enlightenment from 1917 to 1929, also wrote scripts for popular film melodramas often featuring his actress wife Natalia Rozenel.

THE DOLLAR PRINCESS

1 Dated 28 June 1946 but unfinished. A few days later E returned to the main theme of this chapter in 'Katerinki'.

2 See *ESW2*, pp. 255, 373–3, 413n262.

3 Reference to the sets designed by Isaak Rabinovich for the 1933 production of Tchaikovsky's opera *Eugene Onegin*.

4 Hans Fender (1854–1926), German theatre and opera actor, old-school character comic, known for his pointed sense of humour; he worked in Riga at the beginning of the twentieth century. Kurt Busch (1879–1954), German opera actor and director, worked in Riga from 1905 to 1911, as did the actor Fritz Sachsl.

5 This chapter was never written but a plan for it, dated 8 May 1946, does survive. It is headed in English 'The case of the ugly duckling who never really became a swan (never to become a man)'.

KATERINKI

1 Dated 8 August 1946 and written in English, French and Russian. This chapter marks E's third attempt to give an account of his tragic love for an unknown girl. The first was 'The Dollar Princess', which he never completed. A week later, on 4 July 1946, he began a chapter entitled 'From Katrinka to Katlinka', but gave up almost immediately. More than a month later he returned to the subject and gave his memoir the form of a 'discovery' of a romantic love story. As is clear from the text, he wrote his 'fairy tale' in two attempts. Next to the date he wrote: 'At the top of the page a facsimile of an old hundred-rouble note.' These pre-Revolutionary notes were known colloquially as *katerinki* because they bore a portrait of

Catherine the Great. This remark is probably less a reference to the wealth of the 'Dollar Princess' than an allusion to her name and to the name of the girl whom the 'Cathedral Builder' had fallen in love with (according to the draft of 4 July) seventeen years previously.

A POET'S LOVE (PUSHKIN)

1 Undated and untitled. It is very probable that it was written as early as 1944–45 for *Method* or *Nonindifferent Nature,* but later removed for the 'Third Letter on Colour'. Comparison with the unsent letter to Yuri Tynyanov shows that this text is a reworking and fuller exposition of the ideas expressed in that letter in late December 1943. This chapter concludes the cycle dealing with the 'discovery' of the dramaturgy of colour film.

2 Pushkin's sojourn in Odessa in 1823–24 was the last stage in his 'southern exile', which preceded his 'northern exile' on his mother's estate at Mikhailovskoye in Pskov Province. The Black Brook is near St Petersburg and was the scene of the duel that killed Pushkin on 10 February 1837 (Old Style).

3 E was planning a film version of Pushkin's *Boris Godunov* in 1940 but this never came to fruition. Some of his ideas for the use of colour were later deployed in *Ivan the Terrible, Part Two.* See also: 'Pushkin the Montageur', *ESW2,* pp. 203–23.

4 Alexander I ascended the throne in 1801 after the murder, with his knowledge, of his father Paul I. The boyar Boris Godunov was elected tsar in 1598 after the death of Ivan the Terrible's son, Fyodor. Rumours abounded that Boris had been responsible for the murder of Fyodor's brother and legitimate heir, Dmitri. Pushkin used this version of events as the basis of his drama, thus raising the issue of succession to the throne through murder without actually incurring the wrath of the censors.

5 Konstantin K. Danzas (1801–70), school friend of Pushkin and his second for the duel with d'Anthès.

6 At this point E left space for a quotation, probably from Danzas' recollections of the duel.

7 The project for the Pushkin film envisaged a score by Prokofiev in which the 'Requiem' was part of a sequence entitled 'Pushkin Travelling to the Duel'.

8 Pushkin jokingly referred to his wife in this way.

9 Tynyanov wrote an article in 1939 suggesting that the real nameless love of Pushkin's life had been Yekaterina Karamzina (1780–1851), the wife of the Russian historian Nikolai Kararnzin (1766– 1826). E takes this suggestion as the basis for this chapter.

10 Reference to Chapter 15 of Tolstoy's *Hadji Murat*, published posthumously in 1912.

11 Reference to Pushkin's 'minor tragedy' *The Stone Guest*, written in 1830.

12 Tsarskoye Selo, also the site of one of the royal summer palaces, was the settlement south of St Petersburg where Pushkin and his family lived.

13 Tatyana's last remark to Onegin in Chapter 8 of Pushkin's *Eugene Onegin*.

14 E has his chronology confused again here: the poem 'The Gypsies' was begun in Odessa and completed in October 1824 in Mikhailovskoye.

15 A jocular remark by Pushkin.

16 Quotation from a report in verse by Pushkin to Governor General Vorontsov who had sent the poet on a pointless expedition to combat locusts.

17. An untranslatable pun: the Russian term *Bes arabskii* literally means 'an Arab devil' but also alludes to his black African ancestry, since Russians at that time did not distinguish between Arabs and black people.

18 During his exile at Mikhailovskoye, Pushkin was placed under the supervision of the local priest, who provided a model for the monk Varlaam in *Boris Godunov*. Arina Rodyonovna (1758–1828) was a serf and Pushkin's nanny. Olga Kalashnikova, a serf who bore Pushkin a son, was *not* Arina Rodyonovna's niece.

19 Owned by Pushkin's in-laws, the Goncharovs.

20 The well-known rebellious and prophetic cry by Eugene, the hero of Pushkin's poem 'The Bronze Horseman', addressed to the statue of Peter the Great on the Senate Square next to the Admiralty and the River Neva in St Petersburg. E's Pushkin project envisaged a scene in this square, where the Decembrist Uprising took place in 1825, as 'the poet's rebellion'.

21 Lines from Zemfira's song which affirms the right to free love.

22 The ostensible cause of the first challenge to a duel to d'Anthès was the anonymous and libellous 'diploma' sent to Pushkin and his friends which

'elected' him a 'Co-Adjutant (Deputy) to the Grand Master of the Order of Cuckolds, and Historian of the Order'.

23 Fear of popular reaction to Pushkin's untimely death meant that the funeral arrangements were changed at the last minute.

AFTER THURSDAY'S SHOWER

1 Dated 8 August 1946, this chapter is essentially a diary entry written immediately after the death of E's mother. The Russian title 'Posle dozhdika v chetverg' means literally 'After Thursday's Shower' but the phrase is used colloquially to denote procrastination.

2. Vsevolod Emilevich Meyerhold (1874–1940), the innovative theatre director with whom E had worked briefly in the early 1920s. His role in Soviet theatre was somewhat akin to E's role in cinema and it is no coincidence that E later refers to Meyerhold as 'my spiritual father'. Vladimir I. Nemirovich-Danchenko (1858–1949), theatre director, playwright and scholar, was co-founder of the Moscow Art Theatre. Khazby was one of E's pupils. Valentin I. Kadochnikov (1911–42), Soviet film director and animation artist, was one of E's pupils at VGIK. Konstantin S. Stanislavsky (1863–1938), co-founder in 1898 of the Moscow Art Theatre, was the leading exponent of both the theory and practice of psychological realism and naturalism on stage. Yelizaveta S. Telesheva (1893–1943), actress, director at the Moscow Art Theatre, worked as E's assistant for acting on *Bezhin Meadow* (second version), in which she also appeared, and *Alexander Nevsky* and at VGIK.

3 That is, *Que Viva México*!

4 Olga I. Preobrazhenskaya (1881–1971), Soviet film director and actress whose best-known work is *Women of Ryazan* [*Baby ryazanskie*, 1927].

5 In the manuscript E had originally and absentmindedly written his mother's name Yulia but then crossed this out and substituted Telesheva's initials 'Ye. S.', hence, the sense of premonition.

LIFE'S 'FORMULAE'

1 Roughed out on 15 August 1946, this chapter ends in outline form.

2 Marie Corelli (1864–1924) and Victoria Cross, pseudonym of Vivian Cory, were British and American popular writers respectively.

3　Pyotr A. Pavlenko (1899–1951), Soviet scriptwriter who collaborated with E on the screenplays for *Alexander Nevsky* and *The Great Fergana Canal.*

4　*The Chocolate Soldier* was an operetta, first performed in New York in 1909 with music by the Austrian composer and conductor, Oskar Straus (1869–1954), based on the Viennese operetta *Der tapfere Soldat* [The Brave Soldier], which was in turn an unauthorized version of Shaw's play *Arms and the Man*, first preformed in 1894—hence, Shaw's insistence on fidelity to his text.

THE TRUE PATHS OF DISCOVERY

1　On 14 October 1946 E wrote two texts. One, entitled 'The True Paths of Discovery' (here called 'The Tale of the Vixen and the Hare') was written as a memoir and dealt with work on *Alexander Nevsky.* The other, 'Layout', was an illustrated exercise demonstrating the process of creative improvisation. E's notes indicate the links between these 1946 texts and the '*Torito*' section written for the first volume of *Direction* in 1934. For this reason the Russian editors see the pieces grouped here as constituting a cycle of three chapters in the *Memoirs*, rather than an expansion of the textbook, and they have, therefore, taken the title of the reminiscence about *Nevsky* as the title for the chapter as a whole.

2　Giorgio de Chirico (1888–1978), Italian painter who lived in France and was one of the founders of surrealism.

3　*Khovanshchina* was written by Modest P. Mussorgsky (1839–81) between 1872 and 1880 but left unfinished. It was completed by Nikolai A. Rimsky-Korsakov (1844–1908). The opera ends with the Old Believers, who realize that their cause is lost, burning themselves on a funeral pyre of their own making.

4　Reference to Nikolai Leskov's novella *Lady Macbeth of the Mtsensk District*, (1865) on which Shostakovich based his opera.

5　Jules Guérin, member of the far-right Ligue des Patriotes. Paul Deroulede (1844–1914), French writer and politician, founded the Ligue des Patriotes in 1882.

6　Paul Morand (1889–1976), French writer and diplomat of right-wing persuasion, published *1900* in Paris in 1925.

7　Goethe maintained that his works were 'opportune', as was the creative impulse itself.

8 See 'The Two Skulls of Alexander the Great' (1926), *ESW1*, pp. 82–4.

9 It was in fact, or so the anecdote goes, James Watt who was inspired to develop the steam engine from observing the way that steam made the lid on his mother's kettle jump.

10 During the Second Punic War at the Battle of Cannae in 216 BCE, Hannibal and his Carthaginian cavalry outflanked the Roman army and inflicted the worst defeat on the Romans in history: almost 50,000 out of a total of 86,000 men were lost.

11 The headquarters of the Soviet Writers' Union occupied a former masonic lodge between Herzen and Vorovsky Streets in west-central Moscow, next door to the town house that was supposedly the model for the Rostov family mansion in Tolstoy's *War and Peace*.

12 Reference to the volume *Zavetnye rasskazy* [Cherished Tales], compiled by the Russian historian and anthropologist Alexander Afanasiev (1826–71) and published anonymously in Geneva in the 1860s. E had been given this book by Viktor Shklovsky.

13 Franciscan friars of the strict rule. The correspondence was not genuine.

14 German scientist Otto von Guericke (1602–86) constructed the Magdeburg hemispheres, two cups held together by atmospheric pressure once the air has been pumped out from between them and a vacuum created.

15 The reference is to the opera *The Maid of Pskov* [*Pskovityanka*], also known as *Ivan the Terrible*, by the Russian composer Rimsky Korsakov, which received its first performance in St Petersburg in 1873.

16 Dmitri N. Orlov (1892–1955), stage actor who narrated fairy tales on Soviet radio. Dogada is a character in a Russian fairy tale.

THE AUTHOR AND HIS THEME

1 This chapter is composed of two texts dating from different periods. The first is an unfinished autobiographical essay dated 27 October 1944 and the second is an extract from *Method* dealing with the same problem. The Russian editors have included them here because of E's repeated intention to demonstrate the continuity of his subject matter.

2 Sigismund D. Krzhizhanovsky (1887–1950), Soviet literary scholar.

3 Ivan A. Goncharov (1812–91), Russian civil servant and censor who became a writer. The three novels cited were in fact written in the reverse order: *A Common Story* in 1847, *Oblomov* in 1859 and *The Precipice* in 1869.

4 S. S. Van Dine, pseudonym used by American art critic Willard Hunting-
ton Wright (1888–1939), creator of the immensely popular fictional detective Philo Vance, best known for his murder mystery *The Canary Murder
Case* (1929).

P . S .

1 Written in December 1946. With this piece E broke off work on his
Memoirs.